CONTENTS

TO THE STUDENT

As its title suggests, this book offers you two ways to develop your writing: *process and practice*. "Process" means the overall strategy which research has shown is used by the most effective writers, whether students or professionals.

Now we realize that writing is not just a hit-or-miss affair, in which we sit down to produce our best work on the first try. Rather, an essay goes in stages: we think, we jot down notes, we try a first draft, we let it sit, then we improve it in a second draft and later maybe even a third. *Process and Practice* encourages this improvement through revision. In fact the opening chapter demonstrates each step of it, through a sample short essay shown in first draft then in second draft — with a commentary on each change and why it was made. For more on this central philosophy of our text, read "Popular Misconceptions About Writing," pages 2–3.

The "practice" which our title also promises is offered in the large middle part of the book through many sections that each explain a point of editing, then give one or more exercises on it. For example "Editing for Economy" (pages 51–62) shows how to write more in fewer words, then provides four exercises, ranging from easy to difficult, for your practice. These exercises are put together from examples found in the essays of other students: thus they "ring true," probably representing your own writing tendencies.

Your teacher may have the class do key exercises together, or may assign exercises to individuals who will practise certain editing techniques at home. Answers appear in the "Answer Key" at the back (except, of course, for those exercises that are open-ended). This means you can do an exercise on your own any time you need it, whether the teacher assigns it or not, then see how you did. You can also use the book completely on your own, whether you are in school or not.

Many students now write by computer, while many others do not. *Process and Practice* is meant for both groups. Read "Writing by Computer" (pages 30–35) if it applies to you, and as you study the rest of the book be sure to read the computer advice set off in text boxes wherever word processing offers special help with the matter under discussion. If you write with pen or typewriter, just ignore the computer boxes; all the text outside them applies to you.

This book can help you right now, through the "process" and the "practice" it provides. Over the long term, though, another "practice" is essential: reading. If you have always read a dozen or more books a year or the equivalent in newspapers and magazines, you may now be in a position to reach your personal best as a writer. If you have not, you have some practice to do over the holidays, or next summer, or even the next several years. See "A Suggested List of Canadian Readings" on page 187 for titles, and start the long-term practice that will do more than any other single thing to make you the best writer you can be.

Finally, I would like to thank all the students who gave suggestions for this fourth edition, but especially Cate Drum and Ardy Phan, who read the new chapter on computers and made practical comments on it.

R.C.

TO THE TEACHER

Editions of a textbook are like drafts of an essay: each new one should be clearer, more forceful, more useful. We believe this fourth to be our best so far, because it is a response to the experience of students and teachers across the country who have tested the first three in use. It is also a response to the survey in which teachers told us what they especially wanted this time.

■ One frequent suggestion was to revise most of the content of the exercises, while keeping the very strongest examples. We have done so. On average about 80 percent of exercise content is new. We have also adjusted format and sometimes length. The very most important sections, such as "Editing for Economy" and "Editing for the Complete Sentence," still have a diagnostic exercise plus levels 1, 2 and 3. In some sections, though, level 3 has been folded into levels 1 and 2, which each have become longer and now have more difficult items at the end. The result is a very similar range of work spread over fewer pages — which has given us space to add new material without inflating the size and cost of the book.

■ Many of the explanations have also been revised, some expanded, and many examples renewed. For instance the material on clichés, jargon and euphemisms has been augmented, and "Euphemisms" now gives a perspective on the troublesome matter of "politically correct" language.

■ We have replaced the sample short essay with a new one on a more current and urban topic. The first and second drafts are both reproduced, exactly as they came out, and a new paragraph-by-paragraph commentary demonstrates the process of revision by pointing out frankly and honestly why each change was made. The process is not tidied and sanitized, but shown as the human and fallible act it really is.

■ Our third edition had offered a few tips for those using the computer, but, given the strong increase in student use of this technology, we now cover the matter more thoroughly. Our new second chapter, "Writing by Computer," is aimed at those who have recently begun word processing, as well as those who are considering it.

Without undue technical detail, the chapter outlines the main advantages, suggests strategies for learning, identifies pitfalls, then gives an overview of choices in selecting and buying equipment. Emphasis is placed on affordability, because it is apparent that, given the overcrowding of most college and university computer facilities, a high percentage of postsecondary students would like to buy this technology if only they could afford it.

In addition, text boxes containing computer advice are placed throughout the book where word processing offers special help with the matter under consideration. Through this means, students using "WP" can spot them easily, while the other students can ignore them easily. Note also that our chapter on the research essay now includes on-line library catalogues and indexes on CD-ROM.

■ In response to many requests from both students and teachers, we have moved the "answers" of the instructor's manual into the final pages of the text, itself. Few instructors were using the manual, clearly because they knew the material so well that they did not need it. Every instructor we asked approved of this change, so students and also nonstudents could do exercises on their own at home. If you do miss the manual, let us know by writing the publisher. If enough instructors request it, we will bring it back next time.

If you are new to this book, read "To the Student," which points out our dual emphasis of "process" and "practice." The opening chapter, with its demonstrations of prewriting, outline, "discovery" draft and second draft, is meant to begin your course and to be followed in each successive essay written.

Then upon this basis of regular writing, add the editing sections as needed. Some matters, such as "agreement" and "pronoun reference," are so universally needed that you will probably wish to do them in class. Others may best be assigned individually, only to those students whose writing shows a need for them. Our intention in covering numerous aspects of editing is not to promote the composition course as Procrustean bed, with 75 percent of students wasting their time doing an exercise in class alongside the 25 percent who need it. Rather, we present the editing sections as resources to be selected judiciously and used as needed. The main focus of any writing class is to begin writing and keep on writing.

Finally, I would like to thank all the teachers who shared their opinions through our survey. Colleagues at Ryerson Polytechnic Institute have helped in many ways: Gerda Grice, John Keyes, Lionel Willis, Nelles Van Loon, John Cook and especially Marie Dowler, who brought her expertise to bear on the computer chapter. Special thanks to librarian Diane Smith for her advice on research sources. Finally, I cannot bring out a new edition without again thanking my wife, Mary, for her kindness and good sense. Without her I would never have begun the first page of the first book.

R.C.

PROCESS IN THE SHORT ESSAY

How do we write? The answer to that question has changed over the last 20 or 30 years. A great deal of folklore has been thrown out, as research has more and more clearly shown us what really happens when we sit down at the writing desk or the computer. Let's examine some theories of the past that no longer make sense.

Popular Misconceptions About Writing

■ *Misconception 1 Writing is just a matter of inspiration: I either hit it or I miss it.* Most familiar ideas, including this one, contain at least a grain of truth. We all hope for inspiration as we write. But now we know that most good writing does not just strike the paper like a lightning bolt; it is developed through a process of revision. The first try is just a beginning; the second version is better; a third will be better still. As many practising writers have believed all along, "Writing is 10 percent inspiration and 90 percent perspiration."

■ *Misconception 2 Writing is almost totally planned in advance.* Not too many years ago most teachers and students believed (or at least said they believed) that a beautifully reasoned outline was the main task in writing. All the rest was a sort of filling in of blanks. Today we realize that this approach can

paralyze our thought process. Of course a short outline helps, but overplanning can be a straitjacket that leads us to ignore the many good ideas that come to us *in the process of writing.* We now realize that writing is discovery! Some of our best thoughts occur right in the middle of the task.

We take a compass on a journey through the wilderness, and we take an outline on a journey through our thoughts. But the compass cannot foretell every turn and twist of the path. What a dull journey we would take if it could! Do use an outline, especially in longer papers, but leave room for discovery as well. And if your discoveries overwhelm your outline, then your outline may have been weak to begin with. Consider changing it, in the light of what you have learned while writing.

■ *Misconception 3 If I just avoid enough errors, my writing will be good.* We can see where this idea led in the past: we were so nervous about grammar and spelling that we paid too little attention to the main point of writing — our message. Reaching for the dictionary in the middle of writing a passage, we lost our train of thought and spent the next ten minutes chewing our pencil in frustration — especially if we believed Misconception 1, that we either "hit it or miss it" the first time.

We do not have to write in this painful and unproductive way. Now we know that our first draft should go fast. We should be free and open. After all, we are exploring: the goal is to get our ideas safely out on paper, without worrying about how "correct" we are.

2

Then later, once the pressure is off, we tinker with grammar, spelling and style.

This whole book is organized to encourage process in writing. In our opening chapter we deal with the big things: getting an idea, focussing it, trying it out in a quick first draft to see what we have to say, then revising our thoughts.

Then in following chapters we turn to the secondary things: paragraphing, economy of words, clear sentence structure, agreement, clear pronoun reference, spelling, etc. These are all important, because the message will not get through without them. But they are "secondary" because, without a clear message in the first place, even the most "correct" of writing achieves nothing at all — like a pile of good bricks on the ground, waiting to be formed into a house.

What Is an Essay?

The word "essay" comes from a French term that means a "try" or "attempt." Our "attempts" to explore a topic in essay form can be as short as one or two handwritten pages or as long as 20, 30 or even 50 pages. They can be a brief and spontaneous treatment of a subject that we already know, or they can be the product of weeks spent researching in the library.

Since the form of an essay can vary so much, in this book we will be looking separately at two basic assignments: let's call them the *short essay* and the *research essay*. Most of the book explores the "short essay," because that is the form most often practised in composition courses, and because the skills necessary for development of the short essay are the basic skills that underlie the research essay as well.

At the end of this book, after examining the whole process of writing, we will explore the more specialized form of the research essay.

Starting Out: What Is My Subject?

First of all, an essay has a subject. What will you write about? Teachers often solve that problem for you by assigning a topic or choice of topics.

Other times you may answer the question by thinking up your own topic. Later in your life, an employer may demand written reports on specified topics; as a son or daughter, mother or father, you may find your-self writing an "essay" in letter form to explain or solve a difficult problem with a loved one; as a concerned citizen, you may write an "essay" of protest to your member of parliament, your mayor, or the editor of your newspaper; and at crucial times, you may put pen to paper just to learn what you think about something that really matters.

Whatever the subject and circumstances, the hardest part is to *begin*. If you need to choose from a list of topics, begin by comparing. Which topic do you already know something about? Which seems most important? Which do you *like* the most? We do our best writing on topics that mean something to us.

Many teachers, especially in writing laboratories or clinics, will ask students to think up their own topics. Some people love this challenge, for they can finally write what's on their mind; others dread it, for fear they will have nothing to say.

In either case, choosing our own topic is an act that closely simulates our writing tasks in later life once we are outside the classroom. Let's look at a powerful approach to this challenge of creating our own topic.

Priming the Pump: Freewriting

Have you ever tried to get water from an old-fashioned hand pump, but nothing came out? Have you ever sat with a blank piece of paper and a pen, but nothing came out? In the case of the pump, hardly ever is the well dry. The problem lies simply in getting the pump started. Oldtimers will pour a jar of water down the pump to seal the chamber; now their efforts will create a suction that pulls up that cold, clear water.

In the case of that blank paper, the well is not dry either. What needs to be done is a kind of mental priming, so that your efforts will pull up ideas from the depths of your mind.

One of the best priming exercises is **freewriting.** Put a piece of paper and a watch on the desk. For about five minutes, simply write. Write *anything* that comes to mind, even if it seems like mental garbage. Get it down as swiftly as your hand and pen will let you, or if you are at the computer as swiftly as you can type. Then rush on to the next thing that comes to mind.

Do not stop the physical process of writing or typing until the time is up. If the next thought does not come, keep repeating the previous one till it does. At the beginning of it all, if not even the first thought will come, try this: write "The" on the paper. Some word will then pop into your mind to follow "The," and another will follow it, until soon your first ideas are out in the open.

Why write what may seem like garbage? Because we humans are not rational beings. Our thoughts tend to appear not in logical order but in sudden leaps of association. If we begin with a few of these intuitive leaps, we get the juices of thought flowing; we pull the raw materials of writing out into the open where our more logical thought processes can now work on them, shaping them into the logical arguments we wanted in the first place.

Here is an actual, unedited piece of freewriting. It took about six minutes, not five, because the writer got so involved in the emerging subject that she couldn't stop. It is also fairly long, because the writer was racing away at the computer keyboard:

> There are always transit strikes and every year the fare goes up, and for a while a lot of people either quit taking transit or talk about not taking it, and the statistics actually say that fewer people take it. Why not take the car? But when you look at what it costs to operate a car in the big city, it is pretty appalling. Parking, maintenance, insurance, gasoline. And then, we complain about standing in the subway during rush hour, like in the summer when everybody is sweating and you feel like a swim in a cold lakle but you are carrying your stuff and trying to hang 9onto the sweatay bar to keep from falling over as the train swings around a curve. Or the streetcar is even worse because the streets are choked with traffic, and you go so slowly you might get there faster walking. But what if We all took transit? What if they added more lines and more cars? What if the traffic on the streets disappeared? Well, it wouldn't disappear, but what it. . . How could we do it? If raising the fares drives people away, how about lowering them? How about making it free? How about making car drivers pay for the operation of the transit system? Everybody would scream taxes, but what if the life in our city improved?

Note the carelessness of sentence structure in this example: some passages run on and on with "ands," while others are cut off into partial sentences. Note the careless spelling and typos, such as "sweatay" for "sweaty" and "what it" for "what if." In freewriting these are not errors, for the whole point is to get thoughts out in the open as quickly and easily as possible.

This writer was lucky enough to begin with a subject already in mind. She did not have to write a page of free association — jumping from one thought or image to another — before hitting upon the idea of public transit and its opposite, the private car.

Yet this early and spontaneous version of her thoughts is far from the argument she will produce by the end of her second draft. She does criticize cars, but mostly from the point of view of cost. That's a good beginning, enough to get her started. It will get her into the discovery draft, where she will go much further, thinking also of air pollution.

Our writer criticizes public transit, too, but even here in the freewriting has discovered a solution which she will later place at the end of her essay: reduce traffic and improve transit by making car drivers pay. It is surprising how often a piece of freewriting, like this one, reveals the main points of the essay that will follow — how much it "discovers" even before the "discovery draft" begins.

Think of your own experience in starting to write essays: Have you been afraid of the blank page? Has "writer's block" paralyzed you? Freewriting can move you past these common problems. After all, what do you have to lose — five minutes of your time? By ignoring the old myth that writing is all planned in advance, you can take mental shortcuts that may save hours of time. The trick is to **think by writing**.

Even if a required topic leaves you cold, seemingly with no thoughts at all on the matter, you can avoid writer's block by freewriting. Launch into a few minutes of warmup by putting onto that blank page something, anything, that relates to your topic. You will often be surprised at what comes out; you may sense that, even at this stage, the writing has somehow begun.

Priming the Pump: Brainstorming

Brainstorming is like freewriting, with this main difference: it is not a piece of continuous writing but a list of ideas put down in short form.

Suppose the person whose freewriting we have just seen had done brainstorming instead. Thinking of public transit and the private car, she would jot down anything that came to mind, in any order. Even ideas that seemed irrelevant or silly could have joined the list. Some might have seemed random or illogical — but, as in freewriting, what is there to lose? A writer who brainstorms casts a net into the sea: when the catch is pulled in, it may include fish that no one would want to eat. So what? They are thrown back and the good ones are kept.

As you look at our author's page of brainstorming, note the progression of thought. She begins with the transit strike, goes on to the cost of transit, then the crowding and waiting. Now comes the alternative of the comfortable car, but also the

PUBLIC TRANSIT

- strike
- costs keep going up
- no student rate
- crowded, hot - can't get a seat
- wait for bus in winter. Cold
- drive car instead
- comfortable
- insurance - parts - Dad paid $700 for new central computer for his car
- pollution. Air getting worse in Toronto
- greenhouse effect. Winters getting warmer

cost (she remembers her father paying $700 to re-place his car's central computer). Then she gets closer to the core of her eventual essay, as she begins to jot down notes about traffic and air pollution. She even specifies the greenhouse effect, which will get only a mention at the end of her discovery draft, but which in the second draft will expand to become her major point against the car and in favour of public transit.

In these few minutes of brainstorming, the writing has already begun.

Priming the Pump: Cluster Outline

A similar but more concrete device is the **cluster outline.** As in brainstorming, one notes down the ideas as they come, but connects them in a diagram that looks like a model of a molecule. In the cluster outline shown on page 6, the ideas we read in the brainstorming example are expressed in a form that is much more visual.

Note how this approach is better at separating ideas into groups. The writer first puts down the key thought of "public transit" in a circle in the middle of the page. Then around it she jots down other words or ideas it brings to mind, such as "price keeps going up" or "hot, crowded, hang onto poles," and connects them with lines to show relationships.

Note especially how toward the lower left, the thought "driving instead" leads to a great many other thoughts, some positive ("comfortable") and others negative ("expensive" and "creates pollution"). These thoughts about driving, as in an outline, are now grouped: all the comfort together, all the expense together, and all the pollution together.

As our writer looks these over, she can see where the argument is leading, and above all where her main focus will be: on the large group of ideas concerned with pollution. As in freewriting and brainstorming, the writing has already begun.

We have looked at three ways to set our thoughts in motion. Usually one or two will be enough. Do not waste time by using all three on the same project, because to some extent they duplicate each other. Instead, try the one or two that appeal to you the most.

The Thesis Statement

Once we have determined our topic and generated information through freewriting, brainstorming or a cluster outline, we need to limit the scope, and focus the purpose, of our essay. Although our first version is a "discovery draft," after "priming the pump" our discoveries must take place within limits. If we kept on wandering from one interesting thought to the next, we could write forever without getting to the heart of one chosen idea.

A device of control that most writers use, consciously or unconsciously, is the "thesis statement." **A thesis statement is a complete sentence — usually placed near the beginning of an essay — that does two things very clearly: it limits the scope of the topic, and it focusses the writer's purpose.** (*Note*: Some people think a title is a thesis statement. It is not. A title is just a label, usually not even a complete sentence. You do need one, but you need a thesis statement, too.)

Limiting the Scope

Do you realize how short an essay is? A book may contain 100 000 words or more, and a magazine article 2000 to 5000, but a classroom essay can have as few as 500 or even 250. The conclusion is inescapable: **For an essay we must choose either a small topic or a small aspect of a larger one.**

Once a student attempted an analysis of communism, socialism and capitalism — certainly a worth-while topic. But he crammed the whole thing into two pages. When we consider that thousands of entire books have been written on each of these three systems alone, it is obvious what kind of treatment this person was able to afford in such a tiny space: a collection of unsupported generalizations that everyone has heard already, with no further explanation or examples to bring the material alive. The "essay" was worthless.

Yet this same person, as the teacher learned later in conversation, had powerful insights into one of these systems, for he had been a political prisoner in a country which practised it. If he had only *limited the scope* to a small part of the topic — say, his arrest or his trial or a day in his cell — he might have been able to say far more about the system he had struggled against.

Think of writing as photography, and put aside the wide-angle lens that includes too much at a distance.

Look instead through the telephoto lens that brings you up close to a small part of the subject. Select the part most meaningful to you, perhaps the part most characteristic of the whole, and then take your picture.

Focussing the Purpose

A thesis statement gives an opinion. It sets a direction for the essay to follow. It does not just state a fact, such as "Rumania is a small country." We either know that fact already or we learn it as we read the sentence. In either case the idea seems self-contained, "over with" once it is stated — and as a result not very interesting.

By contrast, a lively thesis statement makes a *generalization* — as we said, usually an *opinion*. Remembering his time in prison, our politically minded writer might have said something like this: "I discovered that in Rumania, life in a prison cell was very similar to life in the streets." Now our writer can focus on the lack of freedom in the sordid little cell, on the rats and cockroaches, the dismal food, the brutality of the guards — and through this closeup, given in the short space of an essay, he can also imply an impression of the country in general. In effect, our writer would be saying *more with less*.

Where Does the Thesis Statement Appear?

In a long essay the thesis statement is seldom the opening sentence. First we read a little background information so we can understand the thesis when it occurs. Or we read a paragraph or two designed to trap our attention: perhaps a funny or tragic story related to the topic, a relevant quotation, or a frightening statistic. It is toward the end of this introduction that we normally find the thesis statement, which alerts us to the scope and purpose of the argument to come.

In very short essays, say of two or three or four pages, the writer may feel like just launching out with a thesis statement as the first words. But such a beginning is abrupt. It may fall flat, as the writer of this opening sentence failed to realize:

> In this essay I will show how absenteeism among students is a serious problem.

Rather than starting off by hinting your essay will be a bore, as this writer did, why not begin with at least a sentence or two of preparation? Just as in the longer essay, give a bit of background information, a striking incident, a pertinent quotation or statistic. (See page 37 for more on introductory paragraphs.)

Finally, a few essays begin in suspense, build to a climax, then only at the end hit their readers with a thesis statement to clinch the meaning of the whole thing. This can be powerful when it works. But to use such an approach you must know just what you are doing. Far more widespread is the pattern of thesis statement near the beginning, for, by announcing the topic, limiting the scope and revealing your point of view, you prepare the reader. A good thesis statement, like a highway sign, alerts the reader to what is ahead and directs him or her toward a destination.

NAME _____

Limiting the Scope: Exercise

For each of the general subjects below, supply five "closeups" that limit the scope to a size that might fit a short essay.

Example:

Transportation
    a. rush hour on the subway
    b. bicycle paths in the city
    c. the system of traffic signals
    d. buying a used car
    e. streetcars

1. Crime

    a.

    b.

    c.

    d.

    e.

2. Relationships

    a.

    b.

    c.

    d.

    e.

3. Electronics

    a.

    b.

    c.

    d.

    e.

4. Childhood

    a.

    b.

    c.

    d.

    e.

5. Entertainment

    a.

    b.

    c.

    d.

    e.

6. Government

    a.

    b.

    c.

    d.

    e.

7. War

    a.

    b.

    c.

    d.

    e.

8. Sport

    a.

    b.

    c.

    d.

    e.

9. Immigration

    a.

    b.

    c.

    d.

    e.

10. Business

    a.

    b.

    c.

    d.

    e.

NAME _____

Making Thesis Statements: Exercise

Develop each of your "closeups" from the previous exercise into a generalization that could interest your reader and set a direction for your essay. Don't be afraid to state opinions, as long as they are reasonable enough to support in an essay. And remember that a thesis statement is a complete sentence.

Example (from the general subject of "Transportation"):

   a. Rush hour on the subway

      The best way to endure rush hour on the subway is to invent ways of ignoring other passengers.

   b. Bicycle paths in the city

      A system of bicycle paths through Montreal would reduce traffic accidents, reduce pollution and promote physical fitness.

   c. The system of traffic lights

      The average driver has no conception of the sophisticated planning that produced our system of traffic signals.

   d. Buying a used car

      The risks in buying a used car can be greatly reduced if you know how to spot a lemon.

   e. Streetcars

      The streetcar makes more sense than any other form of public transportation.

1. a.

    b.

    c.

    d.

    e.

2.   a.

      b.

      c.

      d.

      e.

3.   a.

      b.

      c.

      d.

      e.

4.   a.

      b.

      c.

      d.

      e.

5. a.

    b.

    c.

    d.

    e.

6. a.

    b.

    c.

    d.

    e.

7. a.

    b.

    c.

    d.

    e.

8. a.

    b.

    c.

    d.

    e.

9. a.

    b.

    c.

    d.

    e.

10. a.

    b.

    c.

    d.

    e.

Audience: Who Is My Reader?

Another good thing to do before starting the first draft is to **visualize your reader or readers.** Who are they? What approach will work with them?

After all, we adjust the way we talk to our listeners: Would we speak the same way and say the same things to a child and an old person? To a criminal and a judge? To our hockey coach and our member of parliament? Probably not. Neither would we write exactly the same things in the same way to these different people. To match your writing to your audience, ask three questions:

1. *What is my reader's level?* An essay for your professor is one thing. A letter to your school newspaper is another. If your reader is highly educated, you may use demanding vocabulary and complex arguments. But if your audience is at an average level of reading and thinking, control your vocabulary and explain ideas plainly.

2. *What does my reader know?* One look at the number of books in a library will convince us that we cannot learn everything. People specialize: thus the philosopher who cannot repair the faucet, the mathematician who cannot write good English, and the English teacher who cannot calculate the income tax. As you plan an essay or report, recognize such differences: try to estimate your own reader's knowledge of the subject.

Some composition courses allow essays on a wide variety of subjects. You might write on inflation, germ warfare, radar, or digital recording for your English teacher. But watch out: if your own field is electronics, you might load your account of digital recording with terms your poor English teacher has never seen and may not find even in the dictionary. Have pity — if your reader is a nonspecialist, avoid most technical terms and define those you do use. Give background. Explain clearly. Use examples. Otherwise he or she will be lost. (For more on this, see "Jargon," page 75.)

On the other hand, the same approach to a paper on, say, a short story by Neil Bissoondath will be a disaster. Your English teacher will be insulted by elementary explanation of terms she or he has used for 20 years, and will miss the challenge of a complex argument. Therefore estimate, as well as you can, the reader's command of your subject — and write accordingly.

Roberts/Comstock.

3. ***What does my reader believe?*** Are you likely to change anyone's mind by quoting Marx to a banker, the Bible to an atheist, or Henry Morgentaler to a right-to-life activist? Probably not. Be realistic: Do not send your message in a form that is sure to be rejected.

Of course you must tell the truth, but in terms acceptable to your audience. For example, build on assumptions that you and your reader can share. Do not preach to a capitalist that socialism is better — but you can certainly claim that capitalism is not perfect, giving examples such as the Great Depression, inflation, unemployment, the cost of housing, etc. At the end of it all, even the banker may begin to understand another point of view.

> In summary, do not think of your reader or readers in the abstract. Instead, *visualize* the person who will read your essay (or if you are writing for a group, visualize one person who represents that group). Then communicate *person to person*. You may be writing alone at a desk, but in thought you are communicating face to face.

The Discovery Draft

Now let's return to our writer who didn't appreciate the transit strike, who dislikes pollution, and who is looking for a better way to get around the city. She has done **freewriting** (pages 3 to 4), or **brainstorming** (page 4) or a **cluster outline** (page 6) to start ideas flowing. Now she is ready to give those ideas preliminary shape in a thesis statement. Here it is:

> The excitement of the strike soon turned to exasperation as city dwellers realized how important public transit is to their lives.

Notice what a "closeup" this statement is. It does not cover city life in general, or transportation in general, or even the strike in general. Instead, it focusses on a *small part of a large subject*: how Torontonians learned to value public transit, through being deprived of it.

Notice also how this thesis gives the topic a point of view, a *direction*. We already see what the writer thinks of public transit: she likes it. Now as we read the explanations and examples to come, we will be prepared to understand and react to the main idea.

But first let's include one more planning step: an outline. Frankly, we all know people who plunge ahead with no outline at all. This may often work in a short essay, and sometimes even in a long one. But without at least some kind of plan — if only a few words to block out the order of main points — a writer can easily end up like Stephen Leacock's famous horseman who "rode madly off in all directions."

Following the advice of researchers in composition, let's remember that an outline should be short, and should be tentative, because valuable new ideas will probably occur while we are writing the first draft. If they do not fit the plan, we may even change the main point, despite our thesis statement and outline. Remember that writing is discovery! We will recognize and promote this concept by calling our first version the "discovery draft."

Now here is our author's brief and tentative outline. Note that it includes the thesis statement.

THE BETTER WAY
I. *Introduction*
   A. *Opening example: Toronto's transit strike*
   B. *Thesis statement: The excitement of the strike soon turned to exasperation as city dwellers realized how important public transit is to their lives.*
II. *Body: Public transit vs. the car*
   A. *Getting to school during the transit strike*
   B. *Disadvantages of public transit*
   C. *Disadvantages of the private automobile*
      1. *Expenses*
      2. *Pollution*
III. *Conclusion: Make the car drivers pay for public transit*
   A. *To reduce traffic*
   B. *To make transit cheaper and better*

Once the outline is before us, we are ready for a discovery draft. Whether we use pen and paper, or a computer and a wordprocessing program, the tactics are similar. We write or type rapidly, getting ideas out into the open without stopping our train of thought.

If the right word doesn't come, just leave a blank to fill in later. If a word or phrase seems wrong, do not fix it now: just leave it, or if you are writing by hand, underline it so that later you can find it and revise.

If you sense a misspelled word or shaky grammar, again — underline. Leave the dictionary and the handbook on the shelf till later. Write paragraphs naturally, as they come: many will be good in your first draft, and the rest can be adjusted later.

> Finally, leaving room for later revision is essential. Do you want to cram new sentences into microscopic writing in tiny spaces between lines? Of course not, so whether you write by hand or key into the computer, be sure to double- or triple-space now.

Here is the author's discovery draft.

DISCOVERY DRAFT: The Better Way

Last fall there was another transit strike. These seem to happen every two or three years. People got angry at first, because how would they get to work or get to school in a city of this size? Then they worked out their strategies. Employers organized car pools. Neighbours and friends did the same. The GO train laid on a lot more trains, with more cars. People put on running shoes so they could walk a mile, or even three or four, to work. It was almost exciting, as the emergency gave people a sense of adventure. <u>But the excitement of the strike soon turned to exasperation as city dwellers realized how important public transit is to their lives</u>.

The streets were choked with traffic. I tried car pooling to get to class, but had to leave at 7:15 in the morning because my friend starts work at 8:30. Then I tried hitchhiking down Yonge Street. There were plenty of rides, but nobody was going very far before they turned off. And traffic was so slow, because everyone was driving, that I actually saw people walking on the sidewalk gaining on us block after block. One day I put on my most comfortable running shoes and tried to walk the five miles myself, but the pollution from all those idling cars was so thick that my lungs were hurting and I was dizzy by the time I got to my locker. There has to be a better way, I thought to myself.

The Toronto Transit Commission, the TTC, calls itself "the better way." When we are trapped in a stuffed subway car in hot weather, during the height of rush hour, sweating like a pig and hanging onto the slippery bar to keep from falling over when the train starts and stops, we hardly think it is "the better way". We long to take a part-time job and get some money together to buy a car. Then we can speed to school, with our favourite tape on the stereo, and smoke and drink coffee and eat all we want to, without somebody's elbow in our face.

4   But is that actually the "better way"? Look at the economics of it. A decent car, even used, costs at least $8000. Insurance for people our age and in the big city costs $2000 if you're lucky, or up to $5000 a year if you have infractions and drive the kind of little red sports car everyone wants to drive. Then parking in Toronto runs $12 a day and up. Maintenance costs a few hundred a year if you're lucky, but with the older cars students can only afford, you may end up rebuilding or replacing a transmission, or doing other costly work. Then there are gasoline, oil, tires, and more. That makes the price of a TTC ticket, even with its annual increase, seem like pretty small stuff.

5   Then there's the environment. Many people my age have a greater concern than the generation of our parents. We've been exposed to the issues since grade one, and, after all, we are the ones who have to live our futures in this world polluted by all those who went before us. My grandfather says that when he was a boy he used to swim in the Don River. Now it's Toronto's biggest sewer. Now you can't even swim in Lake Ontario half the time. To think that our drinking water comes right out of the lake takes away my thirst. If I could afford it, I'd drink mineral water.

6   Air pollution is probably the worst problem in Toronto though. A study came out a couple of years ago that the very most polluted spot in all of Canada is right along Yonge Street

where I walk from the College subway stop to my classes. On a bad day in warm weather the haze just hangs in the air. It actually makes my lungs hurt. Sometimes your eyes hurt and the tears come just from the sulfuric acid in the air, from all the car exhaust. You can hardly see the stars at night. Up in the Bruce Peninsula where my friends and I went camping last summer, you could see thousands, probably millions, of stars twinkling all over the sky. You could see the Milky Way, like a blanket of stars, across the middle. You could see falling starts, and satellites moving across the sky. They say there are a billion stars in our galaxy and I felt like I was seeing them all.   But back in Toronto, nothing. A purplish haze covers the sky at night, lit up from the lights all over town.

I this the kind of city we want? Public transit has its problems, especially in rush hour. But the number of people who drive their cars create much worse problems. Do we want to choke ourselves to death with pollution? Or is there a "better way"? I say that the old, much criticized Toronto Transit Commission is the "better way." It is the future.   7

How can we make it better? How can we get the drivers off the streets and into the buses, streetcars and subway trains? By sheer economics. By devising a system to make drivers pay for public transit, we will begin to clear the streets of traffic and upgrade the transit system at the same time. One there are more frequent transit vehicles, more people will use them. Most importantly for students, who can hardly pay all their expenses, the fare will be greatly reduced or even gone. If our society can realize the true value of clean air to breathe, and of reducing the greenhouse effect that threatens to disrupt civilization across the world, the true cost of providing transit free of charge to the riders will seem very small indeed.   8

Revising the Discovery Draft

Now put yourself in the place of our writer. After the prewriting, she has taken the plunge into a "discovery draft." Writing it gave a certain satisfaction: she got to complain about some things that were bothering her, and worked her feelings into a more or less coherent form.

In the moments after writing the last word, she may even consider the essay a masterpiece. She may have her family and friends read it, and consider them fools if they do not share her enthusiasm.

But a day later she has lost what we could call the "writer's high." As she looks over the draft more calmly, certain passages bother her. They don't seem as good as they did yesterday. Here is a "fact" that is wrong. And here is an idea that doesn't support the point.

But now another idea pops into her head. Why didn't she think of it yesterday? Our writer reaches again for the draft, and two hours later awakens from another "writer's high" to find the once-neat manuscript covered with revisions. In fact, the new section she has just added on the greenhouse effect is now the showpiece of her argument.

Let's see exactly what she did. Go to pages 21 to 25 and look at the second draft, which has the changes and additions boxed so you can see them at once. Then go to pages 26 to 28, where a paragraph-by-paragraph analysis tells why each change was made, to demonstrate what writers do as they go from one draft to the next.

Nowhere does word processing help the writer more than in the act of revising a draft.

Most users key their discovery draft right into the machine, and do a quick spell check (see page 174); then they print out "hard copy" to edit, because they see words better on paper. If you do this, be sure to double- or triple-space, leaving room for handwritten changes. For printing, select "draft" mode, which is fast and uses less ribbon or ink. If your printer takes single-sheet feed, print on the backs of used paper.

After the first version "cools off" for a day, edit your hard copy as our author has edited her second draft, which follows. (Some people do all their editing on screen, printing nothing but the final version. See if this more direct way works for you, but go back to paper if it does not.)

Whether you edit on paper and transfer handwritten changes to the screen, or edit directly on screen, learn the features of your system that will speed your work. Practice the different commands that backspace, that delete one letter, one word, a whole line, or all the rest of the page. Learn to move blocks of text, so that if you find, for example, that your key point is buried in the middle of the paper, you can switch it to the end without retyping.

While the draft is on screen, exploit the speed of your electronic thesaurus by using it on any word that is not exact enough or direct enough or strong enough or short enough. (See page 27.)

Finally, "save" your second draft under a different "filename" than the first, so you can go back to the first in case you change your mind about something you have revised or removed.

SECOND DRAFT: The Better Way

Last fall Toronto endured another transit strike. People 1
got angry at first, because how would they get to work or get to
school in a city of this size? Then they devised their
strategies. Employers organized car pools. Neighbours and
friends did the same. People put on running shoes so they could
walk a mile, or three or four, to work. Some even got out their
roller skates. It was almost exciting, as the emergency gave
people a sense of adventure. But the excitement of the strike
soon turned to exasperation as city dwellers realized how
important public transit is to their lives.

The day the strike began, traffic choked the streets. I 2
tried car pooling to get to class, but had to leave at 7:15 in
the morning because my friend starts work at 8:30. Then I tried
hitchhiking down Yonge Street, a thing I would never do if the
subway were running. There were plenty of rides, but nobody was
going very far before turning off. And traffic was so slow,
because everyone was driving, that I actually saw people walking
on the sidewalk gaining on us block after block. One day I too
put on my most comfortable running shoes and tried to walk the
five miles myself, but the pollution from all those idling cars
was so thick that by the time I got to my locker I was dizzy and
my lungs were hurting. There has to be a better way, I thought
to myself.

3   The Toronto Transit Commission, the TTC, calls itself "the better way." When we are trapped in a stuffed subway car in hot weather, during the height of rush hour, sweating like pigs and hanging onto the slippery bar to keep from falling over when the train starts and stops, we hardly think it is "the better way." We long to take a part-time job and get some money together to buy a car. Then we could speed to school, with our favourite tape on the stereo, and smoke and drink coffee and eat candy bars all we wanted to, without somebody's elbow in our face.

4   But is that actually the "better way"? Look at the economics of it, for example. A decent car, even used, costs at least $6000. With luck, insurance for people our age in the big city costs $2000 a year, but if one has infractions and drives the kind of little red sports car everyone wants to drive, the bill can reach $5000 or more. Then parking in Toronto runs $12 a day and up. Maintenance costs a few hundred a year if the car is in decent condition. But if the vehicle is one of the oldies that students tend to buy, costly items such as the transmission or the central computer may have to be rebuilt or replaced. Then there are tires, oil and gasoline. Many students have worked so many hours to support the driving habit that they have failed out of school, missing their chance for a satisfying career and the salary that comes with it. That makes the price of a TTC ticket, even with its annual increase, seem like pretty small stuff.

5   Even more important than monetary costs of driving are the environmental costs of driving. Many people my age have a greater concern for this planet than the generation of our

parents has. We've been exposed to the issues since grade one, and, after all, we are the ones who have to live our futures in this world polluted by all those who went before us.

Air pollution, caused mostly by private vehicles, is one of   6
Toronto's worst problems. A study published a couple of years ago in the <u>Globe and Mail</u> concluded that the very most polluted spot in all of Canada is right along Yonge Street where I walk from the College subway stop to my classes. On a bad day in warm weather the haze just hangs in the air. It actually makes my lungs hurt. Sometimes my eyes hurt and the tears come just from the sulfuric acid in the air.

Torontonians can hardly see the stars at night. Up in the   7
Bruce Peninsula where my friends and I went camping last summer, thousands, probably millions, of stars twinkle all over the sky. We could see the Milky Way, like a blanket of stars, across the middle. We could see falling stars and satellites moving across the sky. The Milky Way is our galaxy. Astronomers say there are a hundred billion stars in it, and I felt like I was seeing them all. But back at Yonge and Bloor, the night sky was nothing but a purplish haze illuminated by lights all over town.

An even worse result of air pollution is the greenhouse   8
effect, in which atmospheric carbon dioxide, produced mostly by private vehicles, raises temperatures around the world by trapping the sun's heat. Toronto dwellers experience some of the results. Now in winter their sidewalks are covered with slush instead of proper snow, and those who once went cross-country skiing in parks and ravines can now do so only one or two days

per year.   Toronto summers have always been sultry, but lately for several weeks in July and August they are downright unbearable.

9   More serious are the greenhouse effects that drivers in cities such as Toronto cause elsewhere.   As the increasingly warmed atmosphere melts polar ice, the oceans rise.   Low-lying heavily populated coastal areas like Bangladesh experience more disastrous flooding every year, and will eventually disappear, causing a flow of environmental refugees such as the world has never seen.   Meanwhile the same heat around the world is turning vast areas of marginal farmland into desert.   In countries such as Ethiopia and Somalia, the desert is expanding at such a rate that famine kills ever larger numbers of men, women and especially children.   The city dweller half a world away, in North America, contributes to this every time he or she takes the wasteful car instead of the more efficient streetcar, bus or subway train.

10   Is this how we want to live in our city?   Public transit does have its problems, especially in rush hour.   But the number of people who drive their cars create much worse problems.   Do we want to sacrifice our school performance by working enough hours to support a car?   Do we want to choke ourselves with pollution?   Do we want to kill other people around the world by contributing to the greenhouse effect?   Or is there a better way?   I say that the old, much criticized Toronto Transit Commission is the "better way."   It is the future.

11   But how can we make public transit truly "better"?   How can we get the drivers off the streets and into the streetcars, buses

and subway trains? By sheer economics. | If we devise | a system to make | automobile | drivers pay for public transit, we will begin to clear the streets of traffic and upgrade the transit system at the same time. | Once | there are more frequent transit vehicles, | and once there is more room on them, | more people will use them.

| Students, | who can hardly pay all their expenses, | will find | the fare greatly reduced or even gone. | More importantly, | if our society can realize the true value of clean air to breathe, and of reducing the greenhouse effect that threatens to disrupt civilization across the world, the true cost of providing transit free of charge to the riders will seem very small indeed.

12

Revisions: How and Why

"Revision," literally, means "seeing again." Our writer has "seen again" at several points in the writing process. The short outline was a "re-seeing" of the freewriting and other prewriting activities. The discovery draft was then a "re-seeing" of all the thinking and planning that led up to it, and the second draft is a "re-seeing" of the discovery draft.

For example, not every remark in the cluster outline ended up in the discovery draft. Although it may be true that tourists are charmed by the city's picturesque streetcars, the author's real point became how public transportation solves problems.

On the other hand, though the cluster outline gives only one word to the transit strike, by the time the writer begins her first draft she chooses this dramatic event to attract the reader's attention and to lead into her thesis, the importance of public transit. In fact, even in the second draft she continues to develop this introduction, suddenly remembering the roller skaters and adding them to the hitchhikers and walkers.

More "re-seeing" occurs in the second draft. The closing of the discovery draft really bothered our author as she looked it over the next day: the remark about the greenhouse effect in the very last sentence was too sudden. It seemed to introduce a large new topic, only to drop it without developing it. Now, she thinks, this important point *should* be developed, so she goes ahead and does so. The result is a whole new section, paragraphs 8 and 9, which argues that public transit helps not only those who use it but others around the world as well.

By contrast, while looking over the first draft, our author sees that the part she had liked so much, about her grandfather swimming in the Don River, is irrelevant to her topic. Since she has not been able to blame water pollution on private vehicles, she crosses the whole passage right out, and goes on to air pollution.

> Now let's look at the many smaller cases of "seeing again," to illustrate the range of improvements we can make when revising our own papers. Paragraph numbers refer to the second draft, except where specified otherwise.

■ *Paragraph 1*   Compare the boxed revisions in the second draft to the original wording of the discovery draft. The weak "there was another transit strike" becomes the more direct "Toronto endured another transit strike." Now "devised" replaces "worked out," because "work" appeared also in the previous sentence. Repetition is annoying, thinks our author.

Now she considers her audience: Will the average reader know what the "GO Train" of the first draft is? At first she adds another sentence explaining how this transit company serves the suburbs, and how its employees are *not* on strike. Then she wonders whether this example of public transit continuing to operate will just weaken her essay, making the TTC strike seem less important. Suddenly she crosses the whole passage out. But now she worries about concealing the truth, stacking the cards. Oh, well, she thinks, I'll leave it for now and reconsider it if I have time for a third draft.

Finally, she adds the new sentence on roller skaters, which is more picturesque than the first examples.

■ *Paragraph 2*   In adding "The day the strike began," our author links this paragraph to what came before. The time signal also moves the argument forward. Now the active "traffic choked the streets" replaces the weak and passive "the streets were choked with traffic." Next our author points out how she normally does not hitchhike, so we know what an exceptional event she thinks a transit strike is.

Now she catches a grammatical error: "nobody was going very far before they turned off." Since "nobody" is singular, "they turned" becomes "turning," to eliminate the faulty pronoun "they." Next she adds "too," to emphasize her action in joining the walkers. Finally, she shuffles the second-to-last sentence around, so the dizziness and hurting lungs stand out at the end, instead of the less important locker.

■ *Paragraph 3*   Now "pig" becomes "pigs," to match the plural "we." The quotation mark after "the better way" now goes after the period, where most writers now place it. "Could" and "wanted" are more accurate than "can" and "want," because the action is not yet taking place. Finally, the specific example of "candy bars" now develops the general word "eat." Readers love to "see" the subject, our author thinks.

■ *Paragraph 4*   Now revisions become so numerous that we will examine only the main ones. Note how "for example" helps us see what is coming: the present point about economics is not the whole argument in favour of public transit; there will be other points later. Accuracy is important: the car expenses drop from $8000 to $6000. I don't want to exaggerate, thinks our author; if readers don't believe this figure, they may not believe anything else I say either.

Another consideration is *tone*. Seeing words like "you" and "you're" in the discovery draft, our author decides to make the feeling more formal and objective, so her argument will seem serious. Therefore she removes all the "you"s. But the replacement pronoun "one" is a little stiff. Have I gone too far? she asks herself. Will this sound like a Ph.D. dissertation instead of an argument for the average person? She decides to keep the changes for now, then look them over later.

The biggest change, though, is the addition to the second-to-last sentence of students who may now miss their big chance in life by flunking out of school — all because of the time they spend working to support a car. I'll scare the readers, our author thinks, so they will heed my argument.

■ *Paragraph 5* As we said earlier, the grandfather and the Don River disappear from this paragraph because they seem irrelevant to the topic of transit. The vague words "Then there's the environment" from the first draft now change to a proper transition that puts the "costs" of the private vehicle in a broader context: "Even more important than monetary costs of driving are the environmental costs of driving." In parallelling these two "costs," the whole paragraph is now a transition between major sections of the essay.

The thesaurus has long been a major editing tool. If a word is too vague, too long, too elementary or too scholarly for your audience, or too cheerful or too angry for its context, a thesaurus lists alternatives. If the right word exists, you will spot it and use it.

Now most wordprocessing systems have an electronic thesaurus, not as complete as the old hardbound *Roget's*, but fast enough that the essayist can use it constantly.

Let's see how WordPerfect's thesaurus works. Suppose that five or ten words per page of your discovery draft are not quite right. In WordPerfect, for example, you put the cursor under the first term to check, then press "Alt-F1." Now the bottom half of the screen fills with alternative word choices, and a menu to select them.

The exact way you choose depends on which version of WordPerfect you have, but in all of them you can use either a simple key or mouse command to view alternative words, and sometimes to view antonyms. If you do see a word that fits your meaning or expresses your feeling better, a simple key or mouse command will make it pop into place where the old word was.

Once you get some practice, the electronic thesaurus in WordPerfect or in other wordprocessing programs is so fast that you will want to do much of your editing on screen.

See also page 174 on using the electronic speller.

■ *Paragraph 6* Our author cuts the original paragraph in two, because it looked forbiddingly long. Why discourage readers? she thinks.

Now she adds "private vehicles" to the first sentence, directly blaming them for the air pollution about to be discussed. Let's keep the readers aware of my overall point, she thinks. Now she adds the *Globe and Mail,* to credit her source, but has no idea what issue she was reading. Should she go to the library tonight, do a search, and document the point? If this were a research essay she might have to. But it is not. I'll ask my teacher tomorrow whether this is enough, she tells herself.

Finally, "you" becomes "my": after all it is the writer, not the reader, whose eyes hurt.

■ *Paragraph 7* A number of little changes appear in this second half of old paragraph 6, many to heighten the formality. More "you"s are cut out, although some "we"s still appear, because they seem less conversational. Also the specific intersection "Yonge and Bloor" replaces "Toronto": Let's help the reader "see" this city, thinks our author, in order to highlight its difference from the North.

■ *Paragraphs 8 and 9* As noted earlier, the words "greenhouse effect" in the closing of the discovery draft had really bothered our author. They would surely distract the reader's attention by mentioning a whole new point that was not even going to be covered. Well, *why not* cover it? thinks the writer. "Seeing again," she realizes that the thought of our killing other humans across the planet, just by driving cars, would strongly support her argument for mass transit. So now she writes these paragraphs, even though her outline had never mentioned the point.

She becomes excited, yet uneasy, producing phrases like "a flow of environmental refugees such as the world has never seen." Will the readers think I'm laying guilt on them? she asks herself. Will they resent me and even reject the argument? Yet this matter is crucial, she realizes. Maybe North Americans *do* need to change the way they travel. Let's take the chance, she thinks. Why write an essay at all if you don't have a point to make?

■ *Paragraph 10* One well-known kind of error is typos. Finding one in the first line, our author changes "I" to "Is." More importantly, she realizes that at this point in the argument, where she is reaching her summary, she has left out the point about personal economics and has been vague about "pollution" as well. Now she adds the economics and the greenhouse effect, so the reader takes the weight of the whole argument into the closing.

■ *Paragraph 11* Our author splits this passage into two paragraphs, to make the closing look more accessible. She makes a few other changes as well, for example adding "automobile" to "drivers," in case the reader might think transit drivers are also being criticized. Let's make it clear, thinks our author. She also adds the prospect of "more room" on transit vehicles, to counteract the common objection that transit is crowded.

■ *Paragraph 12* Here our author removes the words "most importantly" from the item about cost. Instead she puts "more importantly" in front of the item about air pollution, to emphasize what, only now in her second draft, she realizes is her strongest point.

Further Drafts?

Our essayist sits back from the writing desk after all these revisions, with a sense of having finished the job. On the other hand, that's the same feeling she had after draft one — and look at all the improvements made since then. Maybe tonight more passages will be wrong, more "facts" untrue, or more new ideas too good to leave out.

Come to think of it, just now while explaining the greenhouse effect, she had thought also of acid rain, another kind of air pollution caused in large part by the car. For a moment she almost began a section on it, too, but then held back. After all, is this a whole essay about pollution? Wouldn't the first point on the cost of driving a car seem off-topic if followed by two big sections on two kinds of air pollution?

But now that she thinks of it, the economic costs already seem almost trivial compared to large numbers of Third World citizens dying just because we drive cars. Why not go all the way? Why not forget the car expenses, and focus only on environmental arguments through the new greenhouse-effect point, and the point yet to be made about acid rain?

But what about my introduction? she asks. Does the transit strike make sense as an intro to acid rain? In fact, does it even make sense as an intro to the greenhouse effect? Maybe I should junk all the pollution and stay closer to the student (*myself*) just trying to get to class!

Wait a minute, she thinks to herself, this sounds like another draft. The essay's due tomorrow, and tonight I have to study economics. What if I just leave the essay? Sure, I could make changes forever, but it's a lot better than it was. I do like it now.

She gets up from her writing desk, puts on her coat, and walks to the door. As she enters the park across the street and gazes up at the trees, she reflects on how complicated life is and how complicated writing is.

Process in the Short Essay: Assignments

Choose any one of the general subjects listed below. Apply the principles and examples of this chapter, developing your subject into a "short essay" (your instructor may specify a length). Complete the following steps of the writing process, or at least those specified by your instructor:

1. *Freewrite* (pages 3–4), *brainstorm* (page 4) or make a *cluster outline* (page 7) of your subject.
2. *Limit your scope* and *focus your purpose* in a *thesis statement* (pages 7–8).
3. *Visualize your reader* (pages 15–16).
4. Write a very short, tentative *outline* (page 16).
5. Write a *discovery draft* (pages 16–19). Be free, spontaneous and quick. Save correction of errors for later.
6. Write a *further draft or drafts* (pages 20–25), improving your argument, your style and your "correctness." The instructor may give specific directions for this stage.

If you are using this book in a class, or a writing clinic or laboratory, your instructor may wish to assign the above process of writing several times during the term (each time, you will of course begin with a different subject). The instructor may assign additional subjects, or may encourage you to come up with your own.

You may begin right off with a first short essay, to immerse yourself in the writing process, even though you have not yet studied all the editing skills discussed in the chapters that follow. Then in later assignments you may apply all the rest of the book that you have studied so far, or you may jump ahead to chapters that you especially need (see the table of contents and the index to this book). But whatever you do, the most important thing of all is to start writing and keep writing.

GENERAL SUBJECTS

1.	*Aging*	11.	*Leisure*
2.	*Business*	12.	*Mass media*
3.	*The city*	13.	*Nature*
4.	*Culture*	14.	*Science*
5.	*Education*	15.	*The sexes*
6.	*Family life*	16.	*Success*
7.	*The future*	17.	*Technology*
8.	*Health*	18.	*Travel*
9.	*Housing*	19.	*Trends*
10.	*Language*	20.	*Work*

Note: Be sure to retitle the subject you have chosen, to reflect the smaller focus you are giving it.

WRITING BY COMPUTER

The way we write is always changing. Over the past generation we have more clearly realized the importance of drafts, and have moved to the "process" way of writing shown in this book. Now for a decade or more an equally profound change has been taking place: writers are putting away the pen and moving to the computer keyboard.

Of course many still prefer the good old way for its directness and simplicity. After all, Shakespeare didn't need a computer or even a typewriter. If you are one of those many people, just ignore the rest of this section. Others would like to try word processing, if only they could afford their own machine or find access to one at school.

The pages that follow are for those who have not yet tried "WP" (word processing) but are thinking of it, and for those who have access to a system but are just beginning to use it. The final section is for those who wish to buy their own system but have not yet thought about what equipment to choose or how to afford it.

Since the field of computers is highly complex and constantly changing, these pages do not attempt to be a technical guide. Rather, they are a starting point: an overview of possibilities and choices.

How Word Processing Gives the Writer Speed and Flexibility

Speed

■ As with a typewriter, you can key material in directly, rather than writing by hand. Take a keyboarding course if you have not already, because through good techniques most people can eventually type three or four times faster than they can write by hand. (Or buy software instruction in keyboarding, which you can practise at home.) *Keyboarding can be ideal for your "discovery drafts."* Have you ever forgotten your second point while laboriously handwriting the first?

■ *Using the computer, you will never again have to retype anything.* You can produce a composition on the screen, then either edit it there or print it out on paper to edit. Between sessions you store the document in the hard drive of your computer or on a floppy disk.

30

Photo courtesy of Ronald Conrad.

Then at any time you can retrieve the document to the screen for further revision and editing. (If you like to do these tasks on paper, do so and then transfer the changes to the screen.) After producing any number of "drafts" this way, you simply order the computer to print out the good copy.

Finally, if a teacher is not satisfied with your work, you no longer "rewrite" but only "revise," calling up the previous version on screen and tinkering with it. *Clearly word processing is ideal for the process system of writing, which we follow in this book.*

■ Many software systems include a spell-check feature, which in a couple of minutes finds almost all spelling errors, except those caused by confusing two correct words such as "there" and "their" or "to" and "too." (See page 174 for details.) Another common feature, the electronic thesaurus, is so fast that writers can afford to use it often to sharpen their word choice. (See page 27 for details.) There also exist grammar-check programs, such as Grammatik and Correct Grammar; but so far such programs are relatively crude, and it appears that future improved versions will take up massive amounts of memory.

Perhaps this array of electronic aids does not seem quite fair; but to be realistic, neither did the calculator a generation ago. Composition teachers usually accept these tools, and even encourage their use.

■ The more complete wordprocessing systems offer shortcuts called "macros," whereby you can program a whole series of keystrokes into only two strokes. With these you can then do things like pop your return address and today's date onto the top of all your letters, or move instantly into a favourite format with all margins, line spacing and choice of typeface ready to go.

Flexibility

■ You can adjust format before, during or after keying in the document. This includes choice of margins all around, choice of line spacing, choice of typeface, centring and such variations as italics and boldface. Have you ever single-spaced an essay on a typewriter, only to be told by the instructor that it had to be double-spaced? With WP, instead of retyping the whole thing, you can change the line spacing in a few seconds.

■ Finally, editing on screen provides a flexibility (and therefore speed) that can truly surprise a longtime pen, pencil or typewriter user:

■ On the screen you can quickly delete — *without a trace* — letters, words, lines or whole sections.

This encourages experimentation and exploration, which are qualities at the heart of the process model of writing.

■ If you add words in the middle of a line, the rest of the text moves to make room. You can insert a whole paragraph or more between parts already written. You can move a section of any size to another place without retyping. In major software programs you can split the screen into halves to do two documents at once, or to move parts of an old one into a new one, without retyping.

Writing by computer, then, offers powerful advantages. Not everyone wants to do it, but at the present rate of change composition students who use this technology will soon be in the majority.

Suggestions for Learning

Whether you are a complete beginner or have some computer experience from school, the task of learning word processing may take time and strategy. Consider the following suggestions.

■ Start learning in good time, not two days before your major essay is due.

■ Check out the student computer facilities that your college or university probably has. Is instruction offered?

■ If you are sitting at home in front of your new machine, and have dared to open your 600-page manual filled with terms that may or may not resemble English, you probably feel some fear. Consider these strategies:

■ Rather than read hundreds of pages before turning the machine on, read just enough to get going, then try it out. Learning to use a computer works best through a combination of three things: *study of the manual, trying things out on the machine,* and *advice from friends* (everyone knows at least one computer whiz who can get a person out of almost any jam).

■ Don't be afraid of ruining the machine or program. They are less fragile than you might think. Try things out. Almost any move you make in most programs is reversible. Though it is possible to wipe out files that you yourself have keyed in, it is almost impossible to wreck files that run the software. At the very worst, you may have to re-install a program from disk, if something you did has caused the program to malfunction.

If your hands are not on the machine, you are not learning.

- For most major software programs of any kind, several different manuals have been published, at different levels of expertise. If you find your official manual hard to use, check out the bookstore or library.

- Most people can learn enough to run a piece of WP software in a few hours. Forget fine points for now; as the months and years go by, you can master other details.

Three Cautions

- Never work on a long document without "saving" it to disk (hard drive or floppy) at regular intervals. (Some programs do this for you automatically.) If you do not save your documents, a power failure or computer "crash" can wipe out hours of your work. Also, never store an important document in your hard drive without also saving a backup copy to a floppy disk — just in case your hard drive "crashes" (ceases to function for any of a number of reasons). In fact, crucial documents, such as long theses, should be protected by making three or even four copies — at least one of which is stored in a different building in case of theft or fire.

- Never plug your computer directly into the wall. Power surges caused by lightning, or even by furnace fans, ovens, air conditioners and other large appliances, could erase crucial data from your hard drive. Instead, buy a high-quality "power bar" (multiple outlet) with built-in "surge suppressor."

Throughout this book, wherever word processing gives the writer special tools to apply the skill under discussion, you will find a text box like this one.

If you are computerized but not very experienced at word processing, read the boxed suggestions and try them. They may save you a lot of time and may well improve your writing.

If you are writing by hand, however, just ignore these boxes. All the text outside them is meant both for those who write by hand and those who use a computer.

- Do not even dream of putting someone else's floppy disk into your machine without checking it for "computer viruses" — purposely destructive or invasive programs. Over a thousand such viruses are on the loose, with names like "AIDS," "Blood-2," "Chaos," "Disk Killer," "Friday the 13th," "Holocaust," "Leprosy" and "Microbes." They will do anything from insulting you on your own computer screen to destroying your software and even hardware. Many schools are licensed to distribute protective virus-detecting software to students. See about this at your campus computer centre.

What Equipment Should I Use?

Almost all schools have computers for student use, and many school computer labs offer instruction, or at least simplified manuals for beginners. Using your school's equipment can save you a lot of money. Then by the time you graduate and get a real job, you can afford a much better system than you might have bought while still in school. But whether computers will be available the week you write your major essay is another question. If there is a chance they might not be, you may want to buy your own.

If you do, you face many choices. One is whether to go for a *Macintosh* system or an *IBM-compatible* system. When the Macintosh first came out, it dazzled the public with "user-friendly" software that worked through "icons" (recognizable symbols) and used a "mouse" (a device that makes inserting data easier and reduces keystrokes). By now, though, software for IBM-compatible systems provides similar options. Either system is fine, but you will find a greater choice of software and of low-cost hardware for the IBM-compatible.

Another choice is between *name-brand* and *generic* computers. When personal computers first became popular most people went for the name brands, for fear of breakdown. Today, though, it is mostly businesses that prefer brands; individuals most often go for a no-name machine at half the price. Generics are put together in a local factory, and contain most of the same standardized chips and other parts as the name-brand machines. Of course any computer may break down, but today's machines, generics included, are surprisingly reliable. Most have a one-year guarantee, which is reasonable because if anything does go wrong in the first few years it usually does so in the first weeks.

A further choice is the size of computer. The standard "desktop" is large but relatively inexpensive, whereas the "notebook," which you can take to class or the library, is costly. If your budget is very tight, consider also the kind of *electronic typewriter* that, though its display is very small, has a floppy disk drive. This gives you memory, which provides the key advantage of any computer: you may revise from draft to draft without retyping.

The student must also decide whether to buy from a *small company* that offers service and help, or an *electronics "supermarket"* with better prices but little or no service and with sales staff who may or may not know their wares. The first-time buyer might well find the personal help and security of the small dealer worth the extra cost. If you go to either the small dealer or the "supermarket," ask yourself: has the dealer been in business a while? Unscrupulous firms have been known to close after a year or so, open again under a new name, and through this manoeuvre make your guarantee worthless. Think also about location. Do you want to take your machine twenty miles for repairs, or carry it down to the corner dealer?

Though computer prices are falling steadily, for most students the price will still be high. A complete starter system with printer may cost from under $1000 to over $2000. Compare ads. The best information in Toronto, for example, comes in the Saturday *Star* and in the free monthly *Toronto Computes!* Now let's look at some choices that determine cost:

■ Among IBM-compatibles, the "286" (the number refers to the power of the processing unit in the computer) that was so popular in the 1980s is widely considered obsolete (though it has more than enough power to run a good wordprocessing system). If the low price is worth the risk to you, consider picking up a used one as its owner moves up to the faster and more powerful "386." However, industry publications call even the "386" obsolete, as the "486" sells in ever-greater numbers and as ever-newer models are in the works.

This is not the place for a detailed discussion of the computer industry; any newsstand can satisfy that need. Besides, products change so fast that much of what these pages say about equipment may be obsolete by the time you read it. Let's put a perspective on your choice, though. Consider which of these alternatives fits your situation:

A. *If money is a problem* Get a used older machine (taking an experienced friend to check it over), or a cheap new basic model, or even the kind of electronic typewriter with a floppy disk drive discussed above. Though you can forget about exotic programs, you can do essays perfectly well with this equipment.

B. *If money is not a problem* Look ahead: Will you want to use a graphic interface such as the

increasingly popular Windows? Will you need to use powerful software in technical courses? Then invest in a "386" or, even better, a "486." Also investigate features such as speed, random access memory (RAM), math coprocessors, etc., which teachers, dealers and friends can explain. Above all, make sure which features are necessary to drive particular software programs. *Choose your software first, then the machine that can run it.* But remember that even if you buy a state-of-the-art computer today, in five years it will be obsolete and will be sold for half the price if it is still sold at all. Unless you need big power now, strategy A may be best till you graduate.

■ Another choice is amount of *memory in the hard drive* (the device inside your computer that stores information). A few years ago 40 megabytes of capacity (enough to store something over 40 million characters) was thought sufficient. It is still enough to run yesterday's software. Today, though, as a result of memory requirements of the ever-larger programs people are using, 120 megabytes is more the standard. By the time you read this the number may be even higher.

Again, weigh your financial situation now against your computer needs in the future. Some people compromise: they buy less memory now and upgrade later to more memory when they have the money. But the problem with this is that by then prices will have come down so much that upgrading seems unreasonably costly compared to just buying a better machine. The solution is not easy. Consult dealers. Especially consult your friends who are computing.

■ The *printer* is often sold separately from the rest of the system. Since laser printers are beyond most students' financial reach, your choice is probably one of these:

■ *A 9-pin printer* Does the job, but characters will not be of letter quality. Noisy. Slow.

■ *A 24-pin printer* Costs a hundred or two more than a 9-pin, but does letter-quality or near-letter-quality work at a somewhat faster speed. Noisy.

■ *An ink-jet printer* Costs a little more than a 24-pin, runs slowly, but is silent and produces work of almost laser-printer quality. Requires fairly expensive ink. Extremely compact, good for those who have a space problem or who plan to travel with a "notebook" computer.

■ Software is also expensive. However, MS-DOS, or DOS for short, the standard program that organizes your commands to other software, is usually sold in a package deal with your new hardware. Get the latest version, which allows you to make commands through visual means, with a mouse, rather than through hard-to-learn keystroke commands, as in the older systems.

■ A wordprocessing system is your other essential software for writing:

   ■ Some package deals include a fairly simple WP system, which will be easy to use, and will offer all the most important features of more sophisticated and expensive systems.

   ■ On the other hand, you might want to invest your time more directly in learning a major system used by the world of employment. At present WordPerfect is the most widespread in the world.

It is expensive, and some people do not find it easy to learn. It will do almost anything you will ever need to do in word processing, though, and your ability to use it will look very good on job applications.

■ Finally, whatever your computer system costs, how do you pay for it? Some colleges and universities offer leasing through major companies. After you have paid a monthly fee for a year or two, as you would with a leased car, you may opt to buy the machine at a price lowered because of depreciation. Some banks make special loans to students who need a computer. How about sharing with a roommate or friend, and splitting the cost? And if none of these suggestions will do, go right back and make the best of your school's computer lab.

THE PARAGRAPH

Everyone has some idea of what paragraphs are: units of thought several sentences long, which are set off from each other by an indented first line (the first word begins several spaces in from the margin). And most people have some natural feeling for how to paragraph: without even thinking about it, they instinctively pause at the end of a passage. They close off that part, mentally take a breath, then indent the next line to signal a plunge into the next phase of their argument.

Our first chapter, "Process in the Short Essay," recommends this approach for your "discovery draft." If we put too much effort the first time through into organizing each paragraph, we might not have enough attention left to generate our argument — to "think by writing." But once our thoughts are safely out on paper, we can look over what we've done and tinker with it.

As you look over the paragraphs you have produced in your discovery draft, see first of all whether you have fallen into one of these traps:

1. *Ignoring paragraphs totally* Some inexperienced writers will crank out a whole essay with no paragraph breaks at all. In effect, their one "paragraph" might be five pages long. After their breathless first draft they must now go back to find the natural breaks in their thought — and signal them by indenting. If they do not, a prospective reader looking at that shapeless mass of words may feel like a climber gazing up at Mount Everest.

2. *Making paragraphs too short and too numerous* Far more common is this weakness. A whole essay of mini-paragraphs only one or two sentences long may not look bad on paper; after all, if your handwriting is big and especially if you double-space, even a tiny paragraph can *look* big.

Certainly paragraphs as short as one sentence or even one word can serve here and there to give special emphasis. But a series of mini-paragraphs will almost always identify an essay that is seriously underdeveloped — that lacks enough detail to be interesting or even clear. People who fall into this trap may unintentionally be following newspaper style. But a good news article is not underdeveloped; it is simply indented after every sentence or two because of the newspaper's narrow-column format. An eight-sentence paragraph in a single column would look so long that it could scare off readers. But in the full-page format of your own typed essay, as in the full-page format of a printed book, it looks fine. Where you need eight sentences to round out a good point, anything less is too little.

3. *Using "block" form in an essay* Some people have more experience writing letters than essays. And since many business letters are written in the "block" style, which separates paragraphs with an extra space instead of an indentation, these people may forget to indent. Just remember that in essays, unlike letters, paragraphs are always indented.

Kinds of Paragraphs

Years ago people's concept of paragraphs was too rigid: textbooks and teachers sometimes gave the wrong idea that every paragraph was structured the same way. Now we realize that nothing could be further from the truth: paragraphs come in many sizes, are organized in many ways and have many uses. Let's look now at each of the major kinds of paragraph.

The Introductory Paragraph

Let's begin with this, since it begins the essay. A short essay may have only one paragraph of introduction, while a longer one may have several. Therefore an introductory paragraph may stand alone or may be part of a series of paragraphs. Whichever is the case, an introduction has two main functions: to *interest* and to *prepare* the reader.

Rather than putting your reader to sleep with a flat statement of intent, tease your reader's curiosity. Note the difference in effect between these two paragraphs of introduction to the same paper.

A.   This essay will be about the shortage of rental housing in Toronto. It will attempt to show some of the difficulties the average student has in finding accommodations in this urban area. It will also discuss the financial problems encountered by these people once they finally do locate a place to rent, and will end by suggesting solutions to the problem.

B.   Last September Torontonians walking through Queen's Park were startled to see three tents, and in front of them several well-dressed persons of student age roasting hotdogs over a campfire. Most residents have heard how scarce and costly rental housing is in Toronto, but the spectacle of university students living in tents under the very windows of the Ontario Legislature raises a serious question: When will lawmakers act to increase the supply of affordable rental housing?

Introductory paragraph A is a bore because it is too general. It does announce its subject, but in a clumsy and official manner. By contrast, paragraph B seduces us with a puzzling story, then turns our attention smoothly from it to the main point: "When will lawmakers act to increase the supply of affordable rental housing?" Throughout, we are stimulated by dynamic terms such as "startled," "spectacle" and "under the very windows of the Ontario Legislature," rather than being deadened by stuffy expressions such as "This essay will be about..."; "It will attempt to show..."; and "It will also discuss...."

Both introductions have a thesis statement, to serve as the basis of the argument that follows, but note how the thesis of introductory paragraph B takes the form of a question — and thus tries to further involve the reader. We have already examined how the thesis statement introduces, focusses and

then guides the essay (see "Process in the Short Essay," pages 7 to 8). Now let's examine more closely the other function of an introduction: to *interest* the reader. Try these widespread techniques in your introductory paragraphs:

■   *Fill in some background information*   Especially if your topic is little known, difficult or unusual, help others relate to it by sketching in the context: give a bit of historical, social or technical background.

■   *Tell an anecdote*   Everyone likes a story. As in the brief account of students camping by the Ontario Legislature, relate a short incident — unusual, perhaps funny or tragic — that leads to your topic. This favourite technique of public speakers works equally well on paper.

■   *Give a quotation*   Use the index of *Colombo's Canadian Quotations* or *Bartlett's Familiar Quotations* to find a good opening. Whether your subject is war, sex, taxes or sport, find out what Shakespeare or Albert Einstein or Margaret Atwood said about it. Then lead from this to your own thesis.

■   *Give statistics that lead in to your topic*   Use the newspapers or consult such collections as the *World Almanac* and *Book of Facts* or the *Canadian Almanac and Directory*. The statistics that best create interest are those that alarm or even scare the reader.

■   *Make an unusual or puzzling statement* that draws readers into your topic. (To introduce the shortage of student housing, we could begin with "It is not easy to study calculus in a tent.") Do not exaggerate or falsify, but do search for an unusual angle that will whet your reader's curiosity.

The "Main" Paragraph

Between the introduction and the conclusion of an essay comes the main part, the "body," which is made up mostly of what we could call "main" paragraphs. Here is where the "main" work of illustrating, explaining, arguing and convincing takes place. Since they do similar work, these "main" paragraphs tend to be alike in at least two ways:

1.   Many or most have a "topic sentence" that announces the point to be developed in the paragraph.

2.   Everything else in the paragraph develops that point.

Let's look more closely at these two features.

The Topic Sentence

Researchers in the field of composition have debunked the old idea that every paragraph has to have a *topic sentence*. In fact, on average, fewer than half of all paragraphs in published writing have one, especially when we consider that many paragraphs have specific uses: introducing, narrating, bridging major sections and concluding.

But a great many of the workhorse paragraphs that do our illustrating, explaining, arguing and convincing in the body of an essay do have a topic sentence and develop it throughout their other sentences. In this sense a "main" paragraph is like a miniature essay: the topic sentence (like a thesis statement) sets out the point which all the rest will support. Let's see how Annie Dillard uses this pattern in a paragraph from her book *Tinker at Pilgrim Creek*:

> Parasitic two-winged insects, such as flies and mosquitoes, abound. It is these that cause hippos to live in the mud and frenzied caribou to trample their young. Twenty thousand head of domestic livestock died in Europe from a host of black flies that swarmed from the banks of the Danube in 1923. Some parasitic flies live in the stomachs of horses, zebras, and elephants; others live in the nostrils and eyes of frogs. Some feed on earthworms, snails, and slugs; others attack and successfully pierce mosquitoes already engorged on stolen blood. Still others live on such delicate fare as the brains of ants, the blood of nestling songbirds, or the fluid in the wings of lacewings and butterflies.

After reading this paragraph, can you reasonably doubt that "parasitic two-winged insects, such as flies and mosquitoes, abound"? Every sentence, by use of example, furthers our understanding of the main point and our belief in its validity. Not one given fact is irrelevant to the topic sentence.

How does a topic sentence work? It normally fulfills these three expectations:

■ *A topic sentence limits the scope of its paragraph* It cuts off a chunk of thought that is neither too large nor too small for treatment in the several sentences of a paragraph. Some subjects are so minuscule or so obvious that to state them in one sentence is enough. A statement such as "I have two legs" is hardly worth building a paragraph around, for it is self-evident.

The opposite case is far more common: a statement that is too large in scope for development in the limited space of a paragraph. Pity the person who begins a paragraph with the words "Many countries are interesting to visit." How many countries does this writer hope to cram into five or eight sentences, and in what ways are they all "interesting"? In fact,

what does "interesting" mean? One reader may expect an account of historical and cultural sites, another an account of bars and nightclubs, and another an account of the characters this traveller met while hitchhiking.

The fact that entire books are written about one country sheds some light on our writer's problem: the topic is far too broad. Let's narrow it down drastically to "Spaniards are the friendliest people I have ever met" or "Camping on the beach in Mexico was the most dangerous thing I have ever done" or "It is easy to get lost in the Paris subway." Now a few good examples will bring these topic sentences alive.

■ *A topic sentence, like a thesis statement, often makes a generalization* We could simply state a fact, such as "Fifty thousand Canadian lakes have died from acid rain," but if we can also give this information a direction (present it as an opinion), it will make for a stronger paragraph: "The fifty thousand Canadian lakes that have died from acid rain are proof that our industrial society is in trouble."

Of course the way you cast your topic sentence depends on the flow of your argument: what you wrote in paragraphs that came before and what you will write in those that come after. For example, you may sometimes need a paragraph of pure fact to develop a preceding part of the argument. But where possible, begin a "main" paragraph with an idea worth supporting, not just a fact alone.

■ *A topic sentence usually occurs at or near the beginning of its paragraph* Thus the reader sees what is coming and is better prepared to deal with it. Annie Dillard's passage about insects is a typical example of this most common of all paragraph forms. It is easy to understand, because a kind of summary in advance tells us what to look for as we pass through the sentences that follow.

If you don't feel like playing it safe, though, this order can be reversed. By putting the details first, and waiting until the end to make the point, you can introduce a suspense that greatly increases the drama of the argument. This approach requires polish. It is best reserved for an occasional special effect.

Unity in "Main" Paragraphs

When a topic sentence is used in a paragraph, it should dominate. **Every single sentence of the paragraph should in some way support the main idea in the topic sentence.** Where does the following paragraph go wrong?

> Three memorable rides have cured me forever of my desire to hitchhike. The first was a speedy trip in an Alfa-Romeo that met its fate on a cliffside road in Spain. We sideswiped a

long truck, were whirled right around and came to rest with one wheel over the cliff. I looked down at the Bay of Biscay as the driver cried over his twisted car. The next was a ride with a wild young Kentuckian who had the most decrepit Chevy I've ever seen. Every time he swerved to make a pedestrian jump into the ditch, my door swung open and I grabbed for the seat to stay aboard. One of the best rides I've ever had, though, was with a family going to Montreal. They let me drive their new Oldsmobile and even bought me lunch at the rest stop. All in all, I've found hitchhiking to be exciting — too exciting for me.

It doesn't take long to see that this writer has given two examples which strongly support the topic sentence, but a third which contradicts it. The result is a weak argument: we're not really sure what this person does think of hitchhiking. Let's replace that third example with one that does support the point. Here's the revised paragraph:

Three memorable rides have cured me forever of my desire to hitchhike. The first was a speedy trip in an Alfa-Romeo that met its fate on a cliffside road in Spain. We sideswiped a long truck, were whirled right around and came to rest with one wheel over the cliff. I looked down at the Bay of Biscay as the driver cried over his twisted car. The next was a ride with a wild young Kentuckian who had the most decrepit Chevy I've ever seen. Every time he swerved to make a pedestrian jump into the ditch, my door swung open and I grabbed for the seat to stay aboard. The third ride was an early morning trip on glare ice. My driver seemed to think his Trans-Am could go twice as fast as anything else on the road. It did: we soon passed all the traffic while sliding *backwards,* on our way to the shoulder where we snapped off two guard posts and sank into the ditch. All in all, I've found hitchhiking to be exciting — too exciting for me.

The Paragraph of Narration

Narration is one of our most natural and attractive ways to communicate: everyone loves a story. In our section "The Introductory Paragraph" (page 37), we saw how the anecdote about students camping in Queen's Park could begin analysis of the scarcity and cost of housing in Toronto. Narrative can also serve other parts of an essay: the *body* and the *closing*.

Often several paragraphs of narration will occur in a row, to tell a story that illustrates a point. In such a case it is clear that individual paragraphs will not have the common "main" paragraph structure of topic sentence and development, but will merely tell

a chunk of the story in time order. Furthermore, if people in the story are speaking, we indent each time the speaker changes. Such a paragraph can be tiny or large, but in either case will be different from the "main paragraph" because its function is different.

Now let's look at a section of narrative paragraphs which might appear in our essay about student housing:

One of the students roasting hotdogs at the fire recounted the experiences that had led him here.

"The week before school began I called to investigate at least 30 rental ads," he said. "Only three places hadn't been taken."

"When I rang the doorbell at the first place the owner opened the door a crack, with the chain still fastened, and looked me over. Then she asked me if I smoked. When I said yes, the door shut in my face."

He continued. "At the second place, I discovered why the rent had not been specified in the ad: it was $800 a month for a one-bedroom apartment."

"At the third place, I thought I had it made. I would split a rental of $1000 a month with two other tenants, for a large three-bedroom apartment. But when I got inside, a large fellow with tattoos was repairing his Harley-Davidson on the living room floor."

The student put his hotdog in a bun and took a bite. "You know where I ended up staying?" he asked. "In my van."

Note how short these narrative paragraphs are and how none but the first contains anything resembling a topic sentence. Also note that although these paragraphs are not standardized and do not argue a point in logical fashion, their overall effect is to provide a strong example that illustrates the main point of the essay: lack of student housing.

Feel free to use paragraphs of narration wherever they work well to support a point. Do remember that a composition made up *entirely* of narrative will usually not be an essay at all; it will be fiction, news, history or autobiography. But shorter sections of narrative can work powerfully to support the meanings of the essays they serve.

The "Bridge" Paragraph

Bridges help to unify a country: they permit us to cross from one part to another. They do the same for an essay. In short papers a "bridge" is just a word or two of transition: "then" or "first" or "next" or "finally" or "in conclusion." Longer essays use not only these but also longer "bridge paragraphs" that move us from one major section to another. Let's examine one:

These eight students are lucky: they no longer study calculus or accounting in a tent, for media coverage of their stunt brought offers of housing from Toronto landlords. But what about the thousands of others who arrived in late August hoping to find a room they could afford? How many are still living in motels or flophouses or even cars, weary of searching for what seems not to exist?

The opening words, "These eight students," recall the opening section of the essay, which told about the persons camped beside the Ontario Legislature buildings. The rest of that sentence reveals how their problem was solved. A transition word, "but," then moves us toward the next point, the fate of other students still looking for a room. And the final sentence gives a preview of that next major section; at this point we expect an investigation, no doubt with examples, of those many students who are still searching.

Perhaps a later bridge paragraph will link this section on unhoused students to a third on solutions open to lawmakers. Like our "bridge" above, it will be short (note that our example has only three sentences). And like our example, it will probably have two parts — one looking backward and one looking forward, like the two sides of a coin.

Bridge paragraphs, then, differ from "main" paragraphs. Their opening statement may resemble a topic sentence, as in our example. But unlike "main" paragraphs, bridge paragraphs do not develop such a statement throughout, for part of the way through comes a shift that moves us on to the next topic. Paragraphs are certainly not all alike. As in architecture, form follows function.

The Closing Paragraph

Like an introductory paragraph, a closing paragraph is special because of its location. You have probably seen how productions as different as a speech, a sermon, a play or a film close at a high point or climax. From symphonies to rock and roll, music ends literally on a "high note," while TV police dramas close with the excitement of a tire-screeching car chase or a shootout. (This approach is not new; have you ever counted the bodies lying onstage in the last scene of *Hamlet?*)

Roberts/Comstock.

Most essays follow this pattern of ending in excitement. What could be worse than a closing paragraph that trails off into minor details? Suppose that our essay on student housing ended like this:

> In conclusion, postsecondary students in Toronto have a serious housing problem that may not improve for several years. By that time, though, today's students will be safely out in the world of employment, and will spend their weekends mowing grass at their houses in the suburbs. They will have forgotten all about their housing crisis, not to mention all the other minor problems that students have from day to day.

This paragraph ignores a major principle: the ending occupies the most prominent position of an essay. Its potential either for impact or for boredom is even greater than that of the introduction. If our closing paragraph or paragraphs do not leave the reader convinced or inspired, we have wrecked the rest of the essay as well, no matter how good it was. Let's look now at an alternative model:

> In conclusion, Toronto's student housing crisis will not go away by itself. Until legislators stop the conversion of rental units to condominiums, and until they encourage the kind of housing that will increase the supply and stabilize the price of rental units, thousands of students will be denied access to a university education. Instead of becoming leaders in society, the prospective students of today may become the unemployed of tomorrow.

Note that instead of trailing off, this closing paragraph rises gradually to its peak of significance in the last words. As it does so, it also moves upward in time from the present to the future. Both these movements merge in the final ominous phrase, "the unemployed of tomorrow," which impresses upon readers the importance of the whole essay.

Although closing paragraphs come in many kinds, most good ones follow closely the upward pattern of our example, like the crescendo of a symphony. Often the best closings end deliberately on a key word. (In fact, keep this technique in mind for all paragraphs: play around with the last sentence until you can place the most important word at the very end, where it will do the most good.)

Now let's examine the most widespread techniques used for the closing paragraph or paragraphs of an essay:

- *Refer to the introduction* Restate or repeat a key part of the opening to give a sense of completion.

- *Ask a question* that either makes your reader think or that has an answer obvious from the content of your essay. Either method will encourage involvement through your reader's participation in the closing.

- *Give a quotation* that seals your argument with the opinion of an authority or that puts your view in more vivid or memorable terms than you could devise yourself. As with introductory quotations, consult the index of *Colombo's Canadian Quotations* or *Bartlett's Familiar Quotations.*

- *Use transition signals* In combination with other closing techniques, use expressions such as "finally," "last," "in summary" or "in conclusion" to prepare the reader for your final words.

- *Reveal the significance* of your argument, as in our sample closing, which points to unemployment as the result of a student housing crisis. Showing the importance of your point will help to convince the reader of the significance of your argument.

- *Give a summary*, but only at the closing of essays so long or complex that your reader may have forgotten key points. Avoid boring repetition; keep any summary short.

- *Draw a conclusion* A "conclusion" is not just an ending, but a diagnosis or verdict on the subject of your essay: taxes should be raised or lowered, abortion outlawed or permitted, nuclear weapons maintained or scrapped, the voting age raised or lowered. Feel free to make any judgment that is rooted clearly in the logic of your argument.

- *Make a prediction* What could be more appropriate than closing a discussion of a subject's past or present with a look at its probable future? (Remember the unhoused students of today who may become the unemployed of tomorrow.) This approach is a good way to "reveal the significance."

Length of Paragraphs

Since paragraphs have different functions and therefore different structures, it is clear that they will also have different lengths. "Special" paragraphs that introduce, narrate, bridge or close an essay can be as short as one sentence, for special effect, or can be several sentences long. Most tend to be short, though — in the range of two to five sentences — because major explanations tend to occur in the "body."

"Main" paragraphs of the body can also vary in length — from one sentence, for special effect, to as many as ten or more sentences in a lengthy explanation. Keep this natural range in mind: if you do not vary the lengths of your "main" paragraphs, your style may be flat or even boring. Aim for an up-and-down effect, like that of waves in the ocean.

On average, though, "main" paragraphs are substantial: from about three to eight sentences. Of course sentences also vary in length, and this in turn affects the length of paragraphs. A tense passage of ten short sentences may result in a fairly small paragraph, while a single very long and involved sentence may create its own long paragraph. (If you have read Victorian novels, you have seen a few of these.)

Whatever the lengths of their sentences, if your "main" paragraphs are too short, you are crippling your impact as a writer. We have already discussed this common flaw of "making paragraphs too short and too numerous" (page 36).

As an exercise, find an essay you have written in the past and actually count the number of sentences in each paragraph. You might be surprised to find that most of your paragraphs are only two or three sentences long, even though your handwriting makes them look big.

Using the graph below, compare your numbers to the number of sentences in the paragraphs from the revised draft of our sample short essay "The Better Way" (pages 21 to 25).

Though variety is achieved by paragraphs as short as four, three or even two sentences, the overall average for "The Better Way" is almost six sentences per paragraph.

Are your own paragraphs big enough? Do they have the depth of detail that allows for clear thought? Do they sparkle with examples, with images, with facts? Or are they "thin"? Do they just limp along half-developed, only half doing their job? Your own sentence count should help you decide. If your paragraphs are "thin," you should take very seriously the exercise on page 49, "Improving 'Thin' Paragraphs." Do it, review it, remember it and in your own essays apply it.

Finally, remember that we save these concerns mostly for the editing process. Do try to generate details as you write your discovery draft, but at that point avoid the tactical error of stopping to rework a paragraph: by the time you get it right, the next things you were going to say may have slipped from your mind. It is later, in the second or even third draft, that we practise carefully the art of paragraphing.

PARAGRAPH LENGTHS IN THE SHORT ESSAY "THE BETTER WAY"
(second draft, pages 21–25)

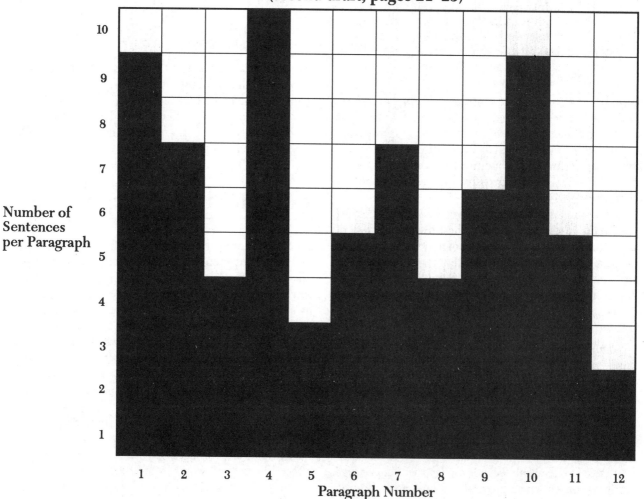

Number of Sentences per Paragraph

Paragraph Number

NAME _____

The "Main" Paragraph: Exercise

*Note how each topic sentence below gives an opinion. Support that opinion with at least four examples. If you disagree with the opinion given, change it and then support your own. In either case, as you fill out **a** through **d**, avoid any material that does not support its topic sentence.*

1. Summer employment is one of the most valuable forms of education.

    a.

    b.

    c.

    d.

2. Canada is an economic colony of the United States.

    a.

    b.

    c.

    d.

3. Going to a movie is a more satisfying experience than watching television.

    a.

    b.

    c.

    d.

4. Automation contributes to unemployment.

    a.

    b.

    c.

    d.

5. Canadian society is truly multi-cultural.

    a.

    b.

    c.

    d.

Devise a good topic sentence to unite each of the following groups of material. Be sure each time to express an opinion.

1. _____

   _____

   a. French fries contain large amounts of oil and salt.
   b. Most milkshakes contain artificial colour and flavour, as well as large amounts of sugar.
   c. Hamburgers are made of fatty beef and served on buns made of white flour.
   d. Soft drinks are basically water, sugar and artificial flavours and dyes.

2. _____

   _____

   a. Bars of metal and even pieces of salt were once used as money.
   b. For thousands of years metal coins were the main source of exchange.
   c. Paper money permitted large amounts of value to be concentrated in easily portable form.
   d. Chequing accounts and then credit cards permitted greater versatility in exchange.
   e. Now "electronic money" — the electronic transfer of credit — permits instantaneous financial transactions and does away with most paperwork.

3. _____

   _____

   a. Car exhaust is a major source of acid rain.
   b. Vast amounts of farmland in North America have been paved over in the construction of streets, highways and parking lots.
   c. Leaded gasoline has produced high concentrations of lead in the air and soil along major traffic arteries.
   d. Carbon dioxide from the internal combustion engine is a major cause of the "greenhouse effect," which has already triggered disastrous changes of climate.

4. _____

   _____

   a. Single-glazed windows are a major source of heat loss.
   b. Heated air leaks rapidly through cracks around doors and windows.
   c. Many houses are insulated poorly or not at all.
   d. Furnaces that need adjustment, cleaning or a new filter can waste a great deal of energy.

5. _____

   _____

   a. Clearcutting of forests, in such places as Vancouver Island, turns old-growth forest into expanses of stumps and trimmed branches.
   b. Heavy rains in British Columbia wash away the soil from clearcut hills and mountains, polluting trout and salmon streams.
   c. Several species of wildlife have become endangered because of clearcutting in British Columbia.
   d. The dried bush left after clearcutting is a major fire hazard.

NAME _____

Topic Sentences: Exercise

Underline the statement that you believe would make the best topic sentence of a paragraph. Remember that opinion is usually stronger than pure fact.

1. a. Chainsaws make a great deal of noise.

   b. The chainsaw is the most dangerous tool that can be operated without a permit.

   c. Some chainsaws now have a chain brake to reduce bucking.

2. a. In Vancouver the lineups for movies are often a block long.

   b. I go to the movies almost every weekend.

   c. The convenience of watching television will never replace the thrill of going to the movies.

3. a. We used to shoot off firecrackers every Victoria Day.

   b. A cousin of mine lost the last joint of his index finger by holding onto a "TNT bomb" too long.

   c. Fireworks are still a hazard to children.

4. a. In today's economy, couples are choosing to have fewer children.

   b. Some families are large, while others are small.

   c. I have three brothers and four sisters.

5. a. Scuba diving can be a safe sport if you know what you are doing.

   b. A scuba diver I know almost drowned when he caught his foot on some old wire at the bottom of a river.

   c. The term "scuba" stands for "self-contained underwater breathing apparatus."

6. a. Ice cream is a popular food.

   b. I often eat ice cream as a snack.

   c. Ice cream contains more chemical additives than almost any other food we eat.

7. a. You see pickup trucks everywhere these days.

   b. City people drive pickup trucks for the same reasons they wear blue jeans and cowboy boots.

   c. Most pickup trucks get worse gas mileage than cars.

8. a. I saw wolf tracks one morning outside our cabin.

   b. The wolf is a large mammal of the northern forest.

   c. It is our prejudice against wolves that leads to their destruction.

9. a. I love hockey.

   b. Hockey is an extremely popular sport in Canada.

   c. Wayne Gretzky is the greatest player in the history of hockey.

10. a.   Medical drugs can be just as dangerous as street drugs.

    b.   I often take two aspirins when I'm getting a cold.

    c.   Drugs sometimes have a negative effect on the human body.

11. a.   In times of inflation, term life insurance is a better investment than straight life insurance.

    b.   I know many people who have life insurance.

    c.   My sister is an insurance agent in Edmonton.

12. a.   The bicycle is the most energy-efficient form of transportation ever invented.

    b.   Someone stole my ten-speed by cutting the chain.

    c.   CCM, Canada's oldest bicycle manufacturer, went out of business a few years ago.

13. a.   I love the smell of pine needles in the early morning.

    b.   Pine trees, like other conifers, keep their needles all year long.

    c.   The Austrian pine has become a favourite of landscapers because it resists urban pollution.

14. a.   Some novels are a bore.

    b.   The more concise a novel is, the more interesting it tends to be.

    c.   *Wuthering Heights* is the first novel we studied in Introduction to Literature.

15. a.   My mother likes a drink or two on a Saturday night.

    b.   Alcohol is a major cause of heart disease.

    c.   Wine is popular around the world.

16. a.   Every morning my grandmother fixed pancakes and sausages on the wood stove.

    b.   Many people are using wood stoves these days.

    c.   Heating with wood is cheap but time-consuming.

17. a.   The geranium is a well-known house plant.

    b.   There are several steps to propagating a geranium by cuttings.

    c.   Geraniums have an unusual smell.

18. a.   My family's lawnmower has a Briggs and Stratton four-cycle engine.

    b.   Lawnmowers are machines often used by homeowners.

    c.   A rotary-type power lawnmower can be dangerous both to the user and to bystanders.

19. a.   Over the last five years, the cost of bread has risen considerably.

    b.   Standard North American white bread is so devoid of nutrients that even mice won't eat it.

    c.   White bread is more popular than brown bread.

20. a.   Many people do crazy things these days.

    b.   Skydiving has been popular for a number of years.

    c.   Skydiving is one of the most dangerous sports ever invented.

NAME _____

Unity in "Main" Paragraphs: Exercise

Revise the following paragraphs to achieve unity of purpose. First underline the topic sentence. Then delete or replace any material that does not support it. If the paragraph does not reflect the topic sentence at all, revise the topic sentence.

1.   Many English teachers dress poorly. They wear blue jeans, corduroy jackets and sandals, as if they were still living in the sixties. Or they wear ragged pants and old baggy sweaters, as if they plan to dig in the garden after class. Or they wear shockingly mismatched colours — blue pants, brown jacket and purple tie — as if they were colour-blind. However, I once had a math teacher who looked even worse: he wore a blue and red plaid jacket, green bow tie and grey and white pinstriped trousers.

2.   Having to share a bedroom with my brother taught me how to get along with others. We each had to respect the other person's half of the room, for example, by not throwing our dirty clothes on each other's bed. We had to take turns cleaning and sweeping. We had to discuss what colour to paint the walls and which posters to put up. Most important of all, we had to be quiet when the other person was trying to study or sleep. As a result of this trying experience, I have learned that it is hard to get along with others. I'm glad that I have left home, because now all the fighting is over.

3.   The Olympics have become a fraud in which innocent victims — the athletes and the general public — are manipulated by business and government. In a cynical bid for world prestige, wealthy nations regiment and train their athletes almost like soldiers. These professional "amateurs" then walk off with the gold medals. In greedy schemes to attract tourists or to encourage construction and investment, municipalities such as Montreal lavish hundreds of millions on Olympic facilities — only to sink their own citizens in municipal debt for decades to come. And worst of all, in a spirit of crass hatred, terrorist groups hatch plans to murder the innocent and idealistic individuals who make the whole event possible: the athletes. Almost as bad is the illegal use of steroids by many of the contestants, both male and female.

4.   Many homeowners plant species of trees that cause problems later on. The Chinese elm that looks so attractive when it is ten feet high soon becomes a sickly monster dropping hundreds of little sticks onto the roof and lawn every time the wind blows. The silver maple that grows so conveniently fast soon becomes a rotten hulk ready to crush a roof or a parked car when a storm rips off its branches or even its trunk. (The sugar maple is much better, strong as well as attractive.) But the ailanthus, the so-called "tree of heaven" that is so delicately beautiful, clogs sewers with its greedy roots and every spring produces flowers that emit a sickening, rotten stench.

5.   The North American free trade pact is an excellent change for Canada's future. Trade will increase dramatically, although most factories now in this country will move south of the border where wages are lower. High-tech jobs, in particular, have already begun to flee, leaving Canada as a supplier of raw materials which will be turned into profits by other nations.

6.   Jogging is an excellent means to physical fitness. Heavy persons should avoid it, though, to prevent a heart attack caused by the sudden overload of violent action. Women are advised to avoid jogging, too, because in some cases the movement can cause the uterus to loosen — a potentially serious medical problem. Bone spurs in the foot, tearing of the Achilles' tendon and deterioration of the knee joint are other common hazards of jogging. Some joggers have even been killed by traffic, because people with jobs tend to run at night when visibility is poor. But all in all, jogging has become one of our most popular forms of exercise.

7.   Splitting wood is a very easy process. First you place a large piece of log on the ground, like a stump, for a chopping block. Then you put the sections of log onto it, which raises them to a convenient level. Whether you are using a splitting maul (a sort of sledge hammer with a blade) or wedges and a sledge hammer, the process is the same. First "trim" pieces off around the outside of the log, then split up the remaining centre. If you try to split a large log right across the middle, your maul or wedge will get stuck. In fact, it may get stuck even in the "trimming" process. When this happens, the best remedy is to use another wedge to get the first one out — but even the second one may get stuck, especially in an unsplittable wood such as elm. Many are the wood-splitters who have resorted to the most desperate remedy of all: the chainsaw.

8.   Driving to work is greatly preferable to taking the bus or subway. First of all, being enclosed by the car affords a privacy impossible to achieve in public transit. Secondly, no matter how long your car is stuck in a traffic jam, you can relax by turning on the radio and having a cigarette. Need we mention the fact that no transit connections, involving lineups in the heat or cold, need to be made by the motorist? And finally, although it is true that driving costs about five times as much as taking the transit, some people can deduct this cost as a business expense.

9.   Most cities do not have enough parkland. It is true that Vancouver has Stanley Park, while Toronto has its huge High Park and a network of exquisite ravine parks — an assembly of land so extensive that it places an undue burden on the taxpayer. But a scarcity of green areas in major cities reduces the quality of life. In parks children can play on the swings or splash in a wading pool while their parents read a newspaper. Pensioners can sit on a bench in the shade and smoke. Vagrants can stretch out on the grass for a nap. And young lovers can stroll down the path to find the privacy so rare in everyday urban life. Yes, we can almost say that the worth of a city is summed up by the quality of its park system.

10.   My favourite job was delivering pizza last summer. The restaurant I worked for made excellent pizza with homemade sausage and generous amounts of cheese. Every night I got a free pizza for supper, plus a soft drink. When five or eight pizzas were ready in their boxes, I would roar around town in my old Pontiac, waving at my friends on the street and collecting big tips from the customers. I also collected ten or twelve traffic tickets, because although I usually drove at twice the speed limit, the boss called me "Speedy" because he thought I was too slow. And one night the clutch went out, costing me $235 in repairs. The boss lent me his van in the meantime, but charged an exorbitant rate for mileage. He was the worst skinflint I have ever seen.

NAME _____

Improving "Thin" Paragraphs: Exercise

The most frequent weakness of paragraphs is "thinness." Add details to develop the following examples into vivid and convincing paragraphs. Write your new versions on a separate page, adding words, phrases or whole sentences of example, image or fact. Remember to follow, all the way through, the direction set by the topic sentence.

1. Having brothers or sisters is not easy. You have to tolerate each other's behaviour, and you must learn to share. But this effort is worthwhile, because it prepares you for your own family life in the future.

2. For many students, car ownership is not worth the expense. The car itself must be paid for, then maintained through costly visits to the garage. Gas and oil are increasingly expensive. Worst of all is the astronomical price of insurance.

3. Many parents dread rock concerts. They worry about the effect of the music on their children. They wonder what kind of people their children will meet. And they wonder whether their children will try new and forbidden experiences in the anonymity of the crowd.

4. American television drama has a heavy influence on our own. Many Canadians think CBC series are boring, and would rather turn to American sitcoms or police shows. Thus Canadian producers are tempted to win viewers by imitating the format and style of the American product.

5. This year's fashions for women are silly. Some of the clothes are unflattering. Others are uncomfortable. Why do we keep spending our hard-earned money on this trash?

6. School cafeteria food leaves something to be desired. It is heavy in starches, grease and sugar. It tends to be overcooked. Finally, it is often expensive.

7. Never before has music been so closely identified with the lives of its fans. People who dress in certain fashions and adopt a particular behaviour tend to favour one kind of music, or even a specific band. This music then becomes an expression of their lifestyle.

8. Computers now control many aspects of our lives. We come under their influence at school, at work and even at home.

9. A good holiday can shake us out of the old rut and show us new paths to follow. Going to other places stimulates the imagination. Meeting new people can teach us a great deal. Why stay at home all the time when there is so much to learn elsewhere?

10. Great numbers of people in other countries admire Canada and, if they had the chance, would move here. Canada is rich in natural resources. It is beautiful. It is relatively unpolluted. Its standard of living is among the highest in the world. Most importantly, it is a nation at peace.

EDITING: THE REST OF THE PROCESS

Now that we have done the "big" things, we turn to the "little" things. Now that we have zeroed in on our topic, our thesis and our audience, now that we have unleashed our ideas in a first draft or two, we move on to the finer points of editing.

This phase covers a lot of ground. Each "little" thing contributes, for good or for bad, to the total effect of an essay. Now we tinker with words, replacing a weak one with a strong one, a vague one with a concrete one. We mend ungrammatical sentences. We change punctuation. We reach for the dictionary. And at the very end we give our good copy the final quality control of proofreading.

Frankly, the process doesn't always follow this plan. We did a bit of word-tinkering and happened to see a few "errors" even in the "discovery" draft. We didn't make an issue of it then, for we didn't want to lose our train of thought. But we took a moment here and there to change a comma to a period or replace "there" with "their." And now that we're set to do all these things in the editing stage, the reverse may happen: a new idea may come rushing out of our mind — just the thing to round off a point that we thought we had already finished. So we may interrupt the "little" things we are doing and for a while move back to the "big" things.

But apart from these exceptions, we now turn our attention to editing — to the material in the following sections of this chapter. Different teachers will use the editing chapter in different ways. Some will select the sections they consider most important, to discuss and to practise in class with exercises. Other will select sections and exercises as needed, according to what they see in essays from the class. Still others will assign sections only to individuals who need a certain skill. Whatever the approach of your teacher, keep four things in mind:

1. Not everyone needs everything in this chapter. If your punctuation is already good, turn your attention to other things such as style.

2. Almost everyone does need certain parts of this chapter that cover chronic problem areas. The two most often needed are probably "Pronoun Reference" and "Agreement."

3. Whatever material your teacher assigns, and in whatever order, remember that you can also use this chapter as a reference. If you feel unsure about commas, look them up. If your teacher has written "cliché" beside your favourite expression, find that section and study it. If your last paper was "wordy," study "Editing for Economy." To find things use the table of contents, the index or simply the "Editing Guide" on the inside back cover.

   If you wish to do exercises on your own, note the answers given at the back of the book.

4. Above all, do not study all the editing sections *before* you write. If we tried to master the "little" before the "big," we'd never get to the first line of our first essay. Start writing, keep writing and apply each new skill as you learn it.

Editing for Economy

As the old saying tells us, talk is cheap. Most people can spend hours talking just for fun, and don't mind afterwards if they hardly remember what was said. But using words to pass the time is one thing; using them to convey a message is another.

In our more serious writing tasks, "talk" is not cheap at all. If we "spend" more than we need to, our message weakens or even dies under a mass of words. But when we use language economically, making every word contribute to the overall message, our writing grows in power. It is easily read, quickly understood and strongly felt.

Using words economically is crucial to other aspects of writing as well. The process of editing an early draft to make it more direct and concise automatically reduces errors in grammar, for the purpose of grammar is also to make our message clear. Give this matter a high priority: edit for economy *before* you edit for the aspects of grammar discussed later in this chapter.

The two worst enemies of economical writing are *wordiness* and *repetition*.

Wordiness

Make every word count. Get rid of those that do not.

A. ***Move swiftly to the main point of an essay*** rather than padding the introduction. Avoid wordy beginnings like this:

> Well, the question I am going to write about raises a lot of problems, and can easily be debated with many people taking either side.

Any question worth writing an essay about "can easily be debated," and in a debate people usually take "either side." The author has wasted words by telling us what we already know, but has neglected to tell us what we do not know: the topic. (See page 37 for more discussion of introductions.)

B. ***Stay on topic*** Give your reader all the explanation needed to understand your point, but do not waste time with information that does not explain it:

> Running promotes health. Excess weight that might someday cause a heart attack is burned off. After a few years, the heart becomes so strong that it may beat as few as 40 times per minute. The muscles become strong and flexible, which enables the runner to cope more easily with the tasks of everyday life. *And running is an inexpensive sport, costing only three or four cents per mile for shoes.*

Saving money has nothing to do with health. Even if the last sentence interests the reader, it wastes time. Let's remove it, then, and perhaps put it into a different paragraph whose purpose is to discuss the cost of running.

C. ***Be plain rather than fancy*** Avoid trying to make your writing seem more important than it is:

> With a college education one looks forward to gaining sufficient knowledge whereby one can assist in the development of society. This education can assist in enlightening the masses of society or even in the utilization of knowledge gained to establish an institution to further scatter abroad information.

(This author would make a fine speech writer for a politician who has to talk for two hours without promising anything.)

> The students who rioted were exterminated from school.

(This writer, pushing her vocabulary too hard, has had her subjects murdered instead of expelled.)

> The smells were sweet to his nasal palate.

(In other words, something smelled good to him. This writer should avoid decorating the message, and instead just deliver it.)

One of the surest ways to weaken your writing is to deliberately choose big words. Some students go through the first draft of an essay replacing small or plain words with long or fancy ones from the dictionary. "Think" becomes "ponder" or "cogitate"; "read" becomes "peruse"; "chew" becomes "masticate." In trying to seem bigger and better than it is, such writing is dishonest, sometimes ridiculous and usually diluted to the point of wordiness. Do use a big word when it fits best, but in general choose the smallest one that exactly fits your meaning.

(For related material, see "Jargon," page 75.)

D. ***Manipulate sentence structure to avoid wordiness*** One student wrote this sentence:

> The flavour of coffee tastes delicious to me. (8 words)

Since we know that coffee has a flavour, we can omit the first three words by using "coffee," rather than "flavour," as a subject.

> Coffee tastes delicious to me. (5 words)

We could further reduce the statement by using "I" as a subject.

> I enjoy coffee. (3 words)

Another student wrote this wasteful message:

The purpose of my composition is to give an explanation of why I do not drink strong beverages. The reason why I do not indulge in strong drink is based on my religious convictions. (34 words)

Note how the second sentence restates much of the first. Let's combine them:

This composition will explain how my religious convictions prevent me from indulging in strong drink. (15 words)

Many people find it easier to cut waste from the computer screen than from the page. Learn how your system deletes not only letters but also whole words, lines and passages.

For example in WordPerfect, press Ctrl-Del to instantly remove a whole word; Ctrl-End to remove a line of type; and Ctrl-PageDown to remove the whole page from the cursor down. Be bold: cut a passage to see if you need it, because the "undelete" function will instantly recall it if you did.

Once these moves are automatic, words shift constantly, moving into gaps left by vanishing waste. Passages shrink in size as they expand in power.

If your system has a thesaurus (see page 27), use it. This tool is so fast that you can afford to check all the flabby words of your discovery draft and replace them with short and strong ones.

Count words electronically. Most word-processing software allows you to do so quickly, either through the speller or through a separate menu. Consult your manual for the commands. Count often, to track your gains in economy.

Is a passage hopeless? Move it down the screen with your "Enter" key, put the cursor in the empty space, and do a quick new version not looking at the old one. If it comes out shorter and better, delete the original.

In summary, word processing frees you up to do the experimenting which is at the heart not only of economy, but of our whole "process" approach to writing.

So far we have less than half the original number of words, but the sentence is still wasteful. Why must "this composition" be mentioned when the reader already knows that this is the author's composition? Why mention "convictions" if they can be assumed from the religion? And why use "indulging in strong drink" instead of the single word "drinking," which in this passage would obviously refer to alcohol? Let's try a new sentence:

My religion keeps me from drinking. (6 words)

E. ***Avoid the passive voice, which is wordy and weak; use the active voice, which is concise and strong***

PASSIVE

The moose was shot by me. (6 words)

ACTIVE

I shot the moose. (4 words)

PASSIVE

The crash was witnessed by five people. (7 words)

ACTIVE

Five people witnessed the crash. (5 words)

Repetition

Saying something more than once is by far the most common way of wasting words. To improve your efficiency and your style, avoid repetition of fact and of vocabulary.

A. ***Avoid stating a fact more than once***

None of us will ever forget the true meaning of Christmas, *and I doubt that we ever will.*

The last seven words are useless because they repeat the beginning. Editing would have helped the writer to avoid this waste.

B. ***Avoid stating a fact that can easily be assumed from another fact you have given***

The chair is green *in colour.*

Since green is obviously a colour, let's get rid of those last two words.

My grandfather always told me, "You have to take a bit but you have to give a bit as well." *This little saying that he told me is still in my memory.*

We already know that the author remembers the saying, since she has just written it down for us. Let's save 12 words, then, by omitting the second sentence.

Radio, television and newspapers use repetitious language so often that certain useful expressions may come to mind as you write. *Avoid these self-repeaters and any like them:*

Photo courtesy of Suzanne Conrad.

absolutely perfect
at this point in time
completely surrounded
consensus of opinion
contributing factor
crisis situation
deeply profound
an emergency situation
end result
equally as good
final conclusion
for the purpose of
future generations to come
in actual fact
many different kinds
mutual agreement
mutual co-operation
my personal opinion
no other alternative
period of time
repeat again
return back
solid fact
sufficient enough reason
truly remarkable

C. *Avoid trying to strengthen a word that is already strong. Intensifiers such as "very," "highly" and "extremely" add nothing to words such as these:*

crucial	*miserable*
definite	*obese*
fascinating	*perfect*
horrible	*tragic*
impossible	*unique*
intriguing	*wonderful*

One person wrote this:

Training a cat to do tricks is *very* impossible.

How can something be more impossible than "impossible"? Let's remove "very" and remember that it is one of the most overused words in English.

D. *Avoid repeating words, especially long ones.* Your message will be more efficient and your style more pleasing.

A sign in a church parking lot proclaimed this:

Parking *permitted* by *permission* only. (5 words)

Naturally, "permission" implies that something is permitted. Let's omit the word:

Parking by *permission* only. (4 words)

The student who wrote this one may have been desperate to meet a required essay length:

The author's *imagination* is very *imaginative*. (6 words)

Not only is the sentence wasteful, but it is irritating to the reader, who is being led in circles. An obvious correction is to remove one of the repetitious words:

The author is very *imaginative*. (5 words)

The word "imaginative," though, is strong enough that we can omit "very":

The author is *imaginative*. (4 words)

Better yet, we could use "imagination" as the subject of a sentence that gets on to the next point:

The author's *imagination* is evident in the fresh imagery of the poem.

Finally, we must recognize that not all repetition is bad. Would the following passage be as effective if the main word occurred only once?

We drive *American* cars, read *American* books, listen to *American* music and go to *American* movies. If our habits do not change, we may someday even become *American*.

This repetition of "American" is deliberate, not accidental. Far from wasting words, it strengthens and emphasizes the message. Feel free to use repetition this way as a device of style — as long as you realize what you are doing.

A dictionary of synonyms, such as *Roget's Thesaurus*, will help you find replacements for a word repeated too often. It will also help you to choose the word that most accurately fits your meaning, a process that tends to make your writing more concise. Buy one of these useful books, available in paperback form, and keep it where you write.

E. *Repetition of similar sounds can be irritating, and in such cases should be avoided*

Population *density* of great *intensity* creates social chaos.

This new version avoids the unintentional rhyme:

High population *density* creates social chaos.

NAME _____

Economy: Diagnostic Exercise

Put an "X" beside each passage that clearly contains wordiness or undesirable repetition.

1. What can I say about culture in Toronto? Well, first it is a multi-cultural culture. _____

2. The front of the building faces north while the back faces south. _____

3. Advertisements give the user of credit cards the image of status and importance when credit cards are used. _____

4. Television is everywhere. _____

5. Proper sitting and standing are very crucial factors in having a healthy back. _____

6. Even though the novel *Erewhon* came under some criticism, the overall opinion was that of a positive one. _____

7. Unfortunately for women, when they get pregnant they have to cause delays in their occupational activities. _____

8. It's very fascinating to see Chinatown at night. _____

9. The difference between a room with plants in it and one with no plants is extremely obvious. _____

10. A fax machine is a machine that can be used as a telephone for transferring documents. _____

11. The house has 16 rooms. _____

12. Swimmers who vary their pace will get very exhausted. _____

13. When you first arrive in North America for the first time, you have an impression of cleanliness. _____

14. The piston is connected to a connecting rod which in turn is connected to the crankshaft. The crankshaft is connected to a large metal disk called the flywheel. _____

15. Vancouver has many drug pushers trying to push drugs. _____

16. People no longer had the freedom they used to have before. _____

17. It is hard to get a job. _____

18. In my opinion, I would advise anyone to choose a front-wheel-drive car. _____

19. Knowledge is crucial to the survival of the investor's investment. _____

20. I remember the sound of the "bang." _____

21. Language is a very fascinating thing. _____

22. Frequently we would often go to play against another team. _____

23. After ten minutes in the cold, I could hardly feel the existence of my limbs. _____

24. Walking is the safest exercise. _____

25. The evolution of the cinema has evolved over the last 70 years. _____

26. Pollution can mortally kill plants, animals and even people. _____

27. Today in industrialized nations, 80 percent of the people live in urban areas, while 20 percent live in rural areas. _____

28. We find that some teachers are negligent of criteria essential to the students' comprehension of a subject. _____

29. In Halifax many crimes happen frequently every day. _____

30. Greece is a beautiful country, with sunshine, olive groves and fantastic nudist beaches for those who like to bathe in the nude. _____

31. Winter is unique. _____

32. Having possession of an automobile is something many people would want. _____

33. Relationships are brief and short-lived. _____

34. The art of homemade wine making has been around for centuries. _____

35. My grandmother once broke her leg. As a result, she limps quite a bit when she is walking. _____

36. The best job I have ever had was at the London Public Library. It was the best job because it was interesting. There were a number of facts that made the job interesting. One of the major facts that made the job interesting was the people who worked at the library. _____

37. Smoking is a major risk in women's pregnancies. _____

38. People use contact lenses instead of glasses because of the positive benefits. _____

39. Economically speaking, eating at home is much more economical than eating out. _____

40. Under free trade, Canadian companies are producing fewer products. _____

NAME _____

Economy: Exercise, Level 1

To chop waste from your draft, examine each word. Does one repeat another? Does one even imply the meaning of another? If so, cross one out. Practise this strategy on the following expressions that were found in actual student essays.

1. truly astounded
2. in the future ahead
3. products produced by industries
4. the final result
5. good advantages
6. emotional feelings
7. cheap in cost
8. very fascinating
9. a true fact
10. at that moment in time
11. very unique
12. merge together
13. 8:00 a.m. in the morning
14. in the coming future
15. our surrounding environment
16. very crucial
17. many different countries
18. self-confidence in myself
19. and etc.
20. $150 dollars

21. quite obvious
22. very fascinating
23. extremely miserable
24. positive self-esteem
25. reappear again
26. easily without any trouble
27. very obvious
28. 600 hundred students
29. very chaotic
30. so crucial
31. rectangular in shape
32. a light green colour
33. quite impossible
34. in the month of June
35. light brown in colour
36. old age people
37. rather unique
38. no other alternative
39. competitive competition
40. in my own personal opinion

NAME _____

Economy: Exercise, Level 2

Improve the economy and style of the passages below by crossing out wordiness and repetition or by rewriting in the space provided. If no revision is needed, write "Correct" in the space.

Example: The room is square ~~in shape.~~

1. Arteries are blood vessels that carry blood.

    _____

    _____

2. The time was 9:30 p.m. at night.

    _____

    _____

3. Immigrants come to Canada with high aspirations of hope.

    _____

    _____

4. An older brother is like a second father.

    _____

    _____

5. Many teenagers' lives have been snuffed out by fatal car accidents.

    _____

    _____

6. Friends are a necessity that we need to have.

    _____

    _____

7. Gravelbourg, Saskatchewan, is a French community of 1800 hundred people.

    _____

    _____

8. Another useful item is the grape crusher, which crushes the grapes.

    _____

    _____

9. Living away from home is a very unique experience.

    _____

    _____

10. The cost of having a television set is expensive.

    _____

    _____

11.   Our public school was a big school.

_____

_____

12.   I have noticed a change in my mental attitude.

_____

_____

13.   My boss was obese.

_____

_____

14.   I could, at this point, carry on and stretch this paper to maybe ten pages, but I'm sure you could easily recognize the padding.

_____

_____

15.   Computers have replaced files.

_____

_____

16.   With a word processor you can erase any paragraph that you don't like and rewrite it again.

_____

_____

17.   The oil vat machines have openings which, when opened, allow the oil to flow into a filtering machine, which filters the oil.

_____

_____

_____

18.   One disadvantage of the assembly line is that the worker on the line is dehumanized and not treated as a living person. Manufacturers and business executives are turning blue-collar workers into things.

_____

_____

19.   There are different credit cards for every type of purchase. Some examples of credit cards are major credit cards, store credit cards and even gasoline credit cards.

_____

_____

20.   The subway must be the worst way to travel around town. Several times I've been literally pulled out of a subway car. On one occasion when I was pulled out of the subway car, at Yonge and Bloor, the man who pulled me out of the subway car ripped my shirt. When the doors began to close, I retaliated and gave him a punch in the face.

_____

_____

_____

NAME _____

Economy: Exercise, Level 3

Improve the economy and style of the passages below by crossing out wordiness and repetition or by rewriting in the space provided.

1.   The heavy lifting was fine with me, but what I really hated was the dirt on the clutches. It was unbelievable to see so much dirt on the clutches. I was always working with the dirt, having only a laboratory coat protecting me from the dirt. My pants were black all the time from working with the dirt.

_____

_____

_____

_____

_____

_____

_____

2.   The sea was calm as I skimmed swiftly and silently over the water's surface on my sailboard, along the scenic coast of an enormously incredible panorama. On one side of me there was an enormously wide and long gold-coloured sandy beach, with huge mountains in the background. On the other side of me was nothing but clear water that seemed never to end.

_____

_____

_____

_____

_____

_____

_____

3.   For my English assignment, I am supposed to describe the best or worst job I have ever had. The topic of the essay has made me think. What is a best or worst job? What has been my best or worst job? I have pondered on the topic for a while, and have come to the conclusion that there is no best or worst job. Any job can be either enjoyed or hated, because all jobs possess both good and bad points. In other words, a job is what you make it.

_____

_____

_____

_____

_____

_____

_____

_____

_____

4. When a fluorescent light is first turned on, the light seems to slowly float through the room. The light from a fluorescent bulb travels at the same speed as the light from an incandescent bulb, but it does not seem to be as responsive. The light from a fluorescent tube is produced by the emission of radiation from the tube. The light that is produced seems to be a pale, dull-blue light. There is very little heat generated from the tube, but a slight humming can be heard from within the tube. The life of a fluorescent tube is much longer than that of an incandescent bulb. The average bulb would last six to twelve months, but most tubes last three to five years.

_____

_____

_____

_____

_____

_____

_____

_____

_____

_____

5. In earlier times people could spend only what they had, but with credit cards the line of credit was introduced. This line of credit is the maximum limit of spending on a credit card. This problem worsened with credit cards that were labelled as gold or platinum because of the unlimited line of credit. Some people have so many different types of credit cards that they need a new wallet to carry them. When customers have a credit card, they can buy merchandise even if they have no money. Does this seem right? All they have to do is just say, "Charge it!"

_____

_____

_____

_____

_____

_____

_____

_____

_____

_____

_____

Editing for Honesty in Language

Good writing is honest. People have many reasons to write. Some want to reveal facts; others want to conceal them. Some want to clarify an issue; others want to cloud it. Most writers want to convince their readers of something, which is a natural human urge. But while some argue by appeals to reason, others bypass this process to play on the reader's emotions.

These attempts to avoid real communication may seem almost acceptable in our world of advertising campaigns and political propaganda, for our exposure to such abuses has been immense. Yet, as you will see in the examples that follow, dishonesty produces not only weak and wasteful writing, but sometimes even dangerous writing.

As you study the clichés, euphemisms, bias words and jargon that follow, you may notice that the categories overlap: euphemisms and bias words tend to be clichés, and jargon tends to be euphemism. Perhaps the reason for this is the very fact that, in different ways, they are all dishonest. *Edit them out of your writing.*

Clichés

A large part of writing honestly is being original. We all know that handing in another's essay as our own is a serious offence, and that anyone who copied another person's book for publication would end up in court. Yet many of us cheerfully repeat other people's expressions every time we write. These worn-out sayings are termed *clichés*, after the French word for a printing plate that mass-produces copies of an original.

Every time we write "sadder but wiser," "few and far between," "a sight for sore eyes" and "hit the nail on the head," we are lazily avoiding the work of being original. Like parrots, we are letting our language slip into preestablished channels, a process that discourages real thought and therefore bores the reader.

It must have taken real imagination for the first person to say for the first time, "I've got butterflies in my stomach." The first listener was probably dazzled by this new image that so clearly described nervousness. But today, when we hear those words for the thousandth time, we don't even think about butterflies. We may not think about anything at all, because repetition has deadened us.

Other clichés describe situations that no longer exist. A sailor once had to "know the ropes," but do we? If not, why do we write it to describe our job driving a taxi or programming computers? People still say "Hold your horses," though for decades we have driven cars. The Black Plague once killed a third of Europe; with today's antibiotics we no longer fear the disease, yet still avoid things "like the plague."

When we no longer "see" what a cliché means, we will unknowingly stick it into ridiculous situations. One student wrote, "Right off the bat, nine seconds into the hockey game, a goal was scored by the guest team." We might be so numbed by the cliché that we do not "see" its image. But if we do, we might wonder what a bat is doing in a hockey game. This example, like the others above, shows the harm that clichés can do: *they keep us from thinking.* For that reason, *avoid them all.*

Are clichés automatic? To answer that question, see how many of the following expressions you can complete without really thinking:

1. *birds of a* _____
2. *blind as a* _____
3. *by hook or by* _____
4. *cool as a* _____
5. *diamond in the* _____
6. *hook, line and* _____
7. *in the nick of* _____
8. *last but not* _____
9. *make a mountain out of a* _____
10. *raining cats and* _____

NAME _____

Clichés: Exercise

Here are some clichés that have appeared in student writing. First identify them, then substitute your own words to fit the meaning. If you see a passage that contains no clichés, write "Correct" in the space.

Example: The first day at work I was ~~bright-eyed and bushy-tailed.~~ *enthusiastic*

1.   I grabbed the front of the toboggan, holding on for dear life.

   _____

   _____

2.   There was never a dull moment at work. I was on my toes day in and day out.

   _____

   _____

3.   The next year I played defence on the soccer team.

   _____

   _____

4.   When June rolled around, Standard Tube hired me and I was ready to put my shoulder to the wheel.

   _____

   _____

5.   The government tried to battle inflation but the unemployment crisis was bursting at its seams like a swollen dam.

   _____

   _____

   _____

6.   Calculus was the last straw. I was bored stiff.

   _____

   _____

7.   Two of my bosom buddies and I found a neat little apartment overlooking English Bay.

   _____

   _____

8.   In this day and age, family members need to touch base with each other each and every day.

   _____

   _____

9.   Rush hour in Toronto fascinates me. The buses and subways cars are jammed like sardines.

   _____

   _____

   _____

10. My new interest in fitness is mind-boggling, because in the past I avoided exercise like the plague.

_____

_____

11. The hustle and bustle of the city takes it toll, and the individual can only grin and bear it.

_____

_____

12. My three weeks in the woods made me realize that life is not a bowl of cherries.

_____

_____

13. I passed my ordeal with flying colours.

_____

_____

14. The bottom line is that parents should be on their toes whenever their children are glued to the tube.

_____

_____

15. Marsha's schools, clothes and even friends were chosen by her parents.

_____

_____

16. Our country is going down the drain. The government is pulling the wool over our eyes, and the public is on the short end of the stick.

_____

_____

_____

17. Day in and day out, we are glued to the television set.

_____

_____

18. A great book shows the whole world and its problems in a nutshell.

_____

_____

19. I was spending money left, right and centre for my entertainment.

_____

_____

20. With spring just around the corner, I'm thinking about a summer job.

_____

_____

21. Life isn't a bed of roses.

_____

_____

22. I was three years old, ready to take on the trials and tribulations of nursery school.

_____

_____

_____

23. It's in my blood to get up and go.

_____

_____

24. I get sick and tired of working the bugs out of the system each and every time.

_____

_____

25. Canada is really and truly at a standstill. It's time to get the lead out, and jump-start the economy.

_____

_____

26. If a few individuals can get away with murder on their tax returns, why should the rest of us toe the line?

_____

_____

27. To think that reckless drivers keep their licences is hard to swallow.

_____

_____

_____

28. Many pets are spoiled rotten.

_____

_____

_____

29. Each and every night I burn the midnight oil.

_____

_____

_____

30. Canada has become a mere imitation of the United States. It is about time for Canadians to stand on their own two feet and start making waves.

_____

_____

Euphemisms

When we use one word instead of another, we choose not only between meanings but also between feelings. Why do we call one person "slim" while we call another "skinny"? Is it because we like the "slim" one better?

Many people think of language as a code, as an objective set of meanings that convey objective truth. But in fact language is as human as we are, reflecting all our emotions and irrationalities. The experienced essayist knows that the same set of "facts" can be made to sound good or bad, cheerful or gloomy, plain or fancy, approving or condemning, all depending on what words he or she dresses them in.

Consider the words people choose to describe their professional roles. Since we all want to feel worthwhile, a janitor is now a "maintenance engineer," a garbage worker is a "sanitary engineer," and a barber is a "hair stylist." An undertaker, who at the time of Shakespeare was called a "grave digger," is now a "mortician" (rhymes with "physician"). Terms like these, which make things seem better than they were, are called *euphemisms*.

Companies naturally hope that we, the consumers, will feel good about their products and services. Euphemisms do the job. When ground beef is "Salisbury steak," when lawnmowing is "vegetation management," when ink is "writing fluid," when glasses are "eyewear," when used cars are "pre-owned" and when hairdressing is "hair sculpture," we spend and companies profit.

Since organizations want us to like them, they choose carefully the words that describe their actions. Companies no longer "fire" but "de-hire" us. They no longer "lose money" but experience "negative economic growth." Governments no longer ask for new taxes, but only "revenue enhancement measures." Armies never "attack" or "kill," but "control" or even "pacify" (literally "make peaceful") the enemy. And now countries making war no longer indulge in propaganda or lies, but only "disinformation."

. . . . I am conducting an exhaustive experimental study into a whole myriad of perceptual stimuli and the apparent effect on the gastronomic behavior patterns of the average householder. I am not just 'stuffing myself in front of the tube.'

Courtesy of The Globe and Mail, Toronto.

For years this desire of individuals and groups to improve their image through euphemisms has grown. In the nineties, though, a new and controversial twist has appeared. We all know that words naming groups of people can be loaded, and that reasonable persons have never used the bad words for those of other races, cultures or gender. But now word choice has become a political struggle. Groups that have felt marginalized, shut out of economic or social or political power, are now using and demanding language that is *"politically correct."*

A whole code of terms has emerged. People who were once "disabled" are now "differently abled." Those who were once rape or incest "victims" are now rape or incest "survivors." Those once said to be "dying" of AIDS are now "persons living with AIDS."

Even names of racial and ethnic groups are changing. For example, those once called "Indians," then later called "native peoples," are now increasingly called "first nations people" — to improve their status by reminding others who was here first.

Considerate persons normally respect the wishes of minority groups by using the suggested terminology. After all, such words are meant to convey kindness and respect, in a society in which everyone belongs to a minority.

Lately, though, some people have grown uneasy about the whole trend, sensing extremism and even totalitarianism in language. The idea of saying "herstory" for "history" or "animal companion" for "pet" reminds them of George Orwell's nightmare novel *1984*, in which a police state literally rewrites the dictionary so that words like "liberty" and "democracy," which once made rebellion thinkable, are now forgotten. Those who object to the new "political correctness" in our own society accuse its proponents, who at first only wanted to improve their image, of now using censorship to tyrannize over others.

So who is right? That is for each one to decide. As an essayist, you can feel good about writing some euphemisms out of kindness to others. Your grandparents may not be "old" but merely "senior citizens." However, there may come a time when you sense you are not writing the truth. When that happens, you must make your own decision, one that is at the same time linguistic and political.

NAME _____

Euphemisms: Exercise

All the following terms are euphemisms. Circle those you would feel comfortable using in an essay, and in the space explain why. Cross out those you would not use in an essay, and in the space explain why. (Of course there is no set of "correct" answers; this exercise is meant to encourage your own awareness and free choice.)

1.   air support (for "bombing")

2.   animal companion (for "pet")

3.   between jobs (for "unemployed")

4.   big (for "fat")

5.   continuing incident (for "uncontrolled disaster")

6.   correction (for a "drop" in the stock market)

7.   developing nations (for "poor nations")

8.   expectorate (for "spit")

9.   eye fashions (for "glasses")

10.   frank exchange of views (for "argument")

11.   golden agers (for "old people")

12. hearing-impaired (for "deaf")

13. involuntary actions (for "firings")

14. low-income neighbourhood (for "slum")

15. negative savings (for "debt")

16. pass away (for "die")

17. perspire (for "sweat")

18. selected out (for "fired")

19. senior citizens (for "old people")

20. sleeping together (for "having sex")

21. special child (for "mentally handicapped" child)

22. starter home (for "small house")

23. terminate (for "kill")

24. upscale (for "expensive")

25. visually impaired (for "blind")

NAME _____

Euphemisms and Their Opposite: Words Biased
Pro or Con: Exercise

If euphemisms can distort truth by making things look better than they are, negative bias words can distort truth by making things look worse than they are. In this exercise practise identifying both extremes, so you can more easily detect and avoid excess bias in your own writing.

Here are 25 words that can be used for "underweight." Write each in the column where you think it belongs. Use the dictionary if necessary.

bony, cadaverous, delicate, emaciated, fleshless, gangling, gaunt, haggard, lanky, lean, raw-boned, scrawny, skeletal, skinny, slender, slight, slim, spare, spindly, svelte, thin, underfed, undernourished, underweight, wizened.

VERY NEGATIVE	NEGATIVE	NEUTRAL	POSITIVE	VERY POSITIVE

Here again are 25 words that can be used for "overweight." Write each in the column where you think it belongs. As above, use the dictionary if necessary.

beefy, big, bulky, burly, chubby, chunky, corpulent, elephantine, fat, fleshy, heavy-set, obese, overweight, paunchy, plump, ponderous, portly, pudgy, rotund, stocky, stout, thick-set, tubby, well-fed, well-padded

VERY NEGATIVE	NEGATIVE	NEUTRAL	POSITIVE	VERY POSITIVE

Jargon

Our society adores technology. Now that we humans have walked on the moon, explored the ocean floor and cooked dinner in three minutes with electronic rays, we find ourselves speaking and writing like the technicians we admire.

Even in nonscientific fields like the arts, many of us borrow technical or showy words to dress up the message. Those who prefer the direct approach describe such language as "bafflegab," "technobabble" or "gobbledygook." Its more common name is *jargon*.

Of course there is a place for technical words. Computer engineers could hardly discuss their work without speaking of "megabytes," "motherboards," "macros" and "merge codes." But now the rest of us cannot hold a meeting without "interfacing" through "input" and "output," and without "accessing" data that falls within our "parameters." A visitor from Mars, hearing this language, might think that humans, themselves, had turned into machines.

At its extreme, jargon takes on the impenetrable and ugly quality of this example which the linguist Mario Pei found at "a great university":

The functional methodology shall be based on an inter-disciplinary process model, which employs a lateral feed-back syndrome across a sanction-constituency interface, coupled with a circular-spiral recapitulatory function for variable-flux accommodation and policy modification.[1]

Do you know what the passage means? Perhaps you were not supposed to. One Toronto executive admits to writing short and plain reports when he has something to say, but long and fancy ones when he does not. On those occasions he seeks not only technical terms but any other intimidating and unclear language, such as "cognizant" for "aware," "impact negatively upon" for "harm," and "in the foreseeable future" for "soon."

Jargon can make a subject appear so important or difficult that the average person will leave it to the experts. In this way institutions such as business and government can hide their true objectives, and professionals such as lawyers and tax accountants can force us to buy their services because, on our own, we cannot understand official documents.

As essay writers we can do better. When we actually *need* technical words, let's use them (making sure to define any term the audience may not know). But in nontechnical applications, jargon leads to wordiness, clichés and euphemisms. It is not clear or even honest. *Avoid it.*

(See page 15 for the related topic of *audience*.)

[1]Mario Pei, *Double Speak in America* (Hawthorn Books, Inc.), © 1973 Hawthorn. All rights reserved.

NAME _____

Jargon: Exercise

Here is some widespread jargon. Translate each example into plain, honest English, using the dictionary or thesaurus where necessary.

Example: due to the fact that   *because* _____

1.   to access   _____

2.   on the back burner   _____

3.   ballpark figure   _____

4.   the bottom line   _____

5.   decision-making process   _____

6.   dialoguing   _____

7.   discussant   _____

8.   feedback   _____

9.   guesstimate   _____

10. hopefully   _____

11. to impact on   _____

12. input, output   _____

13. insightful   _____

14. to interface   _____

15. limited time factor   _____

16. low profile, high profile   _____

17. maximize, finalize, utilize   _____

18. a must   _____

19. optimum   _____

20. parameters   _____

21. parenting   _____

22. at this point in time   _____

23. the principal thrust   _____

24. profit-wise (and most other "-wise" words)   _____

25. shortfall   _____

26. societal   _____

27. stagflation   _____

28. in terms of   _____

29. time frame   _____

30. window of opportunity   _____

Editing for Appropriate Language

As we will see in the next section, "Editing for Complete Sentences," people tend to write as they speak. If you say "could of" and "should of," as most people do in conversation, you might use these same expressions when you write. Though many listeners will consider "could of" and "should of" perfectly correct when you *say* them, readers will certainly view those same words as errors when you *write* them.

Yet it is not accurate to label "could of" as wrong and "could have" as right. Rather, the one form may be *appropriate* to informal speech while the other is *appropriate* to writing. The important thing is not to moralize, considering your own dialect "good" or "bad," but to speak in language appropriate for your listeners and **write in language appropriate for your readers.**

This means that in essays, reports and business letters you will use the same "standard" English that other writers use. Language is a code; you would not try out new dots and dashes while communicating in the Morse Code, so why would you put "nonstandard" expressions into your writing?

Appropriate language in writing also means avoiding the slang that seems so natural when you speak. Napoleon's invasion of Russia may have been a failure, but in your history essay he did not make a "boo boo," "take a spaz" or "get trashed."

Though no linguist would call "standard" English "better" than nonstandard, everyone knows how important a tool it is for success in our society. The main thing is to be practical. Investigate the material that follows, to make sure you are using the standard and appropriate language that will communicate best when you write.

Better yet for the long term, cultivate the reading habit to avoid the trap of writing the way you speak. The more "standard English" you put through your head in the form of other peoples' writing, the more easily and surely you can produce your own. (See page 187 for suggested reading matter.)

Finally, as with other editing, revise for appropriate language *after* you have got the content of your essay safely down on paper.

Standard and Nonstandard English

"Standard" English is what you normally read in a book or periodical, and what well-read persons nor-mally say in conversation. Though "nonstandard" expressions such as "anywheres" or "can't hardly" may be accepted or even expected by some people in conversation, almost all readers — and especially teachers — view nonstandard usages in an essay, report or formal letter simply as errors.

Common sense tells us that although "nonstandard" English may be as appropriate in some situations as "standard" English is in others, if we wish our writing to succeed we must use the standard code of expressions that readers expect. In the list that follows, identify any nonstandard expressions you use in writing, and instead use the "standard" equivalents:

NONSTANDARD	STANDARD
ain't	*is not, am not, etc.*
alot	*a lot*
anyways, anywheres, somewheres	*anyway, anywhere, somewhere*
can't hardly	*can hardly*
could of, might of, must of, should of, would of	*could have, might have, must have, should have, would have*
different than	*different from*
disinterested (meaning "not interested")	*uninterested* ("disinterested" means fair or impartial)
enormity (meaning "hugeness")	*enormousness* (an "enormity" is a terrible wrongdoing)
enthused	*enthusiastic*
hadn't ought	*should not, ought not*
in regards to	*in regard to*
irregardless	*regardless*
_____ *is when*	_____ *is*
a long ways	*a long way*
me and the gang	*the gang and I*
most all	*most, almost all*
the reason is because	*the reason is that*
real good	*very good*
I seen, they seen	*I saw, they saw*
this here	*this*
try and	*try to*
where you are at	*where you are*
youse	*you, all of you*

Slang and Colloquialisms

Everyone knows what slang is: racy, colourful and often poetic language used by people who want to appear up to date or in the know. And colloquialisms are a less flashy kind of slang. Although such language can be vivid and economical, it is more appropriate to a conversation between friends than to a serious piece of writing. How would you like to read a whole book of what follows?

> Well, I was so stiff I nearly turkeyed off from the line, but I decided to wait. I pulled out from the line at 4 a.m. and hailed a limber on the road. Fritz landed a daisycutter and the transport driver done his block and took his hook. He absolutely dropped his bundle, and, to make matters worse, I had started off with a duck's breakfast, but I saw a cookhouse and decided to give it a pop for a binder.[2]

Yes, the passage is written in English, but a restricted English of another time and place. If you had been a New Zealander fighting in World War I, you would understand it. Even Canadian slang, though, can escape us:

> Totally stavers, Joe Buggins blew a bine before he submerged for a zizz.[3]

If you were in the Royal Canadian Navy during World War II, you might recall that "stavers" meant "drunk," "Joe Buggins" was a general name for a sailor, to "blow a bine" was to smoke a cigarette, to "submerge" was to lie down for a sleep and a "zizz" was a nap. The problem, though, is that you were *not* in the Royal Canadian Navy during World War II.

The lesson is obvious: avoid slang when writing for the general reader. You might exclude not only people of a different era or place by the slang that comes naturally to you, but even your next-door neighbour of a different age, background or occupation.

Vagueness is yet another reason to avoid slang in essays, reports and business letters. How can we accurately interpret an expression like the seventies' "far out," which can refer to qualities ranging all the way from good to bad?

Other slang words, such as "goon" and "pig," are so emotionally loaded that they convey a bias unfit for serious writing. Just as bad, many slang expressions are clichés that replace original thought by rushing automatically to mind.

Colloquial language is not quite as vivid as slang and not as restrictive, but is too chatty for essays, reports and business letters. It is the breezy language of conversation, of sports reporting, of disk jockeys and of the lovelorn columns ("If hubby doesn't toe the line for a sweetie like you, he's the dumbest ninny around"). You hardly want to sound like this, or like someone telling stories in a pub, when you are writing an analysis of the symbolism in T. S. Eliot's poems or assessing the future of Confederation. *Instead, choose language appropriate to the situation.*

Finally, putting quotation marks around slang and colloquial expressions does not so much tame them for serious writing as merely call attention to them. Avoid examples like this:

> I believe that our police force is not just a "dinky" one.

A few of the slang and colloquial terms that follow have stayed current for many years; others are long out of date but still used by people who have not changed since learning them; still others will become dated by the time you see them here. Therefore, consider the lists as only a demonstration of what extremely informal language is like, so that you can detect other examples when you write them. The division between slang and colloquialisms is, of course, arbitrary, because even dictionaries disagree as to the status of expressions.

SLANG	COLLOQUIALISMS
bad (amazing)	*blab*
bummer	*brainer*
cheesy	*chill out*
couch potato	*cool*
ego trip	*cop*
geek	*to eyeball*
hardhead	*hangup*
head honcho	*heavy*
humongous	*hick*
nerd	*kind of, sort of*
pig (police officer)	*loser*
psyched	*nitty gritty*
rad	*OK or okay*
to rip off	*pal*
toast	*slob*
to trash	*snow job*
turkey (person)	*street smart*
wasted	*take a spaz*
wicked (amazing)	*thug*
wimp	*veg out*

[2] A. E. Strong of Auckland, New Zealand, quoted by Eric Partridge, *Slang To-day and Yesterday*, 4th ed. (London: Routledge and Kegan Paul Ltd., 1970), p. 287.

[3] *Toronto Daily Star*, June 9, 1945, quoted by Mark M. Orkin, *Speaking Canadian English* (New York: David McKay Co., Inc., 1970), pp. 214–15.

NAME _____

Slang and Colloquialisms: Exercise

Cross out the slang and colloquial language in the passages that follow, and replace it with terms appropriate to a serious essay, report or business letter. If a passage is already free of slang and colloquialisms, write "Appropriate" after it.

Example: My friends thought stealing was ~~okay.~~ *fine*

1. In English class there's this one guy who has a mouth like a hippo, but he's an okay person.

2. When a computer makes a boo boo it's usually a biggie.

3. Pressure drives students bananas.

4. Stopping at the traffic light I noticed a black-and-white pig machine beside me.

5. I am a diehard Leaf fan even when my team is shellacked to the tune of 10–1.

6. Max Beerbohm is not a very serious writer.

7. Some people think gambling is an alright thing to do, but it turns me right off.

8. Saccharin, which was the most widely used artificial sweetener, was shot to pieces after a study showed toxicity in rats.

9. I'm really into the outdoors.

10. When I was in grade school, having the most friends and belonging to the coolest group was where I was at.

11. Mr. Ebert is a really neat old man to talk to if you're into stuff like war stories.

12. My friend drank a little too much of Mexico's pure, clean water and had to spend a whole day in the bathroom by his lonesome.

13. At a party, I feel separated from other people because they begin to feel "high" while I am still "straight."

14. Yesterday in history we yakked for a whole hour about Hitler and his hangups.

15. Don't gripe and beef, just get with it.

16. In a game between Toronto and Philadelphia a few years ago, a Leaf player was sent to the penalty box for fighting. The fans at Philadelphia went "nuts." They tried to get at the Leaf player while he was in the "cooler." They threw beer cans, shoes and eggs at him. They even tried to break the protective glass around the "cooler" so they could get hold of the poor Leaf player. Finally the cops were called to escort the helpless guy to his dressing room and safety from the mild-mannered hockey fans.

17. Many people put down snowmobiles.

18. Usually when one of my friends calls to shoot the breeze I'm up to my eyeballs in homework.

19. Nuclear plants scare the hell out of me.

20. To put it in the extreme, my job was the pits.

21. For a person who exercises regularly, physical work is a "piece of cake."

22. The Leafs are a scared bunch of guys trying not to look dumb.

23. Almost anyone can get married.

24. Well, I took care of the first guy who hassled me but the other two I couldn't handle.

25. My friends are now hooked on the booze and blame it all on their parents.

26. Boy! Christmas is work.

27. To change your image, you must be willing to trash part of your existing wardrobe.

28. Had Darcy not hurt Elizabeth's pride, they could have got it on a lot sooner, but then Jane Austen wouldn't have had anything to write about.

29. By 7 a.m. I was busting my butt down the dirty rows of the tobacco field.

30. Many people who play electronic games don't know what's going on. How many times have you watched people playing a game shout, "All right!" when really they got blown away?

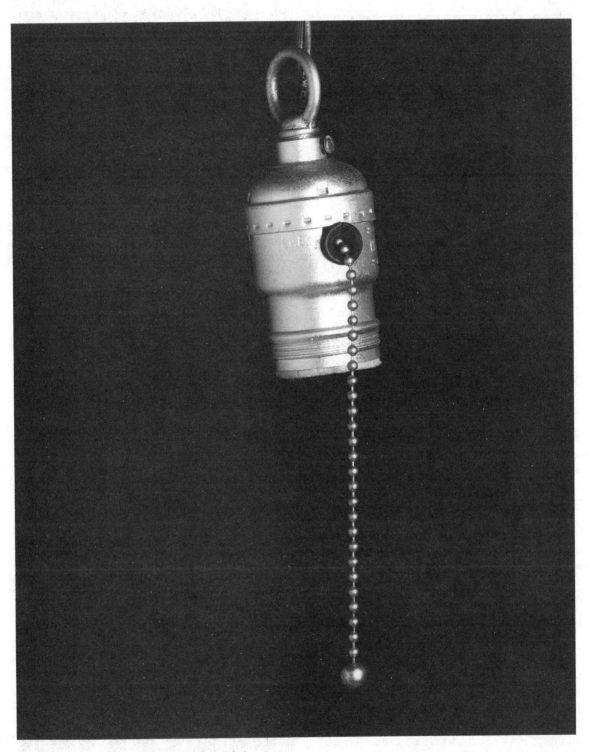

Photo courtesy of Johnson/Camerique Inc. International.

Editing for Complete Sentences

People often talk like this:

"Hungry?"
"Yeah."
"Me too."
"S'noon."
"Got class?"
"No. Cafeteria's kinda busy now."
"So what? Hey, gotta couple bucks on ya?"
"Maybe. Just a minute. Yeah, here."
"Thanks. Let's eat."
"Remember that five from last week?"
"Uh, yeah. Pay ya back next week, eh?"
"Hmmmmm."

Seeing a conversation like this on the page, we recognize its fragmentary nature: a great many words are *left out*. But is there any doubt that our two speakers understand each other? Their words are only one part — maybe the smallest part — of their real communication. As any actor learning a script will realize, those words are accompanied by raisings and lowerings of the voice, by posture, gesture and other body language, and by facial expressions so obvious that a small child could "read" them. And if either person does fail to catch something, a quick "What?" will clear things up. The reason, of course, is that *the speakers are in the same place.*

When they go home to write their essay for English or history or economics, though, they will encounter a totally different situation. If they write as they speak, they may produce "sentences" like these found in student essays:

A love affair that was doomed.
New highways leading to smaller cities.
Although his children encouraged him to retire.
Medicine and law, two rewarding fields.

The reader of these partial statements will hear no voice, see no gesture, ask no question. All he or she will have are these symbols on the page — and in their incomplete form these symbols are not enough to make the message clear.

No wonder, then, that readers expect complete sentences. This tradition is so strong — at least in serious explanatory writing such as essays, reports and formal letters — that an incomplete sentence (or *sentence*

fragment) is usually perceived as a serious error. Here and there we may accept a *fragment* that is deliberately placed for emphasis. But probably the most important step in editing errors out of a manuscript is to revise all accidental fragments into complete sentences.

A word about technical terms: Although technical words can be a nuisance, some are essential. Just as electricians need terms like "diode" and "capacitor" to talk about their subject, we will need a few terms to talk about ours. You know the most important ones already. Learn the rest as you study this section, because you'll need them in later sections.

The essential parts of a complete sentence are one subject and one verb. The subject is what the sentence is about, and the verb tells what the subject does or is.

SUBJECT	VERB
Cars	*pollute.*
Snow	*fell.*
Roger	*sleeps.*
Jane	*studies.*
They	*danced.*
We	*won.*
Honesty	*pays.*
Time	*flies.*

The Subject

The *subject* is a noun or pronoun. A *noun* is a person, place or thing, while a *pronoun* is a word such as "she" or "they" which substitutes for a noun. A sentence with a pronoun as the subject can be "complete" even if we don't know what the pronoun refers to:

They danced.

Of course if nearby sentences do not inform us clearly who "they" are, another error is made: faulty pronoun reference (see pages 128 to 129).

Some subjects, such as "honesty" and "time" in our examples, do not have a physical form. Yet these abstract nouns are "things" because they do exist and we can state what they do:

Honesty pays.
Time flies.

The Verb

The *verb* is usually described as an action word such as "danced" and "flies" in our list of examples. But even in the sentence "Roger sleeps," where there is no obvious action, the verb still tells what the subject *does*. **Other verbs, such as "is," "am" and "are," tell not what the subject *does* but what it *is*:**

Canada *is* the second-largest country in the world.

I *am* a Nova Scotian.

Women and men *are* equal in law.

In statements like these, words of explanation are added to the verb. The verb plus all the words that complete its meaning are together called the *predicate*. We could enlarge our definition of the sentence, then, by saying that a **complete sentence has a subject and a predicate.** Yet that predicate means nothing without its key part, the verb:

Canada the second-largest country in the world.

I a Nova Scotian.

Women and men equal in law.

Some verbs are made of more than one word. Instead of saying "We *won*," we could say "We *have won*." Or we could substitute any of the following and many more:

had won	*may win*
had been winning	*might win*
were winning	*might have won*
could win	*might be winning*
could have won	*might have been winning*
could have been winning	*should win*
did win	*would win*
have been winning	*shall win*
are winning	*will win*
do win	*will have won*
can win	*will have been winning*

Each of these, like a one-word verb, can be called a *complete verb,* and in the sentence each functions like a one-word verb.

Directions and *commands* are exceptions to the normal sentence pattern, since often they have only a verb. The unwritten subject is "understood":

Stop! (*You* stop!)

Begin. (*You* begin.)

Drive carefully. (*You* drive carefully.)

NAME _____

Completing Sentences: Exercise

Add a noun or pronoun to form a subject and thus complete the sentence. Circle the complete verb.

1. A hungry _____ ate my lunch.
2. A large _____ ran down our street.
3. My _____ always chases cars.
4. _____ pollute the air.
5. _____ are usually green.
6. An old _____ slept on the park bench.
7. _____ hopes to be the next prime minister.
8. A _____ attacked the swimmer.
9. My best _____ is Greek.
10. A large _____ climbed the tree.
11. Seven _____ escaped from the penitentiary.
12. A black _____ chased a cat up a tree.
13. The _____ wore a mask in the bank.
14. _____ keeps me awake at night.
15. The _____ was sent to jail for stealing money.

Add a verb to complete the sentence. Circle the subject.

1. I usually _____ on weekends.
2. The team always _____ before the game.
3. The crowd _____ the band.
4. City dwellers _____ too much.
5. His dog always _____ on the chair.
6. I _____ my money in Las Vegas.
7. My sister always _____ her homework.
8. The cat _____ the mouse.
9. After the film we _____ at a restaurant.
10. The police _____ the demonstrators.
11. Many Canadians _____ too much.
12. They all _____ like maniacs at the party.
13. Our dog _____ the burglar.
14. I _____ all night before the final exam.
15. After the game the fans _____ the referee.

Variations on the Sentence

Reverse Sentence Order

The subject usually comes before the verb, an arrangement that helps us to identify both. Do not be confused, though, by the occasional sentence in which the verb comes before the subject:

$$V \qquad S$$

At last *came spring*.

$$V \qquad S$$

In the car *were* five *gangsters*.

Remember that the *subject* is what the sentence is about, while the *verb* tells what the subject does or is. Think of the sentence in normal word order to make sure it has both a subject and verb:

$$S \qquad V$$

Spring came at last.

$$S \qquad V$$

Five *gangsters were* in the car.

Compound Subjects and Verbs

A sentence may have two or more subjects:

$$S \qquad\qquad S$$

Spring and *summer* are the best seasons.

A sentence may have two or more verbs:

$$V \qquad\qquad V$$

Spring *comes* late and *is* short.

A sentence may have two or more subjects and two or more verbs:

$$S \qquad S \quad V \qquad\qquad V$$

May and *June are* beautiful but *go* too fast.

Do not make fragments by separating the parts of a compound subject or verb:

SENTENCE	FRAGMENT
May and June are beautiful.	But go too fast.

Longer Sentences

To discuss sentences longer than our examples so far, we need more concepts:

A. A *phrase* is a word group that does not contain both a subject and a complete verb. Alone, it is a fragment:

waiting for spring
night and day
after the robbery

   To make sense, these must be added to a complete sentence:

$$S \qquad V$$

Waiting for spring, Jane studied *night and day*.

$$S \qquad\qquad V$$

The gangsters escaped *after the robbery*.

   These phrases now do a job, giving more detail to explain the core sentence.

B. A *clause* is a word group that has both a complete verb and its subject:

   ■ An *independent clause* can stand alone as a sentence:

Spring arrived.
Jane studied.
The gangsters escaped.

   ■ A *dependent clause* cannot stand alone as a sentence. By itself it is a fragment:

though spring arrived
while Jane studied
when gangsters escape

   (See pages 91 to 92 for a fuller explanation of dependent clauses.)

C. Longer sentences, then, can be made of several combinations:

   ■ A *compound sentence* has two or more independent clauses, usually joined by words such as "and" and "but":

$$S \qquad V \qquad\quad S \qquad V$$

Spring arrived and summer followed.

$$S \qquad V \qquad\quad S \qquad V$$

Jane studied but Roger slept.

$$S \qquad V \qquad\qquad S \qquad\quad V$$

The police came but the gangsters escaped.

   ■ A *complex sentence* has at least one independent clause and at least one dependent clause:

INDEPENDENT   DEPENDENT
CLAUSE   CLAUSE

Canadians rejoice when spring arrives.

DEPENDENT   INDEPENDENT
CLAUSE   CLAUSE

Since she is determined, Jane studies.

■ A *compound-complex* sentence has two or more independent clauses and at least one dependent clause:

INDEPENDENT   DEPENDENT
CLAUSE   CLAUSE

The gangsters escaped after they robbed the bank, but

INDEPENDENT   DEPENDENT
CLAUSE   CLAUSE

the police caught them at the next bank.

In any combination of clauses, *phrases* such as "at noon" or "in the car" may be added to help explain the clauses.

In summary, it is mainly these patterns that give sentences length, variety and versatility. Remember, though, that any combination of word groups, to be a complete sentence, must have at least one independent clause: as we said at the beginning, *a subject and a verb.*

Causes of Sentence Fragments

Now that we have examined the basic parts of the sentence, let's look at the most common ways in which those parts are omitted or are prevented from doing their work.

A. Fragments can lack a subject or verb, or both, because of *carelessness:*

Am a Blue Jays fan. (no subject)

I a Blue Jays fan. (no verb)

A Blue Jays fan. (no subject or verb)

Such errors are usually caused by time pressures or fatigue, and can easily be caught as you edit. *If you make fragments in this way, be especially careful in your editing and in your proofreading.*

Don't let your eyes glide along the lines. Make them stop at every word, because when you read fast your mind will supply words that your eyes do not see. The correction, then, is of course to supply the missing word:

S V

I am a Blue Jays fan.

B. Fragments can occur when *writing is confused with speech.* As we have seen, fragments that may be fine in speech are errors in serious writing. If you write as you speak, you will make fragments like these:

Maybe.

Just one more point.

Not so good.

Do not rely on speech, then, as your model for writing.

C. Other fragments result from a deeper cause: *unfamiliarity* with more than the most basic aspects of sentence structure. Most people with this problem have not read enough to control their own language in its written form. The long-term solution is to read several hundred books or the equivalent in newspapers or magazines. The short-term solution is to study and apply the points that follow.

Fragments: More Causes and Remedies

Participles, Gerunds and Infinitives

Some words *look* like verbs but are not. Used as verbs, they produce fragments. **A present *participle* is a verb form ending in *-ing*:**

Roger *sleeping.*

This fragment does not state anything clearly because it lacks a real verb. Let's try some:

Roger *is* sleeping.

Roger *has been* sleeping.

Roger *could have been* sleeping.

Do not confuse present participles with *gerunds.* **A gerund looks like a present participle but is used as a noun.** It can be the subject of a sentence:

S V

Sleeping is Roger's hobby.

An *infinitive* is the word "to" plus a verb:

Roger *to sleep.*

This confusing statement is a fragment because the subject, Roger, lacks a real verb. Let's try some:

Roger *wants* to sleep.

Roger *has* to sleep.

Roger *decided* to sleep.

Now the infinitive *to sleep* is part of a complete verb (*wants to sleep*) that completes its sentence.

Fragments caused by infinitives occur most often in lists like this one:

> This essay has three purposes. To describe the computer in its earliest forms. To explain the functions of a modern computer. And to show how mass production has lowered the price of this extraordinary machine.

Let's punctuate the list as one sentence so that the subject and verb, *essay has*, make all that follows complete:

> This *essay has* three purposes: to describe the computer in its earliest forms, to explain the functions of a modern computer, and to show how mass production has lowered the price of this extraordinary machine.

Note that although an infinitive cannot be a complete verb, it can be the subject of a sentence:

S   V

To sleep is Roger's wish.

Relative Pronouns

Relative pronouns (*who, whose, whom, which, that*) can be a problem. As the name suggests, **a relative pronoun *relates* word groups to each other:**

INDEPENDENT CLAUSE	DEPENDENT CLAUSE
Canadians eat too much,	*which* is why they weigh too much.

Make sure, then, that you do not break the *relationship* by putting a period before the relative pronoun:

SENTENCE	FRAGMENT
Canadians eat too much.	*Which* is why they weigh too much.

The resulting fragment is corrected, of course, by removing the period and restoring the comma. Like this one, most fragments involving a relative pronoun are corrected by being joined to the previous sentence.

Sometimes, though, a relative pronoun does not belong in its sentence at all:

FRAGMENT

Surprisingly, with education becoming so popular *that* a university degree is no longer enough to guarantee a job.

Getting a good night's sleep is the best way to avoid errors like this. If you discover such a fragment, remove the relative pronoun:

SENTENCE

Surprisingly, with education become so popular, a university

S   V

degree is no longer enough to guarantee a job.

Subordinators

Certain words can change a sentence to a fragment. **Put before a subject and verb, these words will *subordinate*, or make less important, what follows. We can, therefore, call these words *subordinators.*** They produce the *dependent clauses* which, as we said on page 89, cannot stand alone as sentences. There are several kinds of subordinators:

- ■ *Words of time relationship* as, after, as long as, before, till, until, when, whenever, while
- ■ *Words of logical relationship* although, as if, as though, because, even though, except that, if, in order that, since, so that, though, unless, whereas, whether, why
- ■ *The words "where" and "wherever"*

The examples in the table show how these words can subordinate sentences into fragments.

SENTENCE	FRAGMENT
The sun rose.	*While* the sun rose.
We ate breakfast.	*As* we ate breakfast.
We packed the canoe.	*After* we packed the canoe.
We pushed off from shore.	*When* we pushed off from shore.
The river was high.	*Even though* the river was high.
We entered the rapids.	*When* we entered the rapids.
The canoe hit a rock.	*Where* the canoe hit a rock.
The canoe tipped over.	*So that* the canoe tipped over.
We swam.	*After* we swam.
We could grab a log.	*Until* we could grab a log.
It was fastened to the shore.	*Because* it was fastened to the shore.
We dried out.	*As* we dried out.
We discussed next summer's mountain climbing trip	*While* we discussed next summer's mountain climbing trip.

The sentences on the left make sense because they are self-contained. The fragments on the right do not make sense because their subordinators tell us to expect more. (Read the fragments aloud to sense their lack of meaning.) What should we do, then, to correct the fragments? Let's look at two basic alternatives:

■ ***Remove the subordinator*** This simple method gives us what we began with, the complete sentences on the left. Our fragments are now corrected. But have you noticed how short these sentences are and how choppy they would sound together? Read them aloud: the story will resemble the ones you read in grade one.

Removing a subordinator, then, can correct a fragment here and there. But usually there is a better way:

■ ***Combine fragments with sentences*** You've no doubt noticed how some of the examples belong together logically: one explains another or follows another in time. Subordinators are *signals* that point out these relationships. As you proofread a paper, realize that *a fragment beginning with a subordinator will almost always belong to the sentence before or after it.* Join the two, in most cases just by changing a period to a comma and the following capital to a small letter. This gives us a *complex sentence,* whose pattern we discussed on page 89: an independent clause with a dependent clause. Let's try the pattern, taking a sentence and a dependent clause (fragment) from our list:

DEPENDENT
CLAUSE

S V

The sun rose *as we ate breakfast.*

We can change the order to make breakfast more important than the sunrise:

DEPENDENT
CLAUSE

S V

We ate breakfast *as the sun rose.*

And we can put the subordinator first either way:

DEPENDENT
CLAUSE

S V

As the sun rose, we ate breakfast.

DEPENDENT CLAUSE

S V

As we ate breakfast, the sun rose.

Here is a point that confuses some people: are these last two examples fragments because the subordinator comes before everything else? They sound complete. And they are, because a subordinator affects only the words to which its meaning applies:

SUBORDINATED

S V

As the sun rose, we ate breakfast.

SUBORDINATED

S V

As we ate breakfast, the sun rose.

Note that the subordination usually ends at a comma, after which a subject and verb complete the sentence.

> Since we can usually correct a fragment by joining it to a neighbouring sentence, *we could describe most fragments as punctuation errors: periods in the wrong places.* Don't take this idea to extremes, though, by simply avoiding periods for a fear of making fragments. (The next section will show the bad effects of using *too few* periods.)

Now let's look at a new version of the whole list:

> We ate breakfast *while* the sun rose. *After* we packed the canoe, we pushed off from shore. The river was high. *When* we entered the rapids, the canoe hit a rock and tipped over. We swam *until* we could grab a log fastened to the shore. *As* we dried out, we discussed next summer's mountain-climbing trip.

The story is now correct and reasonably clear. It might do for a diary or postcard, but we can hardly call it a work of art. To become a developed piece of writing it needs all the expansion, focus and purpose discussed in the opening chapters of this book. And if it is to please us with its style, it will then need the kind of extensive editing discussed in the rest of this chapter.

"Correctness" alone is certainly not enough. Our readers do require it, but if the larger purposes of writing are not met, no degree of correctness will convey our message. Eliminating error is essential, but is only one part of the writing process.

NAME _____

Complete Sentences: Diagnostic Exercise

Write "F" in the blank beside each passage that contains a fragment. In sentences already complete, underline the subject and circle the verb.

1. Swimming, the ultimate experience. _____

2. Who are the homeless? They are people just like you and me. All with similar needs and desires. _____

3. Winter is a time when the trees are bare and people wear heavy coats to keep warm. _____

4. Running up the escalator to save those extra seconds, so I could catch the next train. _____

5. Petroleum refineries produce two major things that we need to survive. Fuel and plastics. _____

6. Dancers must be conditioned at all times. In order to avoid injury. _____

7. Forcing seniors to sign over their pension cheques. _____

8. When a couple establishes a family. It would be wisest to have only two or three children. _____

9. The basic sports fan who sits in front of the television set, with eyes glued to the tube, moving only when necessary to grab a can of beer. _____

10. I really believe that some dreams have an effect on us, either good or bad. _____

11. In this present age, teenagers have to overcome the peer pressures around them. The pressures to smoke, to join gangs and to fight. _____

12. Educating new drivers is more important than fining them, because after an accident everything is too late. _____

13. Christmas Eve the worst time to go shopping. _____

14. We began to be friends because we had many interests in common. Such as sports, music and movies. _____

15. Contact lenses shouldn't be worn if you are turning the hamburgers over at a barbecue party. Because smoke may cause pain and burning in the eyes. _____

16. If you are over 50 years old it is no longer easy to find a new job. Competing with younger, more educated people. _____

17. When bringing groceries from a car into a house is a very easy task. _____

18. Ignoring my injured leg, I continued to practise. _____

19. No little brothers or sisters running around driving you up the wall and no older ones to boss you around. _____

20. Although I knew that at some moment I would have to confront my doctor about the swelling and the aching pain in the lower left side of my back. _____

21. The old men who stand on the corner begging for money because they cannot find a job. _____

22. The environment is the hostage and the casualty in all wars, especially when war happens to countries that produce oil.

23. Tae Kwon Do is a study in discipline as well as spiritual and physical growth. A system of self-defence without weapons.

24. After changing into work clothes, which consist of longjohns, two pairs of work socks, a heavy sweater, overalls, a safety belt, a hard hat and safety boots.

25. Almost every day we witness tragedies that happen all over the world, caused by human cruelty. Tragedies that cause the death of innocent people.

26. City people always seem to be late for something. Always trying to get where they're going as fast as possible. Never stopping to see what is around them. Never thinking for one instant how great it is to be alive.

27. Teachers with a master's degree are very bright. Maybe too bright for the high school level, because sometimes they forget difficulties that students have.

28. The show takes us from when Brenda gets her test results. To when her parents find out. To how they react.

29. By not depending on a man for my financial welfare meant that I had to decide how I was going to look after myself.

30. To avoid robbery, it is wise not to wear too many valuables such as jewelry. Especially when you are in New York City.

31. If teenagers don't have strong guidance from their parents, they will follow their peers to seek life on the street. A life full of excitement and danger.

32. Though not all television programs are suitable for children.

33. If war is the last resort, and if the cause is just, then Canada would probably get involved.

34. I usually write a list of things needed for the week. Then cross off all the less important things.

35. People don't realize that the excess food they eat is converted to fat and stored in the body. Thus causing the muscles to decrease in strength and tone.

36. Relationships in which two people become so emotionally tied to each other that they risk losing their personal identities.

37. As I focus the picture in my mind, imagining myself behind a huge office desk, at the helm of a huge company, slouched into a lazyboy office chair, looking out the window on the fifty-first floor of my newly acquired company office tower.

38. Acid rain leaches metals, such as aluminum, from the soils and sediments of the watersheds, separating solid particles from soluble components, and then dumps these metals into the lakes and rivers. Thus increasing the high concentration of metal in the river systems.

39. Classification in the movie industry can be good and bad. Good because it helps us to decide what type of movie we want to see. Bad because it doesn't leave any room for individual or creative movies that cannot fit into the five main rating categories.

40. Crowds of people everywhere in the streets, in the subway and restaurants. The frenzy of people rushing around racing to get to their destination.

NAME _____

Complete Sentences: Exercise, Level 1

Underline all the complete sentences. Correct all the fragments, adding or changing words or punctuation where necessary.

Example: ~~Garbage~~ *I saw garbage* in the streets.

1. Looking out my window, up at the bright twinkling stars.

2. Everyone eager to get off the crowded and smelly bus.

3. The sidewalk cafes give a feeling of romance and intimacy.

4. People pushing each other to get by.

5. "Murder-Ball," a fighting ball game that I will never in my life forget.

6. I was ready to ski the big runs again. Not just the bunny slopes but right to the top.

7. Women or men who are qualified to work at a certain job.

8. My mother, a 51-year-old woman who looks 35.

9. Sports fans, a group of people screaming and yelling when a goal is scored or a penalty is called.

10. Although certain unions should not be given the chance to strike.

11. The reason being that sex and violence sell books.

12. To work your way to the top and feel satisfied once you are there.

13.   I heard screams of fear as the roller coaster unleashed its power.

14.   Winter driving can be hazardous. Especially in snowstorms.

15.   My cousin, who is in her thirties and doesn't want to get married.

16.   In our society with fad diets. People have forgotten the need for exercise.

17.   Deep black smoke poured from the house across the street.

18.   Because the stores open on Sunday.

19.   My father, a professional worrier.

20.   Since many crimes and tragedies are caused by gambling.

21.   When the sun begins to set. The sky changes its colour.

22.   A child loves to listen to stories being told. Whereas older people love to tell stories.

23.   Vancouver is experiencing an employment crisis. Which leaves many people on the streets. Lining up at food banks.

24.   If you peeped into Carol's bedroom you would be shocked. Clothes everywhere, shoes, books, papers everywhere, an unmade bed, a terrible sight.

25.   Cars constantly moving every which way, horns honking and people yelling out of their windows.

NAME _____

Complete Sentences: Exercise, Level 2

Underline all the complete sentences. Correct all the fragments, adding or changing words or punctuation where necessary.

1. Ah, cruising down the Don Valley Parkway in a 1992 Suzuki Jeep.

2. I continually have to remind myself that it's all right not to look like a fashion model. A problem that is shared by many women all over the world.

3. When the doctors finished with my back, they took me to the x-ray department. There they threw me on the table like a sack of potatoes.

4. Every kind of person was downtown that night. Punkers with pink and green Mohawk haircuts, leather fanatics, and men singing songs about dreams that would never come true.

5. Wives and husbands, parents and children, all laughing, chatting and having fun browsing in the stores, looking at exciting new merchandise and making their purchase decisions together.

6. On April 27, 1992 seemed to start like any other day.

7. I saw that we had been hit from behind by a white van. And that the driver was still in the driver's seat taking his seatbelt off.

8. Marijuana, the dried leaves extracted from the female hemp plant grown throughout the world for thousands of years.

9. True education is knowing the reality of life. Knowing people, their culture, their needs. Knowing nature and most of all yourself. Knowing things that you will never be able to find in books.

10. Men should support the women's movement, and women's struggle to participate freely in social life. Because this means there is less and less pressure on men.

11. Hearing the sound of jet fighter engines in the sky, looking up and seeing the fighters diving to bombard you. A few seconds later when the smoke and dust settle down, nothing but blood and dead bodies everywhere.

12. Football and warfare are similar. Even the words used to describe a football game are from the military lexicon. Words like "trenches," "suicide squad," "field general," "bomb" and "enemy line."

13.   As I walked down the street peering in the windows at electronic equipment and fashionable clothing, thinking how nice everything looked, wishing I could have it all.

14.   Arguments cannot be avoided, because everyone in this world has a different background and education.

15.   One of the year's most exciting events occurs in August. When relatives or friends get together and head up the mountain for a big picnic.

16.   The silence of cross-country skiing thrills me the most. To cross mile upon mile of forest without hearing the sound of metal against metal or idling engines.

17.   The pushing and shoving of people trying to get on the subway, packing one another into a boxcar like a herd of cattle going into the city.

18.   Governments forget that small businesses are the biggest employers in the country. And that without their enterprising spirit, many people would not be employed at all.

19.   The essence of any serious addiction is a pursuit of pleasure. A search for a "high" that normal life does not supply.

20.   Oh, yes, the plate of cookies and glass of milk that the children leave out for Santa Claus when he comes on Christmas Eve to bring goodies to fill the stockings and give the presents that he's read about in the letters.

21.   People all around splashing in the water, tanning their bodies on the beach, and couples walking hand in hand along the shore.

22.   Trips with your family create memories. That you can look back on and cherish. Even if you went to see your aunt in Sudbury or drove on the Cabot Trail. It was or can be a time to spend and get to know each other all over again. All in an automobile.

23.   Sandra remained in critical condition while she underwent several operations. The most important being the one on her brain.

24.   I cannot speak of Toronto without mentioning Yonge Street. The longest street in the world. Much action goes on there at night. Especially between Bloor and College. Lots of street kids, prostitutes, drunks, people shopping, others working. A very typical scene on Yonge Street.

25.   When I think of Montreal, I always picture St-Denis Street. Especially between Ste-Catherine and Ontario. That was my favourite place. A very French district of Montreal. Where you can smell the odour of strong coffee and the famous Gitanes cigarettes.

NAME _____

Complete Sentences: Exercise, Level 3

Underline all the complete sentences. Correct all the fragments, adding or changing words or punctuation where necessary.

1. We often hear of parents who leave teenagers home alone to go on holiday. Only to return home and find that some disaster has occurred in their absence.

2. As I walked through the mall looking for that special gift, until it captured my attention.

3. How strange it is to see a lake without life. Its crystal clear waters unable to sustain even the simplest life forms.

4. Every person is equal under the law, and the right to be himself or herself without discrimination based on race, national origin, colour, religion, sex or age.

5. The famous electric can opener with "reliable rotating engine, high speed cutting heads, easy to clean lever, and high quality galvanized steel frame," all guaranteed never to fall apart.

6. The World Tae Kwon Do Federation has developed three major forms of fighting for international championships, with new improved safer methods and rules.

7. Sooner or later almost everybody buys a car. A choice that is difficult to make. An investment that loses money, because the value of the car decreases day by day. A decision that leads to environmental tragedy as well.

8. In the First World children have the right to leave home and become independent as soon as they reach age 16. After which, some would rarely return home to visit their parents. Why, then, would parents want to have any children?

9. Before us was a 15-foot hydraulic rapid waiting to consume our raft. Through excitement everyone paddled wildly, then, pow, we hit, and hundreds of gallons of water rushed over my body. Crushing my chest against the front of the raft, my head bouncing around as if it were in a washing machine.

10. It is important for children to learn to make decisions early. Decisions like which way they should go home. Whether they will stay and play in the schoolyard for a while, instead of having to stand in a line at the front of the school at 3:45 p.m. each day waiting for the bus, and then having to sit in an assigned seat.

11. Has the increase in industrialization changed Canadian values? The values that we are taught from grade six Canadian history books through grade 13 world history. Values that are expressed through all aspects of education and daily life experiences.

12. Acid rain, thousands of dead or dying lakes, pollution in the atmosphere, water and food contamination, disease, birth defects, land and wildlife devastation, the deteriorating economy, war as well as hunger in Third World countries, the Middle East crisis and the possibility of nuclear war.

13. The stages of life are divided into several parts. The child, so helpless and yet so giving. The young teenager, so ardent and so full of optimism. The worker struggling to make a name, so as to be respected in a world where money and power are the true motivations. The spouse and parent, who are true confidants. And then, that final door that we fear, death.

14. Downhill skiing has been a favourite activity of both men and women around this world for a long time. From the beginners on the baby hill, the experienced on the moguls, to the courageous trying helicopter skiing. The challenges and excitement come with the courses and hills skied. The excitement of becoming airborne over jumps and the defeat of losing control in landing. The fact that every time one goes down the slopes, it is a different challenge compared to the previous run. Making downhill skiing exciting and fun.

15. Over the next few days I took numerous tours of the island. The sugar cane fields full of people cutting the canes down by hand to make sugar and sell to the local islanders. All of the banana trees full of ripe bananas ready to be picked, and fields of pineapples growing on the ground in clumps. Driving by on the bus and seeing the cattle along the side of the road, with no fences or restrictions on where they wandered and grazed.

Editing Out the Comma Splice and Fused Sentence

When independent clauses are joined by nothing but a comma, the result is a *comma splice*. When they are joined with no punctuation or connecting words at all, the result is a *fused sentence*.

Some readers now accept the "comma splice" in informal writing. And some novelists, for example Margaret Atwood, even use it deliberately to achieve stylistic effects. But most people who read very much still view as serious errors the *comma splice* and its near-twin, the *fused sentence*.

Although these errors are widespread in student writing, you can overcome them if you learned in the previous section to identify independent and dependent clauses (review if necessary). *In this section we examine four major ways to edit a comma splice or fused sentence out of your writing.*

COMMA SPLICES

1. Spanish is easy, German is hard.
2. I applied early, I got the job.
3. Income tax favours the poor, sales tax favours the rich.

FUSED SENTENCES

1. Spanish is easy German is hard.
2. I applied early I got the job.
3. Income tax favours the poor sales tax favours the rich.

Apart from rewriting the whole thing, there are four basic ways to correct a comma splice or fused sentence:

A. **Put a *period* between the independent clauses:**

1. Spanish is easy. German is hard.
2. I applied early. I got the job.
3. Income tax favours the poor. Sales tax favours the rich.

This method is easiest but seldom best. Rather than joining the independent clauses, it separates them, which prevents you from showing the logic of their relationship to each other. And too many little sentences will make your style choppy.

B. **Join the independent clauses with a *coordinator (and, but, for, or, so, yet)*:**

1. Spanish is easy, *but* German is hard.
2. I applied early, *so* I got the job.
3. Income tax favours the poor, *but* sales tax favours the rich.

Naturally, choose the coordinator that best expresses your meaning. Avoid the general word "and" unless it fits best. (Note that a comma comes *before* the coordinator, not *after*.)

C. **Reduce one of the independent clauses to a dependent clause by putting a *subordinator* before it:**

1. *Although* Spanish is easy, German is hard.
2. *Since* I applied early, I got the job.
3. Income tax favours the poor, *while* sales tax favours the rich.

Choose the subordinator that most accurately expresses your meaning. (For a list of subordinators and a more detailed discussion of their function, review pages 91 to 92.)

(Note that a comma joins the dependent and independent clauses.)

D. **When two independent clauses are closely related in meaning, and especially when they are also balanced in form, join them with a *semicolon*:**

1. Spanish is easy; German is hard.
2. Income tax favours the poor; sales tax favours the rich.

For many people the hardest comma splices and fused sentences to avoid are those followed by certain coordinators called *conjunctive adverbs*:

also	*instead*
anyway	*likewise*
besides	*nevertheless*
consequently	*otherwise*
furthermore	*similarly*
however	*still*
indeed	*therefore*
in fact	*thus*

These words do *not* subordinate. There is no problem when they begin a sentence, but be careful when they *join* sentences. If you punctuate them like subordinators, with a comma before, you will make comma splices; if you put no punctuation at all before, you will make fused sentences. The correct punctuation is a semicolon *before* and a comma *after*:

1. Spanish is easy; *however*, German is hard.
2. I applied early; *therefore*, I got the job.
3. Income tax favours the poor; *however*, sales tax favours the rich.

In many cases another method works better. Use semicolons and most conjunctive adverbs sparingly to avoid a slow and heavy style that will bring yawns to your reader. (See page 113 for more discussion of semicolons.)

Finally, in identifying comma splices and fused sentences in the exercises that follow, concentrate on the independent clauses and their proper joining or separation. Do *not* be distracted by phrases or dependent clauses that may occur before, between or after the independent clauses. These expanded versions of example 1 still contain independent clauses improperly joined:

COMMA SPLICE

Spanish is easy, *because the grammar is uncomplicated,* German is hard.

ONE POSSIBLE CORRECTION

Spanish is easy, *because the grammar is uncomplicated;* German is hard.

FUSED SENTENCE

Spanish is easy German is hard, *because its grammar is complex.*

ONE POSSIBLE CORRECTION

Spanish is easy, but German is hard, *because its grammar is complex.*

Remember: If you change a comma splice by just removing the comma, you create a fused sentence. If you change a fused sentence by just adding a comma, you create a comma splice.

NAME _____

Comma Splice and Fused Sentence: Diagnostic Exercise

Write "CS" in the blank beside each comma splice and "FS" in the blank beside each fused sentence. Some examples are correct.

1. During rush hour the streets of Canton are full of bicycles, the buses travel slowly to avoid hitting them.   _____

2. Jennifer and Tony were high school students they quit school and got married.   _____

3. The night before my driver's test I couldn't eat or sleep, I was in a stupor.   _____

4. In the past, the computer could not do as many things as it can today.   _____

5. I wonder about the countryside, will it be replaced by large buildings and paved roads?   _____

6. The lake was frozen over, some boys had cleared a spot of ice and were playing hockey.   _____

7. My curiosity got the best of me I wanted to know what was happening.   _____

8. The street was covered by snow, the driving was dangerous.   _____

9. Time is money, therefore our time is limited.   _____

10. The basement was dark, a mouldy smell filled the air.   _____

11. There are hundreds of newspapers on the market, with all this variety for the readers there is still something missing.   _____

12. Technology has not solved our problems instead it has created new ones.   _____

13. We are still good friends, unfortunately we don't go to the same school anymore, but we still get together.   _____

14. In law class we study about people's rights, the richer the people are the more rights they have.   _____

15. Children with permissive parents seem to be wild and crazy.   _____

16. I have four roommates, some roommates are messy, others are too neat to live with.   _____

17. Driving a car makes people lazy, for example when they have a vehicle they no longer walk anywhere.   _____

18. Our cedar hedge had been flattened there were tire marks across our lawn.   _____

19. The clock was ticking away with two minutes left in the game we were on our own five-yard line.   _____

20. Let's imagine you are working for a strict and stingy boss, would you work diligently for this person?   _____

21. Finally we arrived at the hospital we checked into the birthing area.   _____

22.   An old woman fell as she crossed the street, but the other New Yorkers near her kept walking; it was only when I offered a hand that she got back on her feet.   _____

23.   All the arguments for stores opening on Sundays are unreasonable; the disadvantages clearly outweigh the advantages.   _____

24.   In high school I had no respect for books, I wrote in them and ripped pages out for reference.   _____

25.   Hail is nothing to be afraid of however, caution is always a good thing.   _____

26.   The scene was horrible and unbelievable, people screamed and were helpless.   _____

27.   If you see something suspicious at your home, don't hesitate call the police immediately.   _____

28.   I couldn't sleep that night, I was anxious for the next day so I could call her and ask her out.   _____

29.   The cost of cleaning up acid rain is high; however, the benefits are great.   _____

30.   I was blind and lost, I wanted to come out from the darkness, but I could not because there was no light to guide me.   _____

31.   Our government cannot be trusted, this country functions as if Parliament did not exist.   _____

32.   On April 27 of each year since the accident, I have held a party to celebrate being alive.   _____

33.   I swung around to catch a guy charging at me I grabbed him and threw him to the ground.   _____

34.   I never inherit money from a rich uncle it is always the person next door who has all the luck.   _____

35.   Finally everything was done, the dentist gave me a cup of water to rinse the blood and dust from my mouth.   _____

36.   A book is just like an old friend whenever we need it, the only thing to do is consult it.   _____

37.   Our mother could not afford to feed all the children; therefore, she decided it would be in our best interests to place us with the Children's Aid Society.   _____

38.   Health problems that come with age are often caused by lack of exercise therefore, it is important to provide exercise to all areas of the body.   _____

39.   In today's modern industrialized world, we can have a wonderful material life, money can seem to buy everything we want, but our heart still lacks something.   _____

40.   A child who feels secure at home will develop a positive character; for example, a child who is loved at home will automatically show love to others.   _____

NAME _____

Comma Splice and Fused Sentence: Exercise, Level 1

Correct the comma splices and fused sentences below. If an item contains no error, write "Correct" after it.

1.   Winter came, the wind was howling outside.

2.   It was exactly 8:00 in the morning people were rushing to work.

3.   I ran toward the back of the house to see what had happened.

4.   I wasn't sure of myself, I thought she would laugh at me.

5.   I could not put pressure on my foot, therefore I could not walk, run or dance.

6.   Oil is a gift of nature, no one can create it but only discover it.

7.   I looked at my fingers they were covered with blood.

8.   Life is like playing chess, in order to be successful, you must be patient.

9.   Even with government help, student finances are tight.

10. Some hockey clubs have three or four goon players however, this strategy may not win games.

11. I was shocked I didn't know what to do.

12. Aging is not under our control, therefore, we should make the most out of life.

13. In a few minutes the dentist came in she put on a mask and a pair of gloves.

14. The night was silent, time stood still, I had no thought of the events going on around me.

15. In the past, bicycles were made to last a lifetime.

16. It was a beautiful July day in Edmonton, there was no sign of rain and not a cloud in the sky.

17. The police force was powerless and half an hour late extra police entered the stadium when the riot was already over.

18. My husband held my hand he was trying to cope with the situation.

19. Don't think that just because you are shy nobody will like you. Think of all those great movie stars, they will admit that they are very shy when they are off the screen.

20. Rush hour was busy, this made the trains very crowded, we must have waited for three trains till we got on one of them.

21. The small town was dead, nothing was on the street except a few dogs chasing a mangy cat.

22. I knew I was caught. The cops came over to where I was hiding, they were very large and very angry.

23. Books are mental food, we can't live without them.

24. Glasses and contact lenses both work well, however, they each have strong and weak points.

25. It is best to remove glasses before playing any sports game otherwise, they will be broken to pieces.

26. Once people reach 65 they are forced to retire, usually they can still contribute to society.

27. In winter the Northern Hemisphere is tilted away from the sun, causing the rays to be spread over a great distance; therefore, the temperature falls.

28. When you write on paper, you may have to write several drafts in order to produce a final copy, therefore a lot of paper will be wasted.

29. New York City was just a mess, there were people living in broken-down houses and run-down apartments, there were potholes in the street and garbage all over the sidewalks.

30. We were about a quarter of a mile away when we heard 10 or 15 shots we turned around to see a wave of human beings heading in our direction. We heard more shots and the wave built, there were women screaming and men shouting as a cloud of dust rose behind them.

NAME _____

Comma Splice and Fused Sentence: Exercise, Level 2

*Correct the comma splices and fused sentences below. If an item contains no error, write "Correct"
after it.*

1. The black belt has nine levels, each level is called a dan.

2. You can't hide from acid rain as long as there is wind, acid rain can reach you.

3. Our cat wouldn't keep still, it would run around in circles, tearing bits and pieces out of the chesterfield
    in an uncontrollable fury.

4. Strength is essential when tactics are fairly even the stronger team will dominate.

5. For a thrill, a laugh, a lesson or a reason for a date, go to the movies.

6. The girl was naive and trusting, therefore she thought it was all right if her date came up to her room.

7. A security guard faces four main problems every day they are the boss, the co-workers, the paperwork
    and the public.

8. No matter what I have done, my parents will never abandon me, they will always be there to guide me.

9. At this point I couldn't handle the pressure, my heart ached to talk to her and be near her.

10. When you drive long distances you never know what can go wrong it could be a flat tire or a blown
    transmission.

11. I was sitting in the front of the stalled van when I saw the signal with my heart pounding I shouted to
    the others, "Get out of the van everybody the train is coming!"

12. Martha and I love to insult each other, the nastier the insult, the harder we laugh.

13. Some critics felt that the novel lacked sustained power, it had inconsistent ideas, some went so far as
    to say that it was a dull book.

14. I loved the scent of the double cheese spewing from the sides of the pizza box, and the grease dripping
    from my fingers was enough to drive me into a frenzy.

15. It does not matter how successful you are if your luck turns bad who knows, you might be the next
    homeless person.

16.   I was the only child who had to be in the house at 8:30, whereas the others could stay out till 9:30.

17.   My Grade 11 geography teacher made us hand in assignments every day whether they were easy or hard did not matter.

18.   Contact lenses must be washed very clean otherwise they will expose the eye to disease.

19.   The clouds were puffy and dark when it started to rain the rain suddenly turned into hail.

20.   We took the F train to downtown Manhattan, when we got off I was almost run over by a police officer he told me to get out of his way the next time.

21.   When going out the subway entrance to get a taxi we were faced with a drug deal going on right before our eyes, in New York this was known as an everyday thing.

22.   Every mountain rose out of the valley, yet each was distinct; some had faces where avalanches had wiped out all the trees, others were bold bare windblown slopes.

23.   The ten-foot-high diving board looked at least 30 feet high. My stomach felt funny, my arms and legs felt all tensed up. I stared down at the water.

24.   I share the bathroom with the other tenant, each time I walk in the first thing I see is a note reminding me to mop the floor if I happen to splash water on it.

25.   Emotional security is more important to the wellbeing of a home than financial security, for example when a child feels loved at home he or she will be happy, even if the family is not financially well to do.

26.   I was talking to another student about the protest when two explosions sent clouds of tear gas into a scattering crowd. This was the little spark that ignited the fury of the people they charged the army with bottles, stones and any piece of metal they could put their hands on.

27.   When I saw 12 members of the Hell's Angels stop, I was scared to death, they asked what had happened and helped to fix the bike. Then I rode with them to the next town and offered them a couple of drinks, the only problem was that their couple of drinks ran my bill up to a hundred dollars.

28.   Pollution is not a new phenomenon, historical records dating back to the thirteenth century record how citizens migrated from London to Nottingham to escape the smoke from wood and coal fireplaces.

29.   The high school system in Canada is very helpful to students, because in school, they can develop their own ability to investigate problems and think through solutions, the education system in Canada helps students become active and independent people.

30.   Being slaves of machines and technology is the price we pay for comfort and progress, we have to stop sometimes to think about our achievements more carefully, we have to realize where we are standing in the present and where we are heading in the future.

Editing for Punctuation

Punctuation marks such as periods and commas may seem unimportant because they are small. Some people view them as afterthoughts, as ornaments to be added here and there ("Let's throw in a comma because the last sentence didn't have one"). But how would you like to read an essay made of statements like this?

> I don't smoke myself because I've tried it and don't get anything out of it.

While it may be true that few people enjoy smoking themselves, what the author had in mind was probably something more like this:

> I don't smoke, myself, because I've tried it and don't get anything out of it.

The great difference in meaning is signified by a small difference in punctuation. As you study the following summary of the major uses for punctuation, always keep in mind that these small marks can powerfully influence your writing for better or worse. If you use them accurately to make your meanings clear, you have taken an important step toward writing well.

Period (.)

A.   Use a period to end a *statement* or *command*:

STATEMENT

> Art is anything you can get away with.
>
> — Marshall McLuhan

COMMAND

> Chop the wood.

B.   Use a period after *most abbreviations*:

> At 3 p.m. Dr. Chan removed Mr. Violi's appendix.

(See "Abbreviations," pages 185 to 186.)

Apostrophe (')

(See "Apostrophes," page 176.)

Comma (,)

A.   Use a comma to separate items in a *series*:

> The most productive vegetables for a small garden are beets, carrots, lettuce, onions, pole beans and tomatoes.
>
> A gardener's rewards are the glow of outdoor exercise, the satisfaction of honest work, the reduction of grocery bills and the taste of fresh vegetables.

(Most people now omit the optional comma between the last two items of a series. Sometimes, however, it must be retained for clarity.)

B.   If an *introductory word group* is long, use a comma to separate it from what follows. If it is short leave it unpunctuated. (Examine the above two sentences as examples of the rules they state.)

C.   Place a comma before the *coordinator of a compound sentence*, unless the first independent clause is short:

> The Laplanders have retained the most primitive culture of any European society, *but* modern Scandinavia has now begun to assimilate them.

> A canoe is fast *but* a kayak is faster.

(Note that the comma occurs *before* the coordinator, not *after*.)

D.   A modifier is "restrictive" if it is necessary to the basic meaning of a sentence and "nonrestrictive" if it is not. *Set off a nonrestrictive modifier with commas* to show its limited relationship to the sentence, but *leave a restrictive modifier unpunctuated* to show how its importance integrates it into the sentence:

RESTRICTIVE

> The Church did not allow children *born out of wedlock* to be baptized.

We know that "born out of wedlock" is a restrictive modifier because without it the sentence takes on a different meaning:

> The Church did not allow children to be baptized.

NONRESTRICTIVE

> The neighbour's children, *born out of wedlock*, lived in poverty.

Although the modifier "born out of wedlock" may be related to the poverty, it is nonrestrictive because the sentence means approximately the same without it:

> The neighbour's children lived in poverty.

RESTRICTIVE

> The Canadian novelist *Morley Callaghan* knocked out Ernest Hemingway in a boxing match.

The modifier is restrictive because without it we would be looking for another sentence to explain who "the Canadian novelist" was.

NONRESTRICTIVE

Morley Callaghan, *the Canadian novelist*, knocked out Ernest Hemingway in a boxing match.

Even if we have never heard of Morley Callaghan, the sentence seems basically the same without the modifier.

Morley Callaghan knocked out Ernest Hemingway in a boxing match.

E. Put a comma after the *salutation of an informal letter*:

Dear Lina,   Dear Ms. Sanchez:

BUT

Dear Dad,   Dear Sir:

F. Put a comma *between the date and year*. A comma is optional between the month and year:

July 1, 1867
July, 1867
July 1867

G. Use a comma wherever necessary to *avoid ambiguity*:

AMBIGUOUS

After drinking the three men played cards. (Did the three men drink or did someone drink them? At first we do not know.)

CLEAR

After drinking, the three men played cards.

AMBIGUOUS

What I really dislike is the size of the city and the people. (Are the people the wrong size?)

CLEAR

What I really dislike is the size of the city, and the people.

AMBIGUOUS

Alcohol in my eyes only adds to people's troubles. (Where is the alcohol?)

CLEAR

Alcohol, in my eyes, only adds to people's troubles.

In some cases, though, a clear and graceful sentence is more easily produced by rewriting than by adding a comma:

What I really dislike is the size of the city and the rudeness of its people.

Alcohol only adds to people's troubles.

H. Some of the worst common errors are made not by neglecting to put a comma where it belongs but by putting one where it does *not* belong. You have already studied the worst error, *comma splices*, on pages 101 and 102. Review that section if necessary.

Another mistake is nearly as bad as the comma splice: letting a comma separate a subject from its verb. *Do not place a comma between a subject and its verb except to mark off interruptions such as a nonrestrictive modifier:*

ERROR

S   V
Our neighbour's *dog, ran* away.

CORRECTION

S   V
Our neighbour's *dog ran* away.

ERROR

S   V
Chapter Three, arouses the reader's sympathy.

CORRECTION

S   V
Chapter Three arouses the reader's sympathy.

CORRECT

S   V
Vultures, the scavengers of death, *circle* their prey before moving in.

(Here the commas between subject and verb are correct because they enclose a nonrestrictive modifier.)

NAME _____

Commas: Exercise

In the passage below, cross out all commas that appear in the wrong places and add all necessary commas that are missing. If a passage contains no comma fault, write "Correct" after it.

Example: I love to cook，myself，and eat at home.

1. As I put my coat on the dentist and receptionist had a brief discussion.

2. Sharon flirted outrageously with Michael and Kenny and Jason flirted with her.

3. Ham radio, has become my obsession.

4. The sediment on the ocean floor, hundreds of metres below sea level is up to 300 m thick.

5. One of my math teachers, helped me learn, to achieve my goal, in the subject, by spending a great deal of time working with me.

6. The activities of juvenile gangs, are most noticeable in the increase of vandalism.

7. My brother grandfather and I had been going to the races since before I could remember.

8. It's no secret that a life of freedom, especially in small and less powerful countries, is a rare commodity.

9. I love to play hockey but, studies come first.

10. Patients must be fed when they are too weak to eat themselves.

11. Our diet should contain dairy products rich in protein and vegetables.

12. Television reaches almost every part of the earth.

13. If you can use cash or make your payments promptly.

14. The peace that broke out when the Cold War ended, did not last.

15. Harsh lighting, produces harsh photographs.

16. I am amused by how fast Hollywood stars fall in love, get married, have affairs, get divorced, fall in love again, get married again and so on.

17. The last step is to record the time drug and dosage on the patient's chart.

18. When rivers lose their velocity suspended particles of clay and silt are deposited creating fertile soils in river deltas.

19. My problems in math started the day I began school.

20. People in Istanbul, seem to think that hamburgers and fries are not worth eating.

21. Alcohol has become a problem for our schools and teachers are deeply concerned.

22. Divorce, like birth and death occurs every day.

23. The truth is that many alcoholics never seek help resulting in their own destruction.

24. As society becomes more and more prosperous, and small cities become big cities, the crime rate also increases.

25.   Players who fight during a game, should be suspended for the whole season.

26.   Once, I placed, a couple of lines on the paper, some thoughts, began to appear.

27.   North Americans, believe in eye contact.

28.   The most sensible preparation for aging, is a life well lived from the beginning.

29.   I make my own decisions concerning where I go, when I come home, what I cook and when I clean.

30.   One thing that really bothers me, is the idea of a large dog being kept in the city.

31.   Once the needle is in the plunger is retracted to check for blood.

32.   Skiing, has become the best way for city people to get into the country.

33.   For hundreds of years English Canada, has had social and political control over Quebec.

34.   If you write a word without being completely sure of how to spell it you may be making a mistake.

35.   Although stubborn Hagar is one of Margaret Laurence's most admirable characters.

36.   Marriage, is a big commitment.

37.   Our friendship lasted for years, within which time we sinned, lied, cried, laughed, argued, shared and grew together.

38.   Erroll, was a nice guy, but he was still immature.

39.   The fastest sports are soccer, hockey football, rugby and basketball.

40.   While Dad was putting the lights on my brothers and I started to place the star on the Christmas tree.

Semicolon (;)

Some people have never used a semicolon and hardly know one when they see it. They are better off, however, than those who overuse and misuse it. This punctuation should be limited to certain situations and even then used sparingly, seldom more than once or twice per page. Overused, the semicolon can make your writing slow and heavy; well used, it can add dignity and precision.

A.   Use a semicolon between independent clauses *not joined by a coordinator*:

■   When the independent clauses are *closely related in meaning*:

Keenly, for the first time, I felt that I was a stranger in a strange land; my heart yearned intensely for my absent home.

— Susanna Moodie, *Roughing It in the Bush*

■   When related independent clauses are *balanced in form*:

Becoming independent is the easy part of a revolution; staying independent is the hard part.

B.   Use a semicolon between independent clauses that are joined by one of these *conjunctive adverbs*:

also	instead
anyway	likewise
besides	nevertheless
consequently	otherwise
furthermore	similarly
however	still
indeed	therefore
in fact	thus

The most heavily exposed parts of the negative receive the thickest deposit of silver; *therefore*, these areas appear darkest.

Note that the semicolon comes *before* the conjunctive adverb and a comma *after*. Putting the comma before the conjunctive adverb would create a comma splice (see pages 101 and 102).

C.   Use a semicolon between *items in a series* if the items have internal punctuation:

If you borrow a garment of any kind, be sure that you will tear it; a watch, that you will break it; a jewel, that you will lose it; a book, that it will be stolen from you.

— Susanna Moodie, *Roughing It in the Bush*

D.   Incorrect semicolons will harm your writing much more than correct semicolons will help it. Remember that apart from separating internally punctuated items in a series, *the only normal function of a semicolon is to join independent clauses*. Avoid other uses:

■   Except for the case of item C above, *do not use a semicolon as a comma*:

WRONG

As the guitar and the drums began to roar; the crowd began to scream.

RIGHT

As the guitar and the drums began to roar, the crowd began to scream.

WRONG

Only two problems; the cost and the danger, limit skiing as a sport.

RIGHT

Only two problems, the cost and the danger, limit skiing as a sport.

■   *Do not use a semicolon as a colon*:

WRONG

There are two groups of unemployed; the undereducated and the overeducated.

RIGHT

There are two groups of unemployed: the undereducated and the overeducated.

Colon (:)

The colon is a vigorous punctuation mark because it strongly directs the reader's attention forward. Use it more often than the slower semicolon but not in every possible location.

A.   Use the colon to *formally introduce a statement or question of your own, or a quotation*:

This is the main point: Censorship is dangerous.

The most basic question to be answered is this: To what extent does government spending increase inflation?

Goethe's most famous words are his last: "Light — more light!"

This is Tallyrand's recipe for coffee:
Black as the devil,
Hot as hell,
Pure as an angel,
Sweet as love.

Of course the comma may also introduce quotations, especially short ones incorporated into your sentence:

On his deathbed Goethe said, "Light — more light!"

B. For *emphasis*, use a colon to introduce even a single word:

Scrooge loved only one thing: money.

C. Use a colon when a *second statement explains a first*:

The climate is changing: by the year 2000 our winters will be noticeably warmer.

D. Use a colon to *formally introduce a series*:

The cylinders of a V-8 engine fire in this order: 1, 8, 4, 3, 6, 5, 7, 2.

Most good writers do not place a colon right after the verbs *is, are, was* or *were*, or after the words *of* or *to*.

WRONG

The causes of inflation *are*: low productivity, high wages and depletion of resources.

RIGHT

The causes of inflation *are* low productivity, high wages and depletion of resources.

RIGHT

These *are* the causes of inflation: low productivity, high wages and depletion of resources.

RIGHT

The causes of inflation *are* as follows: low productivity, high wages and depletion of resources.

E. Put a colon *after the salutation of a formal letter*:

Dear Ms. Sanchez: Dear Lina,

BUT

Dear Sir: Dear Dad,

Question Mark (?)

Although the question mark seems easy to use, it is the source of more than a few errors. Remember to put it where it belongs and guard against putting it where it does not belong. *Place a question mark after a direct question but not after an indirect question:*

DIRECT QUESTION

What time is it?

INDIRECT QUESTION

I wonder what time it is.

DIRECT QUESTION

I asked myself, "Would I help a person being attacked on the street?"

INDIRECT QUESTION

I asked myself whether I would help a person being attacked on the street.

Notice that the direct questions are the exact words of a question, while the indirect ones merely *report* a question. If you would not ask "What time it is?" or "Whether I would help?" then you know that they are indirect and therefore do not require question marks.

WRONG

When I reached home, I asked my mother what was happening? (Omit the question mark after this indirect question *or* make the question direct.)

RIGHT

When I reached home, I asked my mother, "What is happening?"

WRONG

Why is car insurance so high. (The person who wrote this may have sensed that it was a direct question but just forgot the question mark.)

RIGHT

Why is car insurance so high?

Exclamation Point (!)

The exclamation point, the strongest of all punctuation marks, should be saved for the strongest expressions of feeling. Ending a weak or ordinary sentence with an exclamation point is like hitting a tack with a sledge hammer.

A. Use an exclamation point to express *strong emotion* such as fear, anger or sorrow:

"Save me!" he cried, "I'm drowning!"
Ruin seize thee, ruthless King!
                    — Thomas Gray, "The Bard"

Alas! alas! that ever love was sin!
          — Chaucer, "The Wife of Bath's Prologue"

B. Do *not* try to make an ordinary statement exciting by adding an exclamation point. Avoid excesses such as this:

When the fair is about a month away, farmers begin to clean their livestock. First, the cows are hosed down with warm water and soap in order to get their hair as clean as possible! After the hair is rinsed, a blow dryer is used, along with a comb, to get the hair as fluffy as possible! In some places, styling is need to make the hair go the right way!

NAME _____

Semicolon, Colon, Question Mark and Exclamation Point: Exercise

Correct all misused semicolons, colons, question marks and exclamation points. Add punctuation marks where they are needed but missing. If a passage is already correct, write "Correct" after it.

1. A Canadian citizen enjoys many rights and freedoms including: voting in federal and provincial elections, running for public office, travelling outside Canada with a Canadian passport, etc.

2. As soon as I saw my brother; I knew that something was wrong.

3. When was the last time you stopped to appreciate the things around you?

4. Why is it that Canadians go south for the winter, instead of looking for something in their own back yards.

5. In Toronto two of the largest buildings are: the Eaton Centre and Commerce Court!

6. Nowadays the thought of a couple happily married after 50 years is incomprehensible to many people; however, my Grandma and Grandpa Wilcox are living proof of a happily married couple after 50 years of togetherness.

7. Although I was swamped with projects, essays and homework; I now know that the workload could have been worse.

8. Bank robberies are meticulously planned to the finest detail to include: the time of the operation; the getaway route; disguises; choice of bank; and a look at police surveillance in the area.

9. In prison we could play: volleyball, soccer and table tennis.

10. Try to analyze what kind of car you need? Is it for city driving? Are you going to use the car in your work? Do you mind the gas money, or is convenience all you care about?

11. Since I had arrived early and knew the area well; I went to a nearby doughnut shop for a cup of coffee.

12. How we all love to eat!

13. Living with four people I learned two things compromise and respect for others.

14. At a wedding you see bright happy colours such as: red, white, purple, green and pink. At a funeral you see dark depressing colours such as: blue, brown and black.

15. Permissive parents always say "yes"; strict parents always say "no."

16. According to scientists; if our population continues to increase, we will have big troubles.

17. There are five major types of energy. Mechanical, chemical, electrical, atomic and solar.

18. I wonder how families can afford more than one car?

19. On page 71 Dickens describes Stephen "He was a good power-loom weaver, and a man of perfect integrity."

20. In Toronto the most common transportation vehicles are: streetcars, subway cars, buses, automobiles and motorcycles.

21. No matter how early and fast you try to get down to the cafeteria; other students are there before you.

22. As speeders roar past, we wonder what they will hit or whose life they will take today?

23. As consumers we can raise awareness; that many products on the market today are totally useless.

24. Depending on the size of the tree; the roots may be thin or thick!

25. "How are you feeling," Karen asked.

26. Our many travels have included: snorkelling for barracudas in Barbados, parasailing over the roofs of Puerto Vallarte, skiing down the snowy mountains of Jasper and Banff, surfing in the Bahamas, and taking pictures of the tulips in Holland.

27. Drug addiction causes paranoia; a mistrust of others.

28. A hundred years ago a person looking for entertainment could not: turn on the TV, go to a movie, play a couple of hours of racquetball, or lie back and listen to the stereo.

29. "Hey buddy, got any change," is the most frequent comment made today in Halifax.

30. I wonder how bus drivers put up with the rush-hour crowd every day.

31. University students have many responsibilities that take a great deal of time: major research papers; employment; and family matters.

32. The main advantage of working while being a student is: learning effective time management!

33. The younger students walk down the long school halls with open ears, hearing what decisions the graduating students have made; dreaming that someday they will be doing the same thing.

34. Before you even start looking for a car, decide exactly how much money you are able to spend?

35. Many people buy lottery tickets every week; and gamble at the race track every day; because they want to win a lot of money.

36. Seven is the most popular lucky number, while 13 is considered extremely unlucky!

37. In Canada we encounter four different seasons spring, summer, fall and winter.

38. There are two parties involved in an option contract; the writer, who sells the contract, and the holder, who buys the contract.

39. I crave the night life of the city; the bright lights, concerts, movies, cafes, shows and nightclubs.

40. At Yonge and Bloor there are many Chinese, Italian, Canadian, Indian, Jamaican and Japanese fast-food restaurants!

Dash (—)

Like the exclamation point, the dash is overused by those with more enthusiasm than skill. Since it can be put almost anywhere, it becomes an escape from the responsibility of choosing specific punctuation. And while it is dramatic and picturesque, its overuse creates a breathless and even scatterbrained impression. Avoid the dash, then, except on rare occasions when it can achieve an effect better than any other punctuation mark can. These are its best uses:

A.   A dash can set off *parenthetical material* more dramatically than commas or parentheses can:

And then — was it hours or minutes after I arrived? — he opened his eyes.

— Margaret Laurence, *The Stone Angel*

B.   A dash can set off and thus emphasize the *end of a sentence*:

Only one investment will endure forever, will be safe from theft, and will almost always increase in value — land.

Parentheses and Square Brackets ( ), [ ]

Like dashes, parentheses are too convenient. Some writers use them as substitutes for more specific punctuation, while others use them to legitimize irrelevant matter that should be cut from their writing. For these reasons, and because the clutter of parentheses can slow down your reader, this device should be used only when it cannot be avoided.

A.   Use parentheses to *enclose matter that does not fit into the grammatical structure of a sentence*:

Caligula (A.D. 12 – 41) was the most corrupt and tyrannical of all Roman emperors.

B.   Use square brackets in quoted material *as you would use parentheses in unquoted material*:

Angling [fishing with line and hook] may be said to be so like the mathematics that it can never be fully learnt.

— Isaak Walton, *The Compleat Angler*

Since "fishing with line and hook" is an editor's explanation rather than part of Isaak Walton's passage, it is put in square brackets.

Quotation Marks (" ")

(See pages 213 to 214.)

Editing to Avoid the Run-on Sentence

When a sentence grows beyond control, especially if its parts are not closely enough connected, it becomes a run-on sentence. While not quite as serious as its opposite error, the fragment, the run-on sentence is exasperating and confusing.

A.   Change monster sentences by *breaking them into parts,* by *avoiding overuse of coordinators (and, but, for, or, so, yet)* and by *cutting out deadwood.*

How would you like to read a whole essay made of sentences like this?

A hundred years ago people were not as busy as they are today, *and* they could sit down *and* write letters *and* send them to their friends *and* their business associates, *but* in our modern times people are really busy, *and* they find that writing is too much work, *so* they just pick up the telephone *and* make a call to someone else. (63 words)

Connecting many thoughts loosely in one statement is something we do in speech, for we often talk faster than we think. When we write, though, the opportunity to revise leaves us no excuse for unorganized and wasteful language.

In our example not only does the repeated word "and" sometimes fail to make logical connections between the parts, but the confusion has also encouraged deadwood. First let's look at a correction that improves only the connections:

A hundred years ago people were not as busy as they are today: they could sit down and write letters to send to their friends and their business associates. But in our modern times people are really busy. They find that writing is too much work, so they just pick up the telephone and make a call to someone else.

So far, so good. We have cut the monster sentence into three parts. We have also replaced some of the "ands" with more precise connections such as punctuation or more exact connecting words. But now let's look at a more radical revision that also cuts out the deadwood that hid the meaning:

A hundred years ago people had time to write letters, but today we are so busy that we just pick up the telephone. (23 words)

Now we have one sentence of medium length whose parts are so tightly joined that the word "and" never occurs at all. In addition, the message has been shortened and concentrated through removal of meaningless information. For example when we "pick up the telephone" it is obvious that we are going to "make a call to someone else" — so why even write those words? *In avoiding monster sentences, do what you have to: sometimes adding periods or substituting*

> Word processing can provide a strong tool for detecting overuse of "and" — or of any other word.
>
> In WordPerfect, for example, press F2 for "search." Enter the word "and" at the bottom of the screen. Now a simple command (depending on which version of WordPerfect you have) will make the cursor come to rest just after the first "and" in your text, and further commands will quickly do the same for all the other "and"s.
>
> Be aware that WordPerfect may identify "and" as a part of another word such as "land," "hand" or "island." Disregard this the few times it happens. Instead, go on to examine every "and" in your text. Replace those that are too vague or loosely used, substituting exact punctuation or more precise transition words.

better connecting words is enough, while other times only a total rewriting will do the job. (See "Editing for Economy" on pages 51 to 54 for ways to cut out deadwood.)

B. *Join the parts of even short sentences accurately.* In particular, avoid *and* whenever a more specific connection can be made. Our first example had 63 words. This one has only 18 but is still a run-on sentence:

> The goalie has only one job to do *and* that is to keep the opposing players from scoring.

Here the word "and" is illogical: it implies that keeping the opposition from scoring is *in addition to* the goalie's job, when actually it *is* the job. A better connection than "and" would be a colon, since the beginning of the sentence introduces the end:

> The goalie has only one job to do: keep the opposing players from scoring.

> "And" is the most overused word in English. Avoid it except to show that one thing is genuinely *in addition to* another.

NAME _____

Run-on Sentence: Diagnostic Exercise

Write "ROS" in the blank beside each run-on sentence.

1. Some people get married at 16 or 17 and some feel too young to get married at 35 or 40. _____

2. How is it that we spend one-third of our lives in sleep and we still know so little about it? _____

3. An optimist could be losing a game 5-1 with one minute to go, and still think there would be time enough to win. _____

4. If you do not love winter, you are not Canadian. _____

5. Sponsors give financial support for teams, and they want their teams to be winners and not losers. _____

6. A dog knows when you're happy and it shows it's happy too and it knows when you're sad or hurt and it tries to show that it understands. _____

7. I strongly believe that, to have a better world, men must make up their minds to learn to share ideas, household duties and child-care duties, and let women become more active in social and political life and accept women as their equal partners. _____

8. I work in a store and some people come in and charge for items under one dollar. _____

9. A breakfast of bacon and eggs is filled with cholesterol. _____

10. He threw a punch at me trying to catch me off-guard, but seeing it coming I ducked and gave him a shot to the ribs, and feeling him buckle under the punch I knew I had won the fight. _____

11. I passed the first-semester chemistry and took the second-semester chemistry and failed. _____

12. Is it safe to bring children into this world, knowing how many crazy people are out there? _____

13. In my family we have done away with giftgiving, and what we each do instead is to spend one evening during the New Year with each member of the family. _____

14. When you have reached the height of your conformity you have become an adult, and you go out in the world to work and in order to work you must have the proper credentials and attire or you will not be accepted. _____

15. Don't people realize that they're paying big bucks for clothes that are new or different, or have a little designer label on them, and though the price is so high, the clothes may be no better than the ones at Honest Ed's? _____

16. In New York City people cannot walk the streets after 9:00 at night, because they might get mugged. _____

17. In the police stories we watch on television, a crime is committed and the police have a car chase and a shootout and capture the criminal. _____

18. There is one thing that impresses me about country people and that is their appearance. _____

19. I know of an employee who had worked faithfully for a number of years for the company and a pay raise had never been granted. _____

20. There was only one problem with my teachers and that was that they did not know how to teach.   _____

21. When farming was the way of life, a family would have six or seven children.   _____

22. I awoke the next morning and hurriedly looked through the window and realized the sun was shining.   _____

23. There is only one sign of my grandfather's aging, and that is a hearing problem.   _____

24. There are people who want to compete in the business world because this is where their interest lies, and there are others who decide that they would rather compete in athletics, and they pick a sport that they play well or just some sport that they might like just for the challenge or interest in the sport.   _____

25. When inspecting your home for places where burglars may break in, check the basement windows carefully.   _____

26. Some people get their first job at the age of 13 or 14.   _____

27. I saw one thing in Thailand that still gives me the shivers, and that was lizards.   _____

28. I am somewhat clumsy and tend to miss the pass and the ball goes off the field and out of bounds.   _____

29. As I put my luggage in the car it became difficult to hold back the tears, and it soon became impossible, for when my father, with his eyes drenched with tears, uttered the words, "I love you, do the best you can, and if you need anything just call," I began to cry and hug my parents.   _____

30. Many people marry to escape family pressures, to meet financial needs or to achieve status.   _____

31. Most companies are not willing to employ students who must be trained and afterwards the students work for a short time and leave.   _____

32. The youngest of my roommates is called Sue and is still in her teens, and keeps confessing that this is her first time on her own, away from home.   _____

33. Cats are much smaller than dogs and belong more in a home and they're not vicious little things like dogs.   _____

34. Some students have no interest in school at all and would prefer to go out and work for a living and feel that they are accomplishing something as soon as possible.   _____

35. My sister went through a lying phase, and it got to the point where she could not find any more excuses and so she moved out.   _____

36. I had my first date when I was 16.   _____

37. We live in a world of high technology and brilliant minds and with this combination new discoveries are being made.   _____

38. The people of Quebec City tried to be helpful since we could not speak French and there were times when they would ask us for English words so they would be able to communicate with us better.   _____

39. One day I decided to try and get a job and about three weeks later I was doing dishes.   _____

40. I wait at the bus stop and a bus full of people passes me and leaves me stranded for ten more minutes.   _____

NAME _____

Run-on Sentence: Exercise, Level 1

The word "and" is the main cause of run-on sentences. In the passages below, cross out as many "and"s as you can. Replace them with more exact coordinators *(see page 117), with well-chosen* subordinators *(see page 91) or with the right* punctuation. *Where necessary, rewrite in the space.*

Example: I have learned an important lesson in my life; and that is, there is no need to impress anyone.

1.   Love is true AND lust is false.

   _____

   _____

2.   My car is eight years old, AND it still looks and drives like new.

   _____

   _____

3.   I know one thing AND that is to fight.

   _____

4.   Each day a great miracle occurs AND a newborn child enters the world.

   _____

   _____

5.   Bifocals can be helpful AND also dangerous.

   _____

6.   I flicked the switch several times AND no light came on.

   _____

7.   People in the city do not try AND make contact with others.

   _____

8.   If you want to double your money at the races, fold it in half AND put it in your pocket AND just watch.

   _____

   _____

9.   Mom doesn't like it when I talk back AND she gets upset AND I know I have it coming.

   _____

   _____

10. There is one big disadvantage to being single AND that is being lonely.

   _____

   _____

11. The old man tried to cross the street at a crosswalk AND the cars did not even stop.

   _____

   _____

12. Now it is evening AND the sun is setting in the west AND the sky is changing to a clear bright blue.

   _____

   _____

13. Good coaches motivate their athletes AND reinforce their good behaviour AND punish their bad behaviour.

_____

14. If you feel you are hungry enough to eat a horse AND do not want to gain any weight, a Chinese restaurant would be best.

_____

_____

15. The weekend comes AND I can't wait to get out of the house to meet all my friends at Julie's, the local pub.

_____

_____

16. Unfortunately the bank never forgets about you, AND at the end of each month you get your statement.

_____

_____

_____

17. The problem of garbage has existed since the beginning of time, AND only now has it become enormously multiplied.

_____

_____

_____

18. Some students decide to study very little since they have other work to do AND when they write a test they find that they don't know anything AND now they turn to cheating.

_____

_____

_____

19. One myth is that women aren't committed to their work AND they will leave when they get married AND have children.

_____

20. Sometimes in the middle of the night Granny can cough for an hour AND the next day she will be walking around the house with a cigarette hanging from the corner of her mouth again.

_____

_____

21. One officer pulled his gun AND said not to move AND hearing this AND having a gun pulled on me I didn't even want to breathe for fear of my life.

_____

_____

_____

22. I remember one day when one of the little kids in the park would not allow Jack to play checkers AND Jack threw himself on top of the poor kid AND just about crushed him.

_____

_____

23. Soon after the accident, a lady who was driving by stopped AND asked if she could help AND my neighbour put me in the car AND the lady took me the rest of the way home, AND my neighbour brought my dog home.

_____

_____

_____

24. In North America over a hundred people are killed every 24 hours, AND most of them are people who cannot defend themselves from the violent people on the streets AND they would probably still be alive if they had gone out AND learned a martial art.

_____

_____

_____

25. If I can give one piece of advice from my experience in starting a business I would say it is an experience that is very useful AND will build your personality AND it will give you background which will add vision to your life.

_____

_____

_____

_____

NAME _____

Run-on Sentence: Exercise, Level 2

Correct these run-on sentences by substituting more accurate connecting words or punctuation, by crossing out all deadwood, or, if necessary, by completely rewriting in the space.

1. To become an achiever you must try and be optimistic.

    _____

2. In five minutes a slow song came on and I walked across the dance floor and asked her to dance and she said, "Sure."

    _____

3. Many people have big families and not enough income.

    _____

4. The ambulance attendants arrived and put bandages on my head and carried me into the ambulance.

    _____

5. It rained that afternoon, and planning to get a suntan on the beach was out of the question.

    _____

    _____

6. Many people ignore the basics and jump right into the middle and start to learn from there.

    _____

    _____

7. My grandfather's apartment was like a prison because there were metal bars on the windows and five locks on the door and two chain locks.

    _____

    _____

8. People are getting lazier because now most of their work is being done by machines and the people hardly have to use their bodies and put in an effort and get something done.

    _____

    _____

9. The economy before the invasion was very good and people were better off financially and were living peacefully in a quiet atmosphere, enjoying their lives.

    _____

    _____

10. Let's look at the Philadelphia Flyers, a hockey team that plays a very aggressive game whether winning or losing, but when they're losing they maintain their aggressiveness but you notice signs of hatred and revenge in their game, such as the cheap shots and especially the stick coming down on their opponents.

_____

_____

_____

_____

_____

11. We left my house around eleven, because it's just before midnight when the strip really becomes crowded, because that's when the theatres close, or if there's a concert on at the Gardens, it usually ends around midnight, and few people go home right away, because they go for a walk on the strip and meet all the lunatics they can find.

_____

_____

_____

_____

_____

12. When I started a computer business two years ago with my brother, I entered a world full of long hours of working and dealing with every little problem in the job and also worrying about it all the time, which does not happen with regular hours with a series of known responsibilities at a job with the government or a private company.

_____

_____

_____

_____

_____

13. Up ahead my favourite high-speed bend was coming, so I clicked her in 50 and opened the throttle and without warning my bike was all over the place. My back wheel had become loose and before I could stop, it fell off and I went flying over my handlebars and right over the cliff, and I landed in the water next to a big sharp rock, so I feel lucky to be alive today, because when you come that close to death it really makes you think how easily you can be killed through no fault of your own.

_____

_____

_____

_____

_____

_____

_____

14. The story is told in a narrative way with Frederick Henry narrating for us, and giving us a good literary description of the surroundings and happenings at the present time period of World War I by speaking of common occurrences during the war, such as shell-marked iron of different structures which were hit by enemy artillery during the war, which, in part, is being described generally and fluently by our narrator, who is an ambulance driver for the Italian army, who is also an American who, as mentioned earlier, donated or sold his skills and techniques to the Italian Army during this time of hardship for the Italians and other warring peoples who are taking part in the war which is spoken of in the story.

15. A hundred years ago who could possibly have imagined that by pressing a few buttons on a microwave oven you could get your dinner ready in a few minutes (fast instant frozen food!), or that you could get an important document instantly in your hands while it is being faxed from the other side of the world, or that a human heart would be replaced with a plastic one, or that a computer with artificial intelligence would be capable, in the future, of learning from mistakes, or, even more startling, that you could choose the gender of your baby?

Editing for Pronoun Reference

Pronouns are handy. In substituting for nouns, they save time and spare us clumsy repetition. But like other shortcuts, pronouns can also cost us time and even obstruct the message. Therefore proceed with care: **Make a pronoun refer clearly to the word for which it substitutes.**

A. **In essays, reports and business letters, most pronouns must have an *antecedent*** (that is, *a noun or other pronoun to which the pronoun refers*). Otherwise, isolated pronouns such as "he," "she," "they" or "it" cause confusion because the reader does not know what they mean:

In the far North, *they* do very little in winter. *They* stay inside *their* shelters because the weather can kill.

> The pronoun "they" has no antecedent. We can logically assume that "they" refers not to polar bears or caribou but to humans, but to what humans? Native peoples? Southerners stationed in the North? Those who live off the land? Those searching for oil, gas or minerals? *The easiest way to correct such confusion is to replace a vague pronoun with a noun:*

In the far North, *prospectors* do very little in winter. *They* stay inside *their* shelters because the weather can kill.

> Now the pronouns "they" and "their" make sense, because they can refer to the noun "prospectors." Of course, if the author had placed the word "prospectors" in the sentence before the example, or in some cases even earlier, we would have an antecedent to explain the pronouns. But *the antecedent should not be very far away.* The noun "prospectors" at the opening of an essay will not explain the pronoun "they" in the fifth paragraph!

- Sometimes a pronoun merely *seems* to have an antecedent:

Smoking is an expensive habit. *It* burns away as soon as a person lights *it* up, even when *it* is not being smoked.

> Can "smoking" burn away, be lit up or be smoked? By substituting the noun "smoking" for the pronoun "it," we find that "smoking" has only disguised the lack of a real antecedent. Now let's add one:

Smoking is an expensive habit. A *cigarette* burns away as soon as a person lights *it* up, even when *it* is not being smoked.

> Here is another typical error:

In the newspaper, *it* says we will have a spring election.

> "It" seems to refer to "newspaper" until we substitute the noun:

In the newspaper, the *newspaper* says we will have a spring election.

> Since a newspaper can hardly be *in* itself, we see that there is no antecedent. Let's avoid the problem by removing the pronoun:

The newspaper says we will have a spring election.

- Note that *the pronoun "I" needs no antecedent,* because it refers to the person writing. "We" should be explained, though, so the reader knows who else is included.

- Note that *the pronoun "it" may sometimes be used in a general sense without an antecedent:*

It snowed last night.

It takes two hours to eat a good French dinner.

No one but the writer knows how difficult *it* is to fill up blank pages day after day.

B. **A singular pronoun should not refer to more than one antecedent.** The reader does not enjoy guessing at the meaning of a passage such as this:

In football games I have been in fights to prove that my team is stronger and better than the other team, even though *it* is wrong.

> Which is wrong — the fighting, the author's team or the other team? We cannot be sure. *The easiest way to improve such a sentence is to substitute noun for pronoun:*

In football games I have been in fights to prove that my team is stronger and better than the other team, even though *fights* are wrong.

OR

In football games I have been in fights to prove that my team is stronger and better than the other team, even though *my team* is wrong.

Be especially careful to make the pronouns "which," "that" and "this" refer to only one specific antecedent. Since these pronouns can refer to many things — from a single noun to a group of words to a whole sentence or even a paragraph — they must be used with precision. Is the following passage clear?

My boss accused me of taking extra breaks. *This* was ridiculous, because all day long the store was packed with customers.

Which was ridiculous, the employer's accusation or the author's taking extra breaks? We can only guess. Now let's look at a clearer version of both possibilities:

My employer's accusation that I took extra breaks was ridiculous, because all day long the store was packed with customers.

OR

My employer called my extra breaks ridiculous, because all day long the store was packed with customers.

C. **The pronoun "who" refers to a human antecedent. The pronouns "which" and "that" usually refer to nonhuman antecedents.** In conversation and in colloquial writing these pronouns are often confused, but in serious writing avoid referring to a human as a nonhuman or a nonhuman as a human. Here are some typical errors:

A student *that* cheats may not have a good self-image.

The people *which* lack interest in exercise are lazy in their bodies and minds.

A pup is easier to train than an old dog, *who* cannot learn new tricks.

Let's substitute the correct pronouns:

A student *who* cheats may not have a good self-image.

The people *who* lack interest in exercise are lazy in their bodies and minds.

A pup is easier to train than an old dog, *which* cannot learn new tricks.

NAME _____

Pronoun Reference: Diagnostic Exercise

Put an "X" in the blank beside each passage that contains faulty pronoun reference, and underline all faulty pronouns.

Example: Using the word processor is easier than writing <u>it</u> out on paper.   X̶

1. In British Columbia, trees are their main resource.   _____

2. When a thorn scratched my knee, it became infected with gangrene.   _____

3. In my country, the children grow up totally dependent on their parents even after they are married.   _____

4. How many people do we know that are educated yet do not have a job?   _____

5. By talking, it will bring emotions into the open.   _____

6. A computer does what it is told.   _____

7. Crack addicts may kill their parents because they refuse to give them money to buy the drug.   _____

8. At night, try to walk with someone who can protect you.   _____

9. A submarine is like a whale who dives to the depths.   _____

10. At school, teachers should tell teenagers how to be more responsible when they sit behind the steering wheel.   _____

11. If I won a million-dollar lottery, there are several ways I would spend it.   _____

12. In the travel brochures, they will say anything to convince you to go to their resort.   _____

13. Since the earth is tilted approximately 23 degrees, it causes the sun's rays to reach the earth at different angles.   _____

14. Some employers are unwilling to give women expensive training, because they do not think they will get a return on their money.   _____

15. I have always heard that if strangers meet three times in a single day, they are related.   _____

16. The next generation of parents will probably be the same as their parents unless they learn from their mistakes.   _____

17. The coffee table matches the side table except that it is wider and longer.   _____

18. There have been many celebrities that started with nothing but finished with a fortune.   _____

19. Plumbing was a profitable trade, but I didn't want to be one all my life.   _____

20. Many dog owners feel they are real companions.   _____

21. When I was in high school they were trying out a cooperative program.   _____

22. In Quebec City it is very romantic.   _____

23. Unions are dreaded by large companies, and they do everything in their power to keep them out. _____

24. Why do some people have back problems while others do not? Let us consider them. _____

25. The main character is tremendously wealthy and spends a great deal of it on entertaining. _____

26. Every year in the United States more than 800,000 heart attacks occur, and of those only 300,000 survive. _____

27. In a large corporation, they can afford to spend millions on highrises to show off their success. _____

28. If the credit card is used properly, and it is paid in full when the statement arrives, it has many advantages. _____

29. Children's drawings are very important to some child psychologists because, to them, they are signs of their mental and emotional states. _____

30. When the health authorities came to inspect the restaurant, they told Myra and Carol that they needed special permits to operate. _____

31. People who don't have a job may have to go on welfare. _____

32. The people that really get me are those that run up the escalators. _____

33. Traditional English teachers have a lot of knowledge and experience to offer their students, if they take the time to listen. _____

34. The pensioner and his sister hid from their neighbours because they were afraid they would see how poor they were. _____

35. Stores should not be required to close on Sunday because it creates more jobs. _____

36. There are many different reasons why people start taking drugs, but they all have misconceptions about them. _____

37. Once the grapes are chosen, the next step is to crush them with the grinder. _____

38. When I explore Chinatown, I am fascinated by their culture and traditions. _____

39. Some people will cash their pay cheques and spend it all on lottery tickets. _____

40. Women have been sending a clear message to men that they are as good as they are. _____

NAME _____

Pronoun Reference: Exercise, Level 1

Correct all faulty pronoun reference below. In some cases you can just substitute a clearer word. Where this would produce clumsy repetition, though, rewrite the whole passage. If a passage has no errors, write "Correct" below it.

Example: At hundreds of airports ~~they~~ *guards* have dogs sniffing out illegal drugs or bombs.

1. Have you ever asked yourself why they manufacture products that fall apart?

    _____

    _____

2. The tremendous impact threw me into the windshield. My head crashed through as if it were made of paper.

    _____

    _____

3. At the hospital they put ten stitches in my head.

    _____

    _____

4. The individual that wants to be successful must have a dream.

    _____

    _____

5. In Quebec City I met people who were truly nice.

    _____

    _____

6. When travelling with a large family it can be quite expensive.

    _____

    _____

7. Men no longer have to open doors or light cigarettes for women because they are equal.

    _____

    _____

8. People are becoming unemployed because now a computer can do it faster and better.

    _____

    _____

9. In New York City, people supply drugs to innocent children until they get addicted.

    _____

    _____

10. Suddenly, out of nowhere, a car came swerving around the corner before their light had changed to red.

    _____

    _____

11. Shy people are often misunderstood because they do not express their opinions.

    _____

    _____

12.   Even one dollar is a lot for any person that is fighting to make ends meet.

_____

_____

13.   Parents need to inform their teenagers that they can always come to them for help.

_____

_____

14.   In big cities the traffic is unbelievable! They drive recklessly. They disobey rules, don't stop at red lights and speed as if to win an award.

_____

_____

15.   By building tall buildings, it can save space.

_____

_____

16.   The English promised the French that if they joined them they would give them the same powers, but they didn't.

_____

_____

17.   There are many Canadians that travel to the U.S.A. on Sundays to shop.

_____

_____

18.   For consumers, credit cards are useful because they do not have to carry large amounts of money.

_____

_____

19.   During the final exam, a guy sitting in front of me took a pack of cigarettes out of his pocket and lit it up.

_____

_____

20.   There are concerts in Vancouver almost every week, whether they are small bands trying to hit it big or popular rock bands that travel the world.

_____

_____

NAME _____

Pronoun Reference: Exercise, Level 2

Correct all faulty pronoun reference below. In some cases you can just substitute a clearer word. Where this would produce clumsy repetition, though, rewrite the whole passage. If a passage has no errors, write "Correct" below it.

Example: In earlier times, children were the only security parents had ~~when they became old and helpless.~~ *in old age*

1. We turned on the radio to find out what was happening. There was a tornado warning and it was coming in our direction.

   _____

   _____

2. Men who abuse their wives take away what little confidence they had. By beating them, they wear down their self-esteem because they realize they have nowhere else to go.

   _____

   _____

   _____

3. In Quebec City they have buildings that attract crowds of tourists, because they are hundreds of years old.

   _____

   _____

4. In New York a teenager was stabbed to death for trying to save his parents from thugs that were stealing their money.

   _____

   _____

5. It is so easy to walk around a shopping mall, buy a few things here and there, charge it to your card and forget about it.

   _____

   _____

6. One function of parents is to provide spiritual growth for their children.

   _____

   _____

7. I watched the old man walk out to his car, open the door, start it up and drive away.

   _____

   _____

8. After World War II the soldiers that returned home gave rise to the "baby boom."

   _____

   _____

9. After many studies done by the city of Toronto, they decided to ban smoking in bus terminals, subway stations, airports and governmental offices.

   _____

   _____

   _____

10. Some people think television programs are garbage, but we cannot ignore them just because they don't solve the problems in our society.

_____

_____

11. Verbal abuse is the worst aspect of being overweight. Being called "Fatso" or "Porky" is awful, because there isn't anything you can say back to them.

_____

_____

12. By adding a camper to a pickup truck, it can be used for summer enjoyment.

_____

13. The rent of the store site was extremely expensive since it was located in the centre of Toronto.

_____

14. One of the first things I noticed about Vancouver was the huge numbers of homeless people who roam the streets asking for money.

_____

15. Montreal has many different styles of architecture. They do not yet have the computerized "Lego" neighbourhoods that Toronto does.

_____

_____

16. The reason why people put the elderly in retirement homes is that they are uncaring and selfish.

_____

17. In order for the cars behind us to pass the accident, they went into the opposite lane and stared at us as they drove by.

_____

18. The theoretical basis for communism was developed in the nineteenth century. During the twentieth century it became a political system in many countries.

_____

_____

19. Last-minute changes can be made more efficiently with a word processor. It can be done by loading the essay from disk back into the word processor, making the changes, and then printing it out.

_____

_____

_____

20.   Take politics, for example. Most of them can warp language to their advantage, because they can word campaign promises to solicit a variety of interpretations.

_____

_____

21.   Holding a needle and thread over the abdomen of a pregnant woman can supposedly determine the sex of the child. If the needle moves in circles, it will be a girl. If the needle sways back and forth like a pendulum, it will be a boy.

_____

_____

_____

22.   It rained all night and, as a result, caused the tent to collapse.

_____

_____

23.   Miss Scatcherd accused Helen of not washing her fingernails, which was impossible to do since the water was frozen.

_____

_____

24.   After 30 minutes in the oven, the cake is tested by sticking a knife into it. If the knife blade remains clean, then the cake is done. If the knife blade has some batter on it, then it needs cooking for another ten minutes.

_____

_____

_____

25.   In *Brave New World*, they turn on a loudspeaker while the children are asleep. It continually repeats things, so that when the children awaken they are implanted in their minds. By doing this they can teach what they want, when they want it and how they want it. In this way they condition them to turn out the way they want them to.

_____

_____

_____

_____

_____

Editing for Agreement

The English we speak and the English we write can be as different from each other as the clothes we wear to the beach and the clothes we wear to the prom. In editing for agreement, this contrast can grow so sharp that sometimes it almost seems that what is natural in speech is wrong on the page, and what is correct on the page is unnatural in speech.

But there is really no problem unless we blindly take speech as our model for writing. We would all *say* "Everyone ate their lunch," and our listeners would regard this as normal speech. But the same words in the more formal space of your essay would seem illogical, because "everyone" is singular while "their" is plural.

The principles that follow will sharpen your ability to change between the very informal language of conversation and the more logical and exact language of the essay. Pay special attention to the most useful technique of all, the *pluralizing* suggested at the end of item "H."

A subject and its verb must agree in number; that is, they must both be singular or both be plural. A pronoun and its antecedent — the noun to which it refers — must agree in number and in person.

A. *Make a verb agree with its subject, and a pronoun with its antecedent, no matter how many words separate them.* Sometimes it helps to imagine brackets around interrupting word groups such as dependent clauses, to make items that must agree easier to identify:

          S

My first *impression* [of downtown Toronto with

its noise, traffic jams, crowded buses and

                     V
thousands of pedestrians] *was* frightening.

          S

The *slaughter* [of rare species, not to mention

                          V
many more species still undiscovered], *is* still

continuing.

B. *Make related nouns, pronouns and verbs agree even when one or more is outside the independent clause:*

                        N   V   P
I took the job because the *company pays its* employees well. (Here the related noun, verb and pronoun are all in a dependent clause.)

                    N   V
The film left out many *parts* that *were* covered in the book. (Here a verb in a dependent clause is related to a noun in the independent clause.)

      N   P
A *factory* leaves its workers unemployed when *it* closes down. (Here a pronoun in a dependent clause is related to a noun that is the subject of the independent clause.)

C. *Make the subject and verb agree even when their order is reversed.* Occasionally the verb occurs first, which makes the subject harder to identify. Just remember that the subject is what the sentence is *about*, while the verb tells what the subject *does* or *is*. Once you identify the two, making them agree is easy.

               V   S   S
On the desk *are* [not *is*] the keyboard, monitor,

    S   S
mouse and printer.

To double-check your sentence, think of it in the normal word order with the verb following the subject:

       S   S   S   S   V
The *keyboard, monitor, mouse* and *printer are* on the desk.

D. *Singular subjects joined by* or *or* nor *take singular verbs and pronouns:*

Butter or margarine *is* [not *are*] fattening.

Neither salad nor fruit *is* [not *are*] fattening.

Of course if the items were joined by "and," they would form compound subjects that would call for plural verbs:

Butter and margarine *are* fattening.

Where two subjects are habitually treated as a unit, though, the two together are singular:

Bacon *and* eggs *is* my favourite breakfast.

E. *Collective nouns take singular verbs and singular pronouns when the group is regarded as a unit:*

The company *wants* [not *want*] to lower *its* [not *their*] costs.

The government *was* [not *were*] ready to defend *its* [not *their*] decision.

The team *loses* [not *lose*] more than it *wins* [not they *win*].

Although a company, a government or a team may be made up of many people, we are discussing one company, one government and one team. Therefore each is singular. *If the members of a group act separately, though, the group may be treated as a plural:*

The jury *were* arguing about the verdict.

F. *"Indefinite pronouns" are usually singular, even though some may seem plural.*

another	everything
any	neither
anybody	nobody
anyone	no one
anything	nothing
each	one
either	somebody
everybody	someone
everyone	something

Anyone who *is* finished may hand in *his or her* [not *their*] essay.

Someone *has* left *his or her* [not *their*] notebook.

Everyone *is* going with *his or her* [not *their*] friends.

Note: Traditionally the pronoun "he" can represent people in general (as in a group that includes both males and females). Today, though, many people view this as unfair to women. Therefore in the examples above, we have used "he or she" instead of the singular "he" (remember that "he or she" is singular, because both pronouns are joined by "or").

See further solutions to this common problem in the next section, "Editing for Equality of the Sexes in Language."

G. If you are not sure whether a verb is singular or plural, remember that *although the final "s" makes a noun plural, it makes a verb singular:*

SINGULAR

    N V
The bird flies.

PLURAL

    N V
The birds fly.

If you are still in doubt about the number of a verb, apply the "it-they" test. Place the words "it" and "they" before the verb. If singular "it" sounds right with the verb, the verb is singular; if plural "they" sounds right, the verb is plural:

SINGULAR   PLURAL

H. *Be consistent in pronoun use.* Do not change in the middle of a passage from "he or she" to "they":

WRONG

The sensible drinker will have only one or two beers, so *he or she* will not lose *their* self-control.

The student who wrote this sentence forgot that singular subjects joined by "or" take singular verbs and pronouns. Other writers grimly exchange bad grammar for bad style by repeating pronouns:

The sensible drinker will have only one or two beers, so *he or she* will not lose *his or her* self-control.

As was said in the box, the traditional "he" or "his" is no longer the solution. It may be less repetitious than "he or she" and "his or her," but it implies that women do not exist:

The sensible drinker will have only one or two beers, so *he* will not lose *his* self-control.

A better solution is to rewrite the sentence so as to avoid all problems of grammar, style and prejudice:

The sensible drinker will have only one or two beers, to avoid losing self-control.

Note how the statement now has no pronoun problems because it has no pronouns at all! Solutions like these are very direct but not always possible. You will find that the most widely useful solution of all is to *pluralize* from the beginning. Use this method often:

Sensible *drinkers* will have only one or two beers, so *they* will not lose *their* self-control.

I. *A pronoun and its antecedent must agree in person:*

FIRST PERSON
I, me, we, us

SECOND PERSON
you

THIRD PERSON
he, him, she, her, one, it, they, them

In speech and informal writing, the second-person "you" is often used to mean people in general. Yet "you" is in the second person while "people" is in the third person. "You" may even be under-stood by the reader to mean herself or himself, personally:

In the two years *I* worked at the restaurant, *I* was always given a meal, a break and all the pop *you* could drink.

Unless the reader is the person who drank the pop, the writer should stay in first person:

In the two years *I* worked at the restaurant, *I* was always given a meal, a break and all the pop *I* could drink.

> *Note:* There is no such word as *"themself,"* because "them" is plural while "self" is singular. Instead, write the logical and standard term, *"themselves."*

NAME _____

Agreement: Diagnostic Exercise

Put an "X" in the blank beside each passage that contains an error in agreement.

1. In Canada a criminal is eligible for parole after he or she has served one-third of their sentence. _____

2. Everyone introduced themselves to me. _____

3. The streets was filled with people. _____

4. Computer viruses can duplicate themself and move to another system, then duplicate themself again. _____

5. Every day someone behind you pushes and shoves their way into the subway car. _____

6. The number of babies being born continue to decline. _____

7. I take pride in my car. It is great to have your own transportation for your convenience. _____

8. Everyone is unique. _____

9. Neither money nor power provide true happiness in life. _____

10. In the main office are a dispatcher, a sergeant and a staff sergeant. _____

11. Every résumé should have a brief covering letter which shows the company that you know something about them. _____

12. If anyone tried to wander from the camp, they were imprisoned or shot. _____

13. American movies and television programs dominates our Canadian society. _____

14. Nobody wants to have a dump in their neighbourhood. _____

15. The price of goods is so high that some families cannot even buy enough food for their children. _____

16. A pregnant person would start asking themselves questions such as "Is it a girl or a boy?" _____

17. How is one supposed to get experience if they cannot even get a job first? _____

18. My impression of the Ontario landscape was of hilly and rocky terrain. You could see trees for miles around. _____

19. Many drug users cannot comprehend the problems their habit is causing. _____

20. Contact lenses may hurt your eyes if you wear it for a long time. _____

21. Everyone was asking me questions. _____

22. A senior citizen may need a part-time job in sales to keep them active. _____

23. The government is discriminating when they tell store owners to close on Sunday. _____

24. The number of universities and colleges is increasing every year. _____

25. For a few minutes of happiness in gambling, one can lose the fortune which they have built all their lives. _____

26. A person's drive to become rich causes them to lose touch with the important things in life. _____

27. The streets of Montreal was very busy. _____

28. Since economy cars have only four cylinders, it will use less fuel and produce less pollution than luxury cars. _____

29. At the foot of the bed are a desk and a chair. _____

30. In prison I dared not pick a quarrel with anyone, because they could beat me at any time. _____

31. The *Sun* fills their classified section with 20 pages of ads for cars, houses and jobs. _____

32. When the price per share goes up, one sells their shares to make a profit. _____

33. Our society rarely pays attention to alcoholics. _____

34. For any person who is afraid of living by themself, it is nice to have a roommate to accompany you. _____

35. Not everybody has had to deal with the death of someone they care deeply about. _____

36. The orchestra were playing quietly in the background. _____

37. The number of common-law marriages have risen. _____

38. Everybody learns from their experience. _____

39. The more hours you work, the more money one receives. _____

40. Toronto's streets and highways are proof that the number of cars on the roads is increasing. _____

NAME _____

Agreement: Exercise, Level 1

Circle the correct choice in the parentheses.

1. The cost of houses (*are* / *is*) rising rapidly.

2. If anyone drove across Canada, (*they* / *he or she*) would notice a lot of empty land.

3. Jack's entire family (*was* / *were*) overweight.

4. To avoid criminal attack, we must think of methods to reduce the chance of its happening to (*you* / *us* / *him or her*).

5. One of the car's lights (*were* / *was*) burned out.

6. The press earns (*its* / *their*) profit only from the advertisements (*it publishes* / *they publish*).

7. Anyone who denies that (*he or she has* / *they have*) ever flirted just isn't telling the truth.

8. A major nuisance in watching a television program (*are* / *is*) the commercials that interrupt it.

9. Across the street (*was* / *were*) an emergency hydro truck, two fire trucks, three police cars and an ambulance.

10. Neither a husband nor a wife (*are* / *is*) free to break marriage vows.

11. The purpose of the pyramids (*is* / *are*) still unknown.

12. When the temperature falls below the freezing point, no one leaves home without (*their* / *his or her*) winter coat.

13. Every family worries about how to educate (*its* / *their*) children.

14. Without vegetation, the topsoil full of nutrients (*are* / *is*) washed away.

15. Each of us (*has* / *have*) unique abilities.

16. To me, friends are essential. Without them (*you* / *I*) would be unable to function normally.

17. If you like somebody, you will worry about (*them* / *him or her*).

18. The number of abortions (*are* / *is*) increasing.

19. Front-wheel-drive cars are the best for (*their* / *its*) good handling.

20. A variety of weapons (*are* / *is*) used in war.

21. The electronics industry (*is* / *are*) advancing rapidly.

22. Between studs, joists and rafters, reflective insulation (*are* / *is*) used.

23. Retirement is something everyone must face at some point in (*his or her life* / *their lives*).

24. The merchandise in New York City, such as stereos, cameras and other electronic equipment, (*are* / *is*) cheaper than in Toronto.

25. Today the cost of housing makes you think twice. Should (*I* / *you*) move out, or stay with (*my* / *your*) parents?

NAME _____

Agreement: Exercise, Level 2

Cross out each error in agreement and write a correction in the blank at the end of the line in which it occurs. If a passage contains no errors, write "Correct" after it.

Example: The number of white-collar crimes ~~have~~ risen sharply.   *has*

1. I like to read the newspaper, which is where you learn what is happening around you in   _____

   our daily lives.   _____

2. The day I started working for the city of Regina, I was so nervous that my insides felt   _____

   like it was going through a blender.   _____

3. The next time you walk by a homeless person, do not treat them like an animal. Give   _____

   them the dignity and respect they deserve.   _____

4. At one end of the room is the tuner, turntable, speakers and two shelves of albums.   _____

5. Gambling can bring one's life up to heaven or down to hell, depending on how much   _____

   they know about the game and how long they spend practising.   _____

6. The interest rate a company will charge a person to use one of its cards is astonishing. _____

7. I have been to Montreal several times. I like to travel on their subways because it's   _____

   clean and attractive.   _____

8. Either slavery or rebellion are the reaction of a child raised by authoritarian parents. _____

9. If you are neat, then it is hard for you to get along with a person who throws their   _____

   clothes around or leaves their dirty dishes in the sink.   _____

10. What makes hockey bloodier than other major sports is the fact that for 60 minutes of   _____

    playing time, each of the players carries a large weapon in his hands, a stick that   _____

    measures five feet in length and has a pointed tip, the better with which to jab your   _____

    opponent in the gut.   _____

11. An entire industry of cosmetic products have been created to prevent aging.   _____

12. In Canada the government acts as a medical insurance company.   _____

13. Why would one risk going into business for oneself, if not to manage your own business   _____

    the way you wish to, without interference from others?   _____

14. In Toronto no one talks to anyone unless they know them.   _____

15. I will be more careful in choosing a partner for my next relationship. I want someone _____

who can take the initiative in telephoning me, showing their feelings about me and just _____

showing they care. _____

16. Everyone knows that eating fatty foods like french fries, hot dogs and bacon make us _____

overweight. _____

17. As soon as I open the machine shop door the smell of burning steel and oil rushes into _____

my nose and makes me cough. The constant harsh noises hit you like a car. _____

18. The feelings that flow through your body as you soar down the hill are indescribable. _____

19. As I grew older and very attracted to women, the idea of committing yourself to one _____

person for the rest of your life still didn't turn me on. _____

20. One can almost believe that they are actually part of the film as the Dolby stereo sound _____

of an explosion trembles right through your body. _____

NAME _____

Agreement: Exercise, Level 3

Cross out each error in agreement, and correct it above the line in which it occurs. If a passage contains so many errors that it must be substantially reworked, write a new version beneath it. If a passage contains no errors at all, write "Correct" in the space.

Example: Everyone on the boat, including myself, ~~were~~ *was* very nervous about the storm.

1. A willingness on both sides to work problems out, and a steady means of communication, is required to make a relationship work.

    _____

2. The circulatory system is composed of three different types of blood vessels: arteries, capillaries and veins. These link the system, although each perform a different task.

    _____

    _____

3. The government can do several things to reduce dangerous driving by teenagers. First of all, they can be stricter in issuing driver's licences. They can even consider the conduct of the person in high school.

    _____

    _____

4. On the dresser is a small radio and a lamp.

    _____

5. Decorating your room on a low budget can bring headaches and certainly takes patience, but the compliments you'll get and the sense of pride you'll feel every time you look around your room is worth the effort.

    _____

    _____

6. Neither a university nor a community college totally prepares a student for the world of work.

    _____

    _____

7. The more expensive the car, the greater the cost in insurance, because they are more vulnerable to theft and vandalism, and its parts are more costly to replace. Economy cars, on the other hand, are cheaper to insure because its parts are cheaper and because it is less appealing to crooks.

    _____

    _____

    _____

    _____

8. To obtain a handgun in the United States, a person undergoes only a quick police check to ensure that they are not already a wanted criminal. Then they can buy a handgun. The gun does not even have to be locked up. It can be stored in a drawer in your home or the glove compartment of your car, or even concealed on your body. It can be stored anywhere a person might need it in order to protect themselves.

_____

_____

_____

_____

_____

_____

9. My friend told me that her parents' divorce has affected her in these ways: You learn how to take care of yourself. You're more mature than other people. You don't need anyone to tell me what to do. You learn how to be more disciplined. I can stay out to any time but I try to limit myself. I just don't feel good staying out all night. She also mentioned that the most frightening feeling of all was knowing that she misses having her parents asking her what time she will be home or how school was today.

_____

_____

_____

_____

_____

_____

10. As a potential alcoholic walks down the street and sees the terrifying life of skid-row panhandlers, complete with their wine sores and filthy clothes, they confidently say that this would never happen to them because they are different. They do not realize that just a few years ago, the person they are looking at probably had a good job and a happy home life! Then something happened that they couldn't handle, and the drink which had always rescued them now turned out to be their worst enemy.

_____

_____

_____

_____

_____

_____

_____

Editing for Equality of the Sexes in Language

One of the most important social trends of our time has been the rising status of women. Not only do most Canadian women now have a job, but increasing numbers have entered professions formerly dominated by men (such as law, medicine and business), and more and more women have taken management positions.

Since language reflects society, some traditional aspects of English now strike many people as "sexist" — biased against women. To say "policeman" ignores the fact that today we also see women patrolling the streets and driving squad cars. It is only natural that more and more people now say and write "police officer" instead of "policeman," for this more neutral term reflects an equality of the sexes.

Although traditionalists may not yet consider previous usage to be "incorrect," sexism in language is insensitive toward half the human race. Study the following suggestions for your own writing.

A. *Avoid terms that unnecessarily differentiate female from male:*

AVOID	TRY
businessman	*business person, entrepreneur, manager*
chairman	*chairperson, chair, head*
housewife	*homemaker (can signify either a male or female)*
maiden name	*birth name*
mailman	*letter carrier*
man, mankind	*humanity, humankind, humans, the human race, people*
man-made	*imitation, synthetic, artificial*
poetess	*poet*
policeman, patrolman	*police officer*
salesman	*salesperson, clerk, sales clerk*
stewardess	*flight attendant*
waitress	*server, attendant*
woman doctor, lady dentist, woman lawyer	*doctor, dentist, lawyer*

Roberts/Comstock.

B. *Use forms of address that reflect equality of the sexes.* Traditionally we have called a woman either "Miss" or "Mrs.," depending on whether she is single or married. By contrast, we have used the term "Mr." for all men. Some women still prefer the traditional terms; in these cases continue to use "Miss" or "Mrs." But many other women, who resent this unnecessary scrutiny of their personal lives, like to be called "Ms." Respect their wish.

In the past, a woman was often addressed by her husband's full name:

Mrs. Pierre Tremblay

Mrs. Albert Tsang

Avoid this practice, for it implies that a woman's identity is derived only through a husband. Instead, use the woman's own name, preceded by "Ms." — unless she prefers "Mrs.":

Ms. Jocelyne Tremblay

Mrs. Elaine Tsang

(Of course specify her own last name if she does not use her husband's.)

C. *The pronoun "he" should refer only to males.* The tradition of using "he" for a person or persons of unspecified gender now seems prejudiced: it implies that females are less important than males. Examples of traditional sexist usage:

Everyone paid for *his* own dinner. (Assumption: everyone is male.)

A lawyer often has little time for *his* family. (Assumption: all lawyers are men.)

One alternative is "his or her" (to be fair, use "her or his" half the time):

A lawyer often has little time for *his or her* family.

One problem with this approach, though, can be clumsy repetition and wordiness:

A lawyer has not only too little time for *her or his* clients, but also for *her or his* family.

In reaching for a style free of repetition, many people create new errors, this time in agreement:

A lawyer has not only too little time for *his or her* clients, but also for *their* own family. (While "his or her" is singular, "their" is plural.)

A better solution is to use plurals all the way:

Lawyers have not only too little time for *their* clients, but also for *their* own families.

In some cases *an even better approach to this and other pronoun problems is to rewrite the sentence without pronouns at all:*

A lawyer has too little time for either clients or family.

At first it may seem hard to free your prose of sexual bias while still maintaining good style. But remember that there are almost always other ways to word your thoughts. Seek them through revision, as in these examples.

D. *Stereotyping the sexes is a form of bias. Avoid it.* Consider alternatives such as these:

BIASED	NEUTRAL
A welder must protect *his* eyes. (In other words, welders are men.)	*Welders* must protect *their* eyes. (Use plurals to avoid "his.")
A nurse must respect *her* patients. (In other words, nurses are women.)	A nurse must respect patients. (Remove the pronoun.)
	OR
	Nurses must respect *their* patients. (Use plurals.)
There were too many *guys* at the party and not enough *girls*. (In other words, females are only girls.)	There were too many *men* at the party and not enough *women*.
	OR
	There were too many *boys* at the party, and not enough *girls*. (Imply equality by using parallel terms.)

NAME _____

Equality of the Sexes in Language: Exercise

Most of the following sentences contain terms that show bias against women. Replace all sexist usages with unbiased terms. If necessary, revise the whole sentence in the space below. Write "unbiased" under any sentence that needs no work.

1. Within a decade, man will be on Mars.

    _____

    _____

2. When I regained consciousness, a lady doctor was taking my pulse.

    _____

    _____

3. Whether he knows it or not, anyone who drives a car produces acid ran.

    _____

    _____

4. My neighbour is a police officer.

    _____

    _____

5. It takes more than just size to be a policeman.

    _____

    _____

6. The guests were Mr. and Mrs. Edward Turnbull, Mr. Peter Chen, Miss Nancy Donnelly and Mr. and

    Mrs. Antonio Santos.

    _____

    _____

    _____

7. Vacuum cleaner salesmen intimidate housewives by accusing them of having filthy carpets.

    _____

    _____

8. All the executives and their wives came to the party.

    _____

    _____

9.   What was your mother's maiden name?

_____

10.   It took over 5000 man-hours to build the model submarine.

_____

_____

11.   A good secretary keeps her desk neat.

_____

_____

12.   A good foreman is fair to his workers.

_____

_____

13.   All parents have their good and bad moments.

_____

_____

14.   The mailman was late that day.

_____

_____

15.   Forty police manned the roadblocks to catch the fleeing gunmen.

_____

_____

16.   There are 23 girls in my class but only seven guys.

_____

_____

17.   How much should we tip the waitress?

_____

_____

18.   My heart sank when our flight attendant showed how to use the life preservers.

_____

_____

19.   Some con men are never caught.

_____

_____

20.   Every soldier knows how to maintain his rifle.

_____

_____

21.   The candidates are Mr. Frank Johnson, Miss Lise Gagnon, Mr. Joseph Horvath and Mrs. Barry Rossiter.

_____

_____

22.   Mankind is his own worst enemy.

_____

_____

23.   Most consumers avoid shoes of man-made leather.

_____

_____

24.   Any person who skips breakfast is endangering his health.

_____

_____

25.   Our neighbourhood is crowded with young girls and boys.

_____

_____

26.   The farmer often makes too little to cover his own costs, while the middleman in the city grows wealthy.

_____

_____

27.   The chairman tabled the committee's report.

_____

_____

28.   If he studies each day's work on time, the student will have no trouble with exams.

_____

_____

29.   Most of Canada's top businessmen think government spending is out of control.

_____

_____

30.   After a day on the oil rigs, you crave a man-sized dinner.

_____

_____

Editing to Avoid Misplaced Modifiers and Dangling Modifiers

A modifier is a word or word group that explains another word or word group. Place a modifier as close as possible to what it modifies; otherwise it may cause confusion by seeming to explain the wrong thing:

UNCLEAR

> Most people like to relax after a hard day's work *in front of the TV.*

CLEAR

> Most people like to relax *in front of the TV* after a hard day's work.

Sometimes a misplaced modifier creates a ridiculous meaning, as above where the writer claims that people do a hard day's work in front of the TV. In other cases, a misplaced modifier merely obscures the meaning. The carelessly worded first sentence below was supposed to mean what the second one actually says:

UNCLEAR

> I *only* eat out once a week.

CLEAR

> I eat out *only* once a week.

The word *only* is the most commonly misplaced modifier in written English, because it is so often placed carelessly in speech. Remember that the position of words strongly influences meaning. Note how the sentence below changes each time the modifier moves to a new position:

> *Only* I saw the robbery on Saturday. (No one else saw it.)
>
> I *only* saw the robbery on Saturday. (I saw it but did not hear it.)
>
> I saw *only* the robbery on Saturday. (I saw nothing else that day.)
>
> I saw the *only* robbery on Saturday. (There were no other robberies that day.)
>
> I saw the robbery *only* on Saturday. (I did not see it any other day.)

A dangling modifier is a modifier connected loosely or not at all to the word or word group to which it should refer. Thus the modifier may seem to explain the wrong thing. Dangling modifiers are harder to correct than misplaced ones because they cannot simply be moved to another spot; instead, part of the sentence must be rewritten to make the connection.

UNCLEAR

> *While reading this essay,* four people will die of starvation and twenty-four babies will be born somewhere in the world.

If the student who wrote this sentence had specified a reader, the ridiculous idea of dying and newborn persons reading the essay would not have occurred to us:

CLEAR

> *While you read this essay,* four people will die of starvation and twenty-four babies will be born somewhere in the world.

CLEAR

> *In the time it takes the reader to finish this essay,* four people will die of starvation and twenty-four babies will be born somewhere in the world.

UNCLEAR

> *When driving,* the most important part of the car is the brake. (Is the brake driving?)

CLEAR

> *To drivers,* the most important part of the car is the brake.

Not all dangling modifiers seem as ridiculous as the ones above. Do not let them escape undetected just because, like the one below, they are relatively easy to interpret:

UNCLEAR

> At home, *when doing my homework,* there aren't any noisy parties to bother me as there are in the student residence.

Since the author has used the words "*my* homework" and "to bother *me,*" we probably will not imagine that a noisy party is doing the homework. Yet the sentence leaves us with the uneasy feeling that we are guessing at its meaning. If the author would refer more directly to herself or himself by saying "when I am at home" and move the words "student residence" closer to the "noisy parties" that occur there, the sentence would become clear:

CLEAR

> *When I am at home,* the noisy parties at the student residence cannot distract me from my homework.

NAME _____

Misplaced and Dangling Modifiers: Diagnostic Exercise

Write "MM" in the blank beside each sentence that contains a misplaced modifier, and underline the misplaced modifier.

1.   Active sports involve a lot of competition, such as soccer.   _____

2.   Children flock to see Santa Claus by the dozens.   _____

3.   Years ago I think back when my friend offered me a cigarette at a party.   _____

4.   If you are like most people, a mortgage will be the largest debt of your lifetime.   _____

5.   I moved to Bayside with my parents when I was 13 years old from the city of Ottawa.   _____

6.   All students are not necessarily the same.   _____

7.   Pills are virtually used for everything.   _____

8.   By staying home you can save transportation money.   _____

9.   As a child, my father told me that the world is a cruel place to be in alone.   _____

10. For many people, losing weight is a difficult problem.   _____

11. A camera can only focus sharply on one object at a time.   _____

12. Hailstones only reach 2.5 cm in diameter.   _____

13. Since I was an only child, my parents wanted to protect me.   _____

14. Car rental is only possible through credit cards.   _____

15. Some programs of study are only available in community colleges.   _____

16. It takes my mother only three minutes to drive to work.   _____

17. Drinking is said to be a bad habit by many doctors.   _____

18. When I was four, my parents and I moved into a new house.   _____

19. There is no city that has no crimes at all in this world.   _____

20. When I was a kid I lived with my grandmother, a lovely lady who would let me do anything I wanted to, for a few months.   _____

Write "DM" in the blank beside each sentence that contains a dangling modifier, and underline the dangling modifier.

1.   After waiting two hours in the lobby, the doctor spent less than two minutes on me.   _____

2.   Looking at my nephew watching television, he seems to be in a trance.   _____

3.   Living on the farm in southern Ontario, winter tends to be cold and harsh.   _____

4. At the age of 13 years, my entire life changed when my mother filed for a separation. _____

5. After a few months of cleaning a dentist's office, the dentist recommended me to her bookkeeper, so I was able to clean the bookkeeper's office too. _____

6. Dogs make good household pets because they are used for protecting the house while away for the day. _____

7. After driving into the middle lane, the truck slowed to a stop. _____

8. When I stroll down a busy city street, accompanied by a blaring walkman, my attention is distracted from my physical environment. _____

9. After being introduced to the class, everyone was nice to me. _____

10. Mothers tend to treat boys and girls differently when small. _____

11. After hearing what had happened, my blood began to boil as an irrational madness for revenge surged through my body. _____

12. Going through Grade 12, the teachers began to demand more work. _____

13. After I finish one or two drinks, my brain feels very light. _____

14. Loose bindings will cause the skis to fall off while standing up and skiing. _____

15. By recycling paper, thousands of square kilometres of forest will be preserved. _____

16. As I recalled my lessons, I didn't feel like attempting anything difficult. _____

17. After spending three hours shivering and trying to stay warm, the storm subsided and we quickly headed for camp. _____

18. When feeling depressed or lonely, a dog is always at your side wagging its tail. _____

19. After writing tests and quizzes, the board of education agreed to let me attend Grade 12 at York Memorial High School. _____

20. When driving in a big city like Montreal, parking is always a problem. _____

NAME _____

Misplaced and Dangling Modifiers: Exercise, Level 1

Revise these sentences, correcting all misplaced or dangling modifiers. If a sentence has no error, write "Correct" in the space.

Example: ~~As~~ When I was a teenager, Agatha Christie was my favourite novelist.

1. By simply repeating commands, my dog eventually understood what I wanted him to do.

    _____

    _____

2. The regiment brutally attacked the enemy, when asleep, with rifles and hand grenades.

    _____

    _____

3. Glasses can be a burden, especially when competing in hockey or football.

    _____

    _____

4. Standing on the beach, the water gently rippled over my toes.

    _____

    _____

5. When watching a one-hour show, as many as six food commercials can come on.

    _____

    _____

6. Barrie is a quiet town when browsing through the main street.

    _____

    _____

7. While downhill skiing, your expenses can run into the hundreds of dollars.

    _____

    _____

8. At the age of four, my parents separated.

    _____

    _____

9. I only lost my first game.

    _____

    _____

10. There should be only one system of weights and measures.

_____

_____

11. The media people only talk about teams that lose, not teams that win.

_____

_____

12. Using a word processor, the usual speed is around 65 to 75 words per minute.

_____

_____

13. Now at the age of six months, we take the dog everywhere we go.

_____

_____

14. After finishing breakfast the house is straightened up.

_____

_____

15. It was at the age of eight when my father first took me on a hike through the woods.

_____

_____

16. Thinking about Los Angeles, Hollywood is the first thing that comes to mind.

_____

_____

17. In living common-law, a child is considered illegitimate.

_____

_____

18. Now old people are told by their children what to do.

_____

_____

19. I was discouraged from speaking the truth by my lawyer.

_____

_____

20. Walking along Robson Street, a major thoroughfare like Yonge Street but half the length, the trendy shops sell the latest fashions and souvenirs for tourists.

_____

_____

NAME _____

Misplaced and Dangling Modifiers: Exercise, Level 2

Revise these sentences, correcting all misplaced or dangling modifiers. If a sentence has no error, write "Correct" in the space.

1. Sitting in the waiting room, looking through an old coverless issue of *National Geographic*, the dentist approached me.

    _____

    _____

    _____

2. This summer I worked as a computer-controlled milling machine programmer.

    _____

    _____

    _____

3. Nearing the top flight of stairs, my nostrils detected the familiar stale stench of the gym.

    _____

    _____

    _____

4. I called the personnel manager on the phone, and by making a good first impression she called me for an interview.

    _____

    _____

    _____

5. By taking a closer look at your immediate environment, the causes of acid rain will become clear.

    _____

    _____

    _____

6. Most students employed during the school break are able to work only three or four months.

    _____

    _____

    _____

7. In prison one is only allowed a certain amount of time to go outside into a yard surrounded by a fence, or else to sit and read in the cell.

    _____

    _____

    _____

8. Garage doors can either be opened sideways or upward.

    _____

    _____

    _____

9. The music on the album was both recorded on stage and in the studio.

_____

_____

10. Money management is a crucial skill, when budgeting for postsecondary education.

_____

_____

11. Racing into a high-speed corner at 150 km per hour on a motorcycle, many things are going through the biker's head.

_____

_____

12. By the time I had spent an hour underwater, the cold was setting in.

_____

_____

13. While jogging, tissues in the uterus have a tendency to stretch or tear, which weakens the walls, thus creating problems in childbirth.

_____

_____

14. While observing all the fascinating shapes of coral in the water, odd peeping fish began to crowd around my feet.

_____

_____

15. Companies along the lakefront dump their hazardous wastes into Lake Ontario, without having been treated.

_____

_____

16. Stephen Leacock was born in England in 1869. At the age of seven his family moved to Canada and settled on a farm near Lake Simcoe.

_____

_____

_____

17. Young pregnant teenagers out of wedlock think the best thing to do for their problem is get married.

_____

_____

_____

18.   Living at the corner of Jarvis and Carlton, the growl of engines, screech of tires and shriek of horns blend together in a roar so loud that at times it shakes the windows.

_____

_____

_____

19.   Meeting my unit supervisor was next, who coordinated the ward's daily activities.

_____

_____

20.   Before getting married I believe that both the woman and man have to look ahead to make sure they are doing the right thing.

_____

_____

21.   After the man received his money, he rushed out of the bank and vowed that he would never return.

_____

_____

22.   One day, while motoring down Eglinton Avenue with my wife, we were discussing our future.

_____

_____

23.   It seems that when reading the newspaper today, a story can always be found on a large company being caught for polluting the environment.

_____

_____

24.   After gaining some composure and getting my two feet on the ground, Peter and I started talking about exactly what went wrong.

_____

_____

25.   Sitting on the bus, tears came to most people's eyes as they thought back to the joyful life they had led before the rebels took over the country.

_____

_____

26.   When becoming financially independent, responsibility and money management come into play when simply working and saving up for an item like a stereo set.

_____

_____

_____

27.   Many workers die shortly after being pensioned off because of a lack of interest in other things.

_____

_____

28.   The bride had long white gloves made of lace on her hands.

_____

_____

29.   Two hundred years ago, half of the newborn babies died from any number of childhood diseases. With today's medical knowledge, the threat of death to an infant has almost been eliminated.

_____

_____

_____

30.   Having immigrated to Toronto nine years ago from Santiago, Chile, the amazement of experiencing two vastly different city lifestyles has been thrilling.

_____

_____

_____

Editing for Parallel Form

Closely related parts of a sentence should fit harmoniously together. Like a red fender on a blue car, the wrong kind of word or word group in a sentence can ruin the effect of the whole.

Consider this example:

> My boss was furious. She wanted to know why I was late, why I hadn't phoned, and *you'd better get serious about this job!*

While we can guess that the person who must get serious about this job is the author, the sentence would be clearer and the style more harmonious if we made a change:

> She wanted to know why I was late, why I hadn't phoned, and *why I wasn't serious about this job.*

Now we have a series of three indirect questions, rather than the start of a series interrupted by an independent clause. We have a sentence written in *parallel form.*

A. Items in a series should be *parallel in form.* For example, if one is a noun they should all be nouns; if one is a verb they should all be verbs; if one is in past tense they should all be in past tense.

WEAK

> Three ways to prevent burnout are having an active social life, eating a balanced diet and regular exercise.

BETTER

> Three ways to prevent burnout are *having* an active social life, *eating* a balanced diet and *getting* regular exercise. (All present participles.)

BETTER

> Three things that prevent burnout are an active social *life*, a balanced *diet* and regular *exercise*. (All nouns)

BETTER

> Three ways to prevent burnout are *to socialize* often, *to eat* a balanced diet and *to exercise* regularly. (All infinitives)

If the items of a series are *parallel in form*, they should also be *related in logic*:

Santa Claus, an old Christmas legend, is a reality to young children. He is an old gentleman in a red suit, black boots, white beard, a big belly and eight flying reindeer pulling a sleigh.

Santa Claus may be an old gentleman *in* a red suit and *in* black boots, but is he *in* a white beard? Is he *in* a big belly? Is he *in* eight flying reindeer? Let's make some changes:

He is an old gentleman *in* a red suit and black boots, *with* a white beard and a big belly. Eight flying reindeer pull his sleigh.

> Split up a list, as above, if the items are not closely enough related to be parallel in form.

B. Word groups that are paired by *contrast, alternation or another relationship* are most effective when parallel:

WEAK

> I thought *I would save my money* but instead *a financial loss occurred.*

BETTER

> I thought *I would save my money* but instead *I lost it.* (Note that "it," a pronoun, parallels "money," a noun. Note also that putting a paired statement in parallel form can save words.)

Photo courtesy of Suzanne Conrad.

WEAK

The advantages of public transit are *low fare* and *the environment is saved.*

BETTER

Public transit helps us *to save* money and *to protect* the environment.

BETTER

Public transit *saves* us money and *protects* the environment.

C. In *comparisons*, parallel form is especially important. Lack of it can produce a "faulty comparison" like this:

An airplane takes a shorter time reaching its destination than by driving a car.

To prevent the airplane from driving a car, let's omit the unparallel item, *by driving:*

An airplane takes a shorter time reaching its destination than does a car.

Better yet, let's save words by recasting the whole sentence:

An airplane is faster than a car.

Best of all, let's scrap the sentence because everyone knows that an airplane is faster than a car. Another person wrote this:

The heart of a child beats faster than an adult.

In other words a *heart* is beating faster than a *person*. Let's add the pronoun *that* to parallel the noun *heart:*

The *heart* of a child beats faster than *that* of an adult.

NAME _____

Parallel Form: Exercise 1

One item in each series is not parallel to the other items. Cross it out, then substitute an item that is parallel.

Example: eating
          drinking
          ~~talked~~ *talking*
          sleeping

1. see
    hear
    feel
    touching
    taste

2. tall
    wide
    thick
    heaviness

3. to write
    speaking
    to read

4. confidence
    authority
    skilfully
    judgement

5. yellow
    large
    green
    red

6. frying
    baking
    to roast

7. steer
    shifted gears
    park
    accelerate

8. lack of exercise
    excess of food
    drinking too much

9. newspapers
    books
    magazines
    going to the movies

10. to skate
    skiing
    swimming
    dancing

11. Spain
    France
    Italy
    Ireland
    London

12. under the table
    after dinner
    in the closet
    behind the chair

13. Monday
    Wednesday
    April
    Saturday

14. honesty
    intelligent
    integrity
    loyalty

15. beaten
    vanquished
    overpowered
    losing

16. to plough the soil
    planting the seeds
    to cultivate the earth
    to harvest the crop

17. Chevrolet
    Ford
    Harley-Davidson
    Oldsmobile

18. love
    hate
    jealousy
    friendliness
    angry

19. hockey
    football
    playing tennis
    basketball

20. spring
    June
    fall
    winter

NAME _____

Parallel Form: Exercise 2

Change the faulty sentences so that each is parallel in form. Retain all the facts, but in each case use the method of revision that seems best. If the form is already parallel, write "Parallel" in the space.

Example: In my free time I listen to records, go to movies and take long walks.

1. My brother prefers luxuries like eating good food and nice clothing.

    _____

    _____

2. In Canada we have snow, rain, sun, cloudy, wind, warm and cold.

    _____

    _____

3. The walkman can be worn while skiing, taking a bath, working out, jogging, cycling, walking, relaxing, suntanning, boating or even swimming.

    _____

    _____

    _____

4. Like many of the schools in Trinidad, we all had to wear uniforms.

    _____

    _____

5. My office position requires me to answer phone calls, filing charts, using the computer to assist me in reaching the information that I need, and to retrieve charts for nurses and doctors.

    _____

    _____

    _____

    _____

    _____

6. The role of women in supporting the family is as important as men.

    _____

    _____

7. Some cars are sporty models, luxury, family, economic, trucks and vans.

    _____

    _____

8. The television habit is as hard to break as taking drugs.

    _____

    _____

9. If teachers lack the basic skills to teach a language, then so will the students.

    _____

    _____

10. A voice said over the P.A. system that the train was arriving and stand behind the yellow line.

_____

11. I enjoy skating, swimming, dancing, parties, walking in parks and a few hobbies.

_____

12. As a small child I was very spoiled: I was the only daughter, the only granddaughter and the only niece.

_____

13. My favourite newspaper is the _Toronto Sun_: it's small, easy to read, the horoscope and the sports section.

_____

14. We have many stereotypes of "bike" riders: black leather jackets, big black boots, long thick chains and of course tough and mean.

_____

_____

15. The cost of keeping a car is worse than keeping a child.

_____

16. Today there are three types of parents: permissive, strict and wealthy.

_____

17. The rent of newer buildings is much higher than older buildings.

_____

18. High-society people have the best of everything. Even the clothes they wear are of higher quality than the average person.

_____

19. I feel that an exciting essay can be written by being prepared, writing about a topic that interests both you and your audience, using many examples, don't repeat yourself, don't use flowery words and have a well-structured essay.

_____

_____

_____

_____

20. Gangs rape, steal and kill.

_____

_____

21.   The constant noise and work of a factory can be similar to a high school.

_____

_____

22.   The Sunday paper, unlike the other days of the week, has many entertaining articles about interesting people, which is a welcome change from the regular auto accidents and disasters.

_____

_____

_____

23.   Having the luxury of your own car gives you many privileges: car radio, control of the temperature, and you may eat and smoke.

_____

_____

24.   The population of New York City is much larger than Toronto.

_____

25.   In renting a condominium one is faced with certain restrictions: no pets, no overnight visitors, need for permission to do decorating and the noise level should be kept low at all times.

_____

_____

_____

26.   With a good roommate you may not have to argue over who will do the dishes, do grocery shopping or cleaning the apartment.

_____

_____

27.   Commuting to work by car is less complicated than the public transit system.

_____

28.   Life in the city is very different from the country.

_____

29.   Some people feel that to lose their job is to lose their life.

_____

30.   Narrow-minded people still look down on a woman who lifts weights, works on a car engine or speaking her thoughts freely.

_____

_____

_____

Editing for Spelling and Related Matters

A couple of generations ago, many teachers and students believed spelling to be one of the major writing tasks. It seemed almost as important as the argument, itself — despite the fact that major authors such as Keats and Hemingway had been terrible spellers.

Today we realize that attention to spelling comes at the *end* of the writing process. After the main work of focus and development has been done in the early draft or drafts, we check over the spelling as a kind of "quality control" — much as the manufacturer of a well-engineered car looks over the paint job to make sure there are no scratches to mar the finish.

In summary, good spelling has little to do with the quality of your argument, but poor spelling can quickly ruin the best of essays by giving an overall poor impression. Consider these errors, which were found in student writing:

bathtube	*soup opera*
deadicated	*suck-seed*
drink a bear or two	*supperpower*
escapegoat	*toe truck*
law biting citizen	*viscous circle*
the Mid-Evil age	*well fear cheque*
pair tree	*who nose?*

Whether such errors make the reader laugh or cry, one thing is certain: they will distract the reader from your message.

Commonly Confused Words

Notice that all the above mistakes occurred when one word was confused with another. Not every error is made this way, but the worst and most frequent are. *Make sure that you know the difference, then, between the following commonly confused words.* Their definitions are not given here because you have a dictionary:

accept / except	*its / it's*
advice / advise	*know / no / now*
affect / effect	*lead / led*
are / our	*loose / lose*
bare / bare	*moral / morale*
brakes / breaks	*passed / past*
breath / breathe	*peace / piece*
buy / by	*personal / personnel*
capital / capitol	*principal / principle*
clothes / cloths	*quiet / quit / quite*
coarse / course	*right / wright / write*
council / counsel	*role / roll*
desert / dessert	*sight / site*
do / due	*than / then*
emigrated / immigrated	*their / there / they're*
farther / further	*thorough / threw / through*
hear / here	*to / too / two*
heroin / heroine	*weather / whether*
hole / whole	*were / we're / where*

"Strange how all six of your previous employers left the 'C' out of the word 'excellent.' "

NAME _____

Commonly Confused Words: Exercise

Circle the correct choice in the parentheses.

1. A person must (*accept / except*) all that life has to offer, both good and bad.

2. Mom warned us not to eat all the candy, but we ignored her (*advice / advise*).

3. Oil slicks in the ocean have a devastating (*affect / effect*) on wildlife.

4. The presence of parental love can (*affect / effect*) the child's ability to love others.

5. How do dreams change (*are / our*) lives?

6. I am so attached to my cat that I cannot (*bare / bear*) to part with it.

7. Some people get all the (*brakes / breaks*).

8. When oil is applied to the water, increasing the surface tension, the mosquito larvae can no longer poke their tubes up into the air to (*breath / breathe*).

9. A beginner will go to the nearest sports shop and (*buy / by*) every piece of equipment in sight.

10. Saint John's is the (*capital / capitol*) of Newfoundland.

11. One of the most important preparations for cross-country skiing is selection of light (*clothes / cloths*) that can be worn in several layers.

12. By the time I finished high school, I had never had a (*coarse / course*) in art.

13. A municipal (*council / counsel*) tends to be divided into prodevelopment and antidevelopment factions.

14. Large parts of Africa are turning into (*desert / dessert*).

15. Let's give credit where credit is (*do / due*).

16. In 1982 my parents (*emigrated / immigrated*) to Canada.

17. I swam laps in the pool till I thought I could go no (*farther / further*).

18. Old people feel isolated because they cannot (*hear / here*) well.

19. Desdemona is a tragic (*heroin / heroine*).

20. My sister ate the (*hole / whole*) pizza.

21. A dog is faithful to (*its / it's*) owner.

22. You never (*know / no / now*) what can happen.

23. Through the example of their parents, children are (*lead / led*) to cheat in society.

24. To (*loose / lose*) a game is to learn a lesson.

25. Police associations say that even the most disciplined force cannot function well if the (*moral / morale*) is low.

26. A year (*passed / past*) before Stephen Leacock found himself teaching at Upper Canada College.

27. I wanted a (*peace / piece*) of the action.

28.   Three days after I was hired, the (*personal/personnel*) manager called me to her office.

29.   I was not one of those troublemakers who were always sent to see the (*principal/principle*).

30.   The hours past midnight are best for studying, because everything is (*quiet/quit/quite*).

31.   At university, students have to (*right/wright/write*) exams as long as three hours.

32.   Professional athletes are (*role/roll*) models to thousands of children.

33.   Many students lose (*sight/site*) of their goals.

34.   Skinheads dress differently (*than/then*) others their age do.

35.   (*Their/There/They're*) stood my husband with the knife firmly in his hand, waiting to plunge it into the intruder.

36.   The police are hard workers. (*Their/There/They're*) not out on the streets slacking off.

37.   My friends and I used to go on trips (*thorough/threw/through*) the wilderness.

38.   More and more coaches and athletes take a friendly match of football (*to/too/two*) seriously.

39.   (*Weather/Whether*) to take a part-time job depends on many factors.

40.   When students (*were/we're/where*) asked to name the prime ministers of Canada, some of them mentioned John Kennedy.

Your Own Spelling List

If you are like most people, perhaps 90 percent of your spelling errors are the same 20 or 30 words misspelled every time you write them. *Therefore, the most direct way to improve your spelling is to make a list of all words you misspell in assignments, and study the correct spellings until you have mastered them.* Have a friend test you on your list, then again on only those words from the list that you still cannot spell. You'll be surprised how quickly you can learn them all.

_____

_____

_____

_____

_____

_____

_____

_____

_____

_____

_____

_____

_____

_____

_____

_____

_____

_____

_____

_____

_____

_____

_____

_____

_____

_____

_____

_____

One Hundred Words Often Misspelled

Since people tend to misspell the same words, you may find the list that follows to be useful. Before you study the words, have someone test you on the list. Then study only those words that you have misspelled.

accommodate	disappear	persistent
achievement	disappoint	piece
acquaintance	disastrous	playwright
acquire	dominant	possess
across	embarrass	predominant
adequately	emperor	preferred
a lot	environment	prejudice
all right	even though	prevalent
among	exceed	privilege
analyze	existence	pronunciation
argument	experiment	psychology
athlete	fascinate	quantity
attendance	fiery	receive
available	forty	recommend
basically	government	resistance
believe	harass	restaurant
beneficial	heroes	rhyme
category	imagination	rhythm
committee	independence	seize
compatible	knowledge	separate
completely	laboratory	similar
conceive	leisure	sincerely
condemn	loneliness	studying
conscience	maintenance	subtle
consistent	material	surprise
controversy	necessary	tendency
convenient	noticeable	tomorrow
deceive	obedience	tragedy
definite	occasion	truly
dependent	occurred	unnecessary
description	opponent	villain
desirable	perceive	weird
destroy	permanent	
dining	perseverance	

Preferred Canadian Spelling

No one who has read very much can fail to note that the British spell certain words one way, the Americans another, and that Canadians are torn between the two.

Most Canadians, especially in the middle and eastern provinces, continue to use the mainly British spellings they were taught in school. Thus they work in *centres* such as the Toronto Dominion Centre. They get paid by *cheque*. After they *labour* they watch their *colour* TV set or perhaps go to a *theatre*.

Yet when some Canadian newspapers write the words *center*, *check*, *labor*, *color* and *theater*, we may not sense those spellings as "foreign," even though they are American. Not all newspapers agree. Those that adhere to the *CP Stylebook* employ mostly American spelling, with exceptions such as "centre" and "cheque." On the other hand, the *Globe and Mail* has recently changed back to "Canadian" spelling, because readers wanted it. Most Canadian book publishers continue to use Canadian spelling.

A large hardbound dictionary still gives the most complete data for spelling and other aspects of word use. However, the many students who have turned to word processing find electronic spellers easy to use, versatile and above all fast.

For example, WordPerfect allows us to quickly check the spelling of a word, a page or a whole essay. It also counts words. Pressing "Ctrl-F2" brings up the command menu at the bottom of the screen, and the user can take it from there.

Electronic dictionaries have both strong points and weak points. Since they are so fast, our normal strategy of leaving spelling for the last draft is no longer useful. Why not just fix spelling the moment the discovery draft is done? After all, the work now takes only a minute or two; if a whole page is later scrapped, you will not have lost your time. The manuscript looks cleaner, so drafts in hard copy are easier to edit.

But electronic spellers so far have one serious drawback: since they work by checking each word on the page against a list of words in memory, they can tell that "recieve" should be "receive," but cannot tell whether "to," "too" or "two" is the right or wrong choice.

Since confusing one word with another is one of the worst sources of spelling error, be sure to master "Commonly Confused Words" at the beginning of this section, and be sure to apply it before printing out your good copy.

See also page 27 on using the electronic thesaurus.

What is the essayist to do? Though some teachers mark American spellings as errors, calling American spelling wrong is no more logical than saying that Spanish is better than German, or vice versa. Rather, the spelling you employ is a cultural choice. Both systems are "correct," but ours may be preferable on other grounds.

Many Canadians are concerned about the influence the powerful American culture now has on our nation. They see American movies in every theatre, American TV programming in every home, American magazines filling every newsstand and American hamburgers and soft drinks feeding Canadians across the country. If you share these concerns, you will probably want to maintain the Canadian spellings you learned in school. The gesture may be small, but is a symbol of larger things.

If you make a mistake, though, it will not be in choosing a "wrong" form but in mixing "correct" forms. *Be consistent*: *do not write* colour *and* color *in the same composition.* Here are three more principles to observe:

■ Avoid the common error of extending Canadian forms to words in which they are not used, as in writing *authour* for *author* or *amoung* for *among*.

■ Observe the limits to the *-our* form in Canadian usage: *honour*, *honourable* but *honorary*; *labour*, *labourer* but *laborious*; *vigour* but *vigorous* and *invigorate*. When you are in doubt, consult the table that follows.

■ Although "Canadian" forms are based on British spelling, do not let avoidance of American forms lead you to use British forms which are eccentric in Canada. Avoid spellings such as these: *amongst*, *whilst*, *connexion*, *gaol*, *kerb*, *tyre* and *waggon*.

To help you apply consistently the system that you choose, here is a list of the most common differences between Canadian and American spelling. Try to use only one side or the other, and consider the reasons why that side might be the Canadian.

CANADIAN USAGE	SHARED USAGE	AMERICAN USAGE
armour		*armor*
behaviour		*behavior*
colour, colourful		*color, colorful*
favour, favourite		*favor, favorite*
fervour		*fervor*
flavour, flavourful		*flavor, flavorful*
harbour		*harbor*
honour, honourable	*honorary*	*honor, honorable*
humour, humourless	*humorist, humorous*	*humor, humorless*
labour, labourer	*laborious*	*labor, laborer*
neighbour, neighbourhood, neighbourly		*neighbor, neighborhood, neighborly*
odour, odourless	*odoriferous, odorous*	*odor, odorless*
rigour	*rigorous*	*rigor*
vapour	*vaporize*	*vapor*
vigour	*vigorous, invigorate*	*vigor*
calibre	*calibration*	*caliber, calibre*
centre	*central*	*center*
fibre	*fibrous*	*fiber, fibre*
litre		*liter*
lustre	*lustrous*	*luster, lustre*
manoeuvre		*maneuver*
metre	*metric*	*meter*
spectre	*spectral*	*specter, spectre*
theatre	*theatrical*	*theater, theatre*
kidnapped, kidnapping, kidnapper		*kidnaped, kidnaping, kidnaper.*
shovelled, shovelling, shoveller		*shoveled, shoveling, shoveler*
travelled, travelling, traveller		*traveled, traveling, traveler*
worshipped, worshipping, worshipper		*worshiped, worshiping, worshiper*
mould (for casting), moulding, moulded		*mold, molding, molded*
mould (fungus), mouldy		*mold, moldy*
smoulder		*smolder*
defence, defenceless	*defensive*	*defense, defenseless*
offence	*offensive*	*offense*
cheque, cheque book, chequing account		*check, check book, checking account*
plough, ploughing		*plow, plowing*

Five Spelling Rules

Although at first the study of individual words is the fastest and most direct way to improve your spelling, the technique becomes less efficient once you have eliminated the most frequent misspellings. You use too many words to study them all.

A partial solution to the problem is rules. Some languages, such as Spanish, have a logical system of spelling in which universal principles ensure correct spelling of almost any word, even an unfamiliar one. We are less fortunate. English is such a mixture of other languages that some of our spelling rules contradict each other, and most have numerous exceptions. Learning the rules may improve your spelling, but probably not as much as you would like. And the process of applying lengthy rules to every tenth or twentieth word will certainly not help you finish your essay before midnight.

In case they will assist you, though, here are five of the clearest and most useful spelling rules. If you would like more, entire books about spelling are readily available in paperback form.

A. Put *i* before *e*, except after *c*
    Or when sounded like *a*
    As in *neighbour* or *weigh*.

Examples of *i* before *e*:
belief, chief, piece, priest, relief

Examples of *e* before *i*:
ceiling, deceive, eight, receive, their

Exceptions to the rule:
either, foreign, height, neither, seize, weird

B. When you add a *prefix*, do *not* change the spelling of the root word:

dis + appear = *dis*appear
dis + satisfy = *dis*satisfy
im + possible = *im*possible
im + moral = *im*moral
mis + lead = *mis*lead
mis + spell = *mis*spell
un + afraid = *un*afraid
un + noticed = *un*noticed

C. When you add a *suffix* beginning with a vowel to a word root that is accented on the last syllable or that has only one syllable, and if the root ends in a single consonant preceded by a single vowel, then double the final consonant of the root:

bat + *ed* = batt*ed*
begin + *ing* = beginn*ing*
control + *ed* = controll*ed*
occur + *ence* = occurr*ence*
omit + *ing* = omitt*ing*
prefer + *ed* = preferr*ed*
rap + *ed* = rapp*ed*
run + *ing* = runn*ing*

D. Drop the final *e* when the suffix begins with a vowel:

lose + *ing* = los*ing*
come + *ing* = com*ing*
use + *ing* = us*ing*
imagine + *ary* = imagin*ary*
separate + *ion* = separat*ion*
ice + y = *icy*

Exceptions (to keep *c* or *g* soft): advantageous, changeable, enforceable, outrageous, noticeable

Exceptions (to avoid mispronunciation): eyeing, hoeing, mileage

Keep the final *e* when the suffix begins with a consonant:

achieve + *ment* = achieve*ment*
excite + *ment* = excite*ment*
live + *ly* = live*ly*
lone + *ly* = lone*ly*
sincere + *ly* = sincere*ly*
use + *ful* = use*ful*

Exceptions: argument, probably, truly, wholly

E. A plural is normally formed by adding *s*, but *es* is added when another syllable results:

ONE SYLLABLE

tree	*trees*
lake	*lakes*
cloud	*clouds*
star	*stars*

ONE SYLLABLE	TWO SYLLABLES
ash	*ash*es
branch	*branch*es
fox	*fox*es
match	*match*es

Apostrophes

We'll discuss the apostrophe here, because although it is a punctuation mark, its misuse is a kind of spelling mistake. Hardly an essay is written that does not contain one such error, and some contain dozens. Remember these principles:

A. Use the apostrophe to signify *contraction*:

I am = I'm
you are = you're
he is = he's
we are = we're
they are = they're
it is = it's
who is = who's
is not = isn't
do not = don't
cannot = can't
should not = shouldn't
I would = I'd

B. Use the apostrophe to show *possession*:

- In a singular possessive, the apostrophe goes before the final *s*:

The single parent's responsibility is doubled.

- In a plural possessive, the apostrophe goes after the final *s*:

Most parents' greatest concern is for their children's happiness.

Note that the word "children" above is already plural without an *s*. In such cases the apostrophe follows the plural ending, and an *s* comes last to show how the word is pronounced: *children's*. Two more of the most common words in this case are *women* (*women's*) and *men* (*men's*).

- The possessives *its* and *whose* never take an apostrophe, although the contractions *it's* and *who's* do. Many errors are made by people who don't know the difference:

POSSESSION

The snake reared *its* head.

Not: The snake reared *it's* (*it is*) head.

I know *whose* work this is.

Not: I know *who's* (*who is*) work this is.

CONTRACTION

It's snowing (*It is* snowing.)
Who's there? (*Who is* there?)

C. The apostrophe is *not* used with every word that ends in *s*. Many errors are made by writers who have thought that since the apostrophe sometimes goes with the final *s*, it must always do so.

- The apostrophe does not form a plural:

ERROR

Student's from high school's, college's and university's were looking for summer job's.

CORRECTION

Students from high schools, colleges and universities were looking for summer jobs.

- The apostrophe does not form a third-person verb:

ERROR

A politician make's new promises whenever election time roll's around.

CORRECTION

A politician makes new promises whenever election time rolls around.

NAME _____

Apostrophes: Exercise

Whenever you find an apostrophe error below, write the correction, with the word in which it occurs, in the blank at the right. Write "C" after any sentence that is correct.

Example: The sun's ra~~ys~~ become more direct in spring.   *rays*

1. All pet's should receive more sympathy than they do.   _____

2. For entertainment Oshawa has movie theatres, ice rinks, roller arena's, nightclubs   _____

    and all sorts of gym's to work out at.   _____

3. The Beatles influence and popularity will live as long as rock and roll exists.   _____

4. The present art of producing with an assembly line system has come a long way   _____

    since it's introduction.   _____

5. As I plunged into the water, its cold temperature chilled every bone in my body.   _____

6. Its exciting to see a great horse thundering down the track.   _____

7. The only way to reduce student's financial problems is to increase their grants and   _____

    loans.   _____

8. Students who are 18 and over are the one's who need money the most.   _____

9. Thousands of people fish Ontario's lake's and river's each year, but how many will   _____

    take a minute to consider the result's of fished-out waters?   _____

10. Driving a motorcycle give's one a sense of independence, because the rider know's   _____

    people are watching.   _____

11. People who have no confidence in their own work will try to use others ideas.   _____

12. Politic's is what get's everyone talking and moving in this world.   _____

13. Parent's moral values are passed on to the next generation.   _____

14. My parent's emigrated from Greece.   _____

15. The Rolling Stones' music was unique for its time.   _____

16. After each goal the team that was scored against get's possession of the ball behind   _____

    it's net.   _____

17. Its a holiday to escape from work and see who can catch the most fish.   _____

18. It's my parent's duty to take care of me; they are legally required to.   _____

19. She see's only his good qualities. _____

20. What drains peoples' energy is the accelerating rate of change. _____

21. Solar system's have a sun and various numbers of planet's. _____

22. Are Canadian's ashamed of their own country? _____

23. A person who's on LSD may see the ceiling of the house crash in. _____

24. There are many owner's club's for most sports cars. _____

25. Newtons Second Law of Motion helps the swimmer to conserve energy. _____

26. Illness can be the minds expression to withdraw from lifes stress's and strains. _____

27. We'd go to my grandparents house each year because it wasn't really Christmas _____

    anywhere else. _____

28. The four-cycle system is what most automobile engine's are based on. _____

29. When Nick sees the Buchanan's reaction to Myrtle's death, he develops a sense of _____

    moral responsibility. _____

30. Animals such as rabbit's, monkey's and cat's are being used for meaningless experi- _____

    ments. _____

31. The arteries' main function is to carry oxygenated blood. _____

32. It was Labour Day when all the delayed thought's of moving finally hit home. _____

33. When children see their favourite player's using sticks to jab and spear other _____

    players, the next thing you know, the children are imitating. _____

34. Anyone who has run for a few year's on the road has no doubt experienced a dete- _____

    rioration of the knee's. _____

35. Elizabeth realized the faults of her parent's marriage. _____

36. At colleges and universities, drinking has become part of the system. _____

37. True punk rockers wear safety pins through their nose's or cheek's. _____

38. A newborn child see's the light for the first time. _____

39. My mothers parent's don't travel at all. _____

40. All over the world we are confronted with the same problems in womens lives. _____

Capitals

Since capitals, like apostrophes, tend to be sensed as an aspect of spelling, we'll discuss them here.

All student writers know the main principles of capitalization, but a surprising number do not know all the ones they may need in an essay. Study carefully any rule below that you do not already know.

A. Use a capital to *begin a sentence, a word group standing for a sentence* and *a line of regular poetry*:

Our big cities are no longer safe.

Yes. Of course. No doubt about it.

The wrinkled sea beneath him crawls;
He watches from his mountain walls,
And like a thunderbolt he falls.
        — Tennyson, "The Eagle"

B. Capitalize the beginning of a *direct quotation* if it is a sentence or a word group standing for a sentence:

According to Aristotle, "Poverty is the parent of revolution and crime." (The quotation is a sentence.)

He shook his head and said, "Over my dead body." (Even though the quoted word group is not a sentence, it is meant to function as one.)

"I'll have roast duck," she said, "with mixed vegetables and salad." (The "with" is not capitalized because it does not begin a new sentence.)

Ben Jonson wrote that Shakespeare knew "small Latin and less Greek." (The "small" is not capitalized because the quoted words are only part of Jonson's original statement.)

C. Capitalize *proper nouns*:

- Names of persons, nationalities and languages:

Sheila Copps	Scottish
Louis Riel	Spaniard
Canadian	speak French
Australian	an English course

- Academic courses whose names are not derived from languages are normally not capitalized:

psychology		English
history	BUT	French
calculus		Latin

- Specific places:

Montreal	Bloor Street
Prince Edward Island	Cabbagetown
Canada	the Maritimes
the Fraser River	the North (referring
The Rocky Mountains	to a region, not just a direction)

- Names of organizations:

Red River Community College
Mount Allison University
Roman Catholic Church
Bruce Trail Association
Parliament
Maple Leaf Glass, Ltd.

      BUT

a community college
a university town
went to church
a hiking trail
parliamentary procedure
the glass company

- Days of the week, months and holidays, but not seasons:

Tuesday	Easter
Saturday	Passover
January	spring
August	winter

- Titles of books, magazines, newspapers, plays, films, musical compositions, poetry, short stories, articles and essays. Capitalize the first word and all others except for connecting words (such as *a, an, the, and, or, but, in, on, by*) that have no more than five letters:

Book: *Such a Long Journey*
Magazine: *The Idler*
Newspaper: *The Vancouver Sun*
Play: *Hamlet*
Film: *King Kong*
Song: "Yesterday"
Poem: "Fern Hill"
Short story: "A Field of Wheat"
Article or essay: "Exaggeration as a Comic Device in the Novels of Mordecai Richler"

(Names of periodicals and titles of books, plays and other long items are italicized as you see above. You can probably italicize, too, if you use a word processor. But if you type or write by hand, symbolize italics by *underlining*. Titles of short items such as songs, poems, short stories, articles and essays are not underlined but are *put in quotation marks* as you see above.)

■ Words of family relationship when used as names or with names:

I congratulated Mother.
There was Father.
Uncle Charles
Aunt Mary

    BUT

I congratulated my mother.
There was our father.
My uncle was named Charles.
Mary is my aunt.

■ Titles appearing before a name or used alone as a form of address:

Professor Haddad
Doctor Stavros
Captain Rousseau
Hello, Professor.
Thank you, Doctor.
I agree, Captain.

    BUT

a professor
my doctor
an army captain

NAME _____

Capitals: Exercise

Add the missing capitals wherever necessary, but avoid creating unnecessary ones.

1. a friend of mine, frank, once told me that he had been behind a mac's store smoking a cigarette when all of a sudden a police officer approached and asked him where the pot was hidden.

2. during the hockey game, the mother of one of the opposing players stood up from her seat and yelled as loudly as she could, "kill that little worm!"

3. in the first year of the program, students have to take accounting, economics, geography, mathematics, english, management, business law and psychology.

4. canadians have long been concerned with developing the north, but only recently with protecting it.

5. my parents bought a house north of the business district, within a five-minute walk of an elementary school, a middle school, a high school, a mac's milk store and a shopping centre.

6. on a bright summer morning, the first monday of july, we got in our canoe and started down the missinaibi river.

7. who has seen the wind?

    neither you nor i;

   but when the trees bow down their heads

    the wind is passing by.

        — christina rossetti, 1872

8. in high school one of my english teachers spent two months on *hamlet*.

9. in addition to containing beef and/or pork, wieners may contain water, flour, milk solids, salt and preservatives such as sodium nitrite, which has been known to cause cancer in laboratory animals.

10. cruise ships have many facilities such as bedrooms, swimming pools, lawn tennis courts, dancing halls, movie theatres and bars.

11. lady macbeth, a strong-willed character who was capable of influencing macbeth to murder his king, brought about her breakdown and death by her own ambitions.

12. john osborne was born on december 12, 1929, in london, england.

13. in today's modern society, people's morals and values are changing, so divorce, birth control and abortion are more easily accepted.

14. j. d. salinger's best short story, "for esmé — with love and squalor," shows how destructive war is to human feelings.

15. when i began high school i really got involved in soccer.

16. i arrived in trinidad on monday and began my search for a job on tuesday.

17. stephen leacock once wrote, "the essence of humour is human kindliness."

18. in his *biographia literaria*, coleridge refers to "that willing suspension of disbelief for the moment, which constitutes poetic faith."

19. mackenzie king said, "the promises of yesterday are the taxes of today."

20. blaise pascal called humans "the glory and the shame of the universe."

21. the driver stopped the bus to jump out and take a look. he was immediately followed by the spaniard, two mexicans, hugh, geoffrey and yvonne.

22. when the canadian dollar sank in value, foreign automobiles such as the volvo, volkswagen, toyota, subaru and honda rose sharply in price.

23. the national hockey league rules committee brought in new rules which prohibited players from being overly aggressive.

24. my mother speaks french, portuguese and english.

25. i have noted that math teachers do not dress as well as english teachers.

26. to depict their toughness, hockey players are given names such as "hammer," "battleship," "tiger" and "bulldog."

27. one of the fastest-growing religions in the world is islam.

28. in each of mordecai richler's earlier novels, *the acrobats, son of a smaller hero* and *a choice of enemies,* the hero is an artistically inclined canadian with a deep dislike of canadian culture and a conviction that the society he lives in is a fraud.

29. as a faithful expression of the theme found in the play, the movie fortune and men's eyes was the epitome of success.

30. "well, doctor," i said, "since you agree with the other doctors, i suppose we had better go ahead with the operation."

Abbreviations

Use abbreviations sparingly. When you write a.m. and p.m. instead of *ante meridiem* and *post meridiem*, you are helping your readers by saving their time. But when you cram into your essay every abbreviation that you can think of (Can., Alta, N.S., Tues., Feb., GT, CB, ASA, LCBO, PC, PCV, etc.), you are doing anything but helping them. To decipher all these letters can take longer than to read the words themselves.

See if you can put the words to the following common abbreviations into the blanks. (The answers are on page 225.) If such abbreviations give you trouble, you can see how they would also give your reader trouble.

1. *CEO*   _____
2. *CPI*   _____
3. *GIC*   _____
4. *GST*   _____
5. *ICU*   _____
6. *NDP*   _____
7. *RAM*   _____
8. *R&D*   _____
9. *RN*   _____
10. *SASE* _____

Do use abbreviations to avoid repetition. For example, after naming the United Nations Educational, Scientific and Cultural Organization once in an essay, have mercy on your reader by referring to it the next ten or 20 times as UNESCO.

And if you are writing a technical report for specialists to read ("Simulation of Control Systems on an Analogue Computer" or "Shear Flow in Closed Single-Cell and Multi-Cell Systems"), do use any abbreviations customary in the field, especially in tables and charts.

But in the kind of general classroom writing that is expected in courses such as English, history and philosophy, use abbreviations only where you can hardly avoid them. Here are some principles to guide you:

A. Abbreviate these titles before a name: *Mr., Mrs., Ms., Dr., Rev.*

Mr. Violi
Mrs. Fitzwilliams
Ms. Wyatt
Dr. Chen
Rev. Scott

Such titles are spelled out, though, when used alone:

Well, Doctor, what are my chances?

Other titles are usually not abbreviated even before a name:

Professor Beauchemin
Mother Teresa
General Montcalm
Sir George

B. Abbreviate names of private or public organizations if the abbreviation is well known and customarily used. Do write out the full name, though, the first time you mention an organization.

RCMP	UN
ITT	INCO
BBC	RCA
CIA	YWCA
OPEC	CBC

C. Abbreviate academic degrees:

B.A.	M.D.
B.S.	Ph.D.
M.A.	D.Ed.
M.S.W.	D.D.

D. You may abbreviate certain geographical names:

U.K.
U.S.A.

Other geographical names (countries, provinces, counties, cities) are not abbreviated except in addresses.

E. Abbreviate certain terms from the Latin:

■ Words that specify time periods:

a.m.	b.c.
p.m.	a.d.

■ Certain terms used in academic writing:

cf. (compare)	i.e. (that is)
e.g. (for example)	q.v. (which see)

■ That overused term, *etc.* Use *etc.* only to signal actual items that you know but choose not to include, never to hide what you do not know. Avoid statements like this:

The major crops of British Columbia are apples, etc.

Symbols and Numbers in the Metric System

Although the Imperial system of weights and measurements is still used in some areas of our daily life — as when we tell our height in feet and inches, or our weight in pounds — the metric system has become the norm in Canada for most other uses. Even when we write an essay, we may need to know the standard metric abbreviations, officially called "symbols," and how to use them.

When numbers are spelled out, terms of measurement used with them are also spelled out; when numbers appear as figures, the terms of measurement appear as symbols. Thus in technical writing or in any charts and tables where a great many numbers are used, you will probably use figures and symbols. But where numbers occur less frequently, as in most essays, you will probably write out both numbers and terms of measurement.

EXAMPLES

A piece of steel 0.25 cm thick, 1.75 m wide and 3.15 m long is welded to the frame.

The average fingernail is about one centimetre wide.

The following table gives the most common metric terms and the symbols for them. The symbols are identical in both singular and plural uses, and unless they occur at the end of a sentence, are written without a period.

LENGTH

kilometre	km
metre	m
decimetre	dm
centimetre	cm
millimetre	mm

AREA

square kilometre	km^2
hectare	ha
square metre	m^2
square decimetre	dm^2
square centimetre	cm^2

VOLUME

cubic metre	m^3
cubic decimetre	dm^3
cubic centimetre	cm^3
kilolitre	kL
litre	L
millilitre	mL

MASS

tonne	t
kilogram	kg
gram	g
milligram	mg

TEMPERATURE

degree Celsius	°C

Our traditional 24-h day and its parts are of course not metric, but are wisely being retained:

TIME

day	d
hour	h
minute	min
second	s

The metric system specifies some new principles for the use of numbers:

- A zero is put before a decimal fraction:

  0.9144 m

- A space, rather than a comma, separates groups of three digits. Numbers of only four digits are not separated:

  1 000 000 g   1000 g

- Only numbers 10 (or 11) and over are expressed in figures.

  five kilograns   75 kg

Reading: The Key to Spelling

On the average, North Americans read less than one book a year, perhaps because they watch four hours a day of television. By the time they graduate from high school they have spent more hours in front of the "tube" than in the classroom. They may know a great deal about how to catch a bank robber, apply a half nelson or estimate the price of a refrigerator, but one thing they will probably not know is how to spell.

By contrast, people who have read a book or two a month (or the equivalent in magazines or newspapers) from childhood to adulthood have seen each word so many times that, with rare exceptions, their own spelling is automatically correct.

Reading is the long-term solution to spelling problems and to other writing problems as well. The great majority of people who read regularly will eventually become much better in spelling, grammar and style than those who do not.

Although the process takes several years, it is the only way to profoundly improve your writing. *Therefore, if you do not have the reading habit, consider acquiring it.* Subscribe to a magazine or two in a field that interests you. Read a newspaper regularly. Keep a couple of good books by your TV chair. If you do not have time to read now, start during the Christmas holidays or the summer break. And if you have not enjoyed reading in the past, don't let that stop you: practice increases proficiency, and proficiency increases enjoyment.

A Suggested List of Canadian Readings

(Novels except where noted otherwise.)

Cat's Eye, Margaret Atwood

The Handmaid's Tale, Margaret Atwood

A Casual Brutality, Neil Bissoondath

A North American Education (short stories), Clark Blaise

Klee Wyck (autobiographical sketches), Emily Carr

La Guerre, Yes Sir! Roch Carrier

Storm of Fortune, Austin Clarke

Fifth Business, Robertson Davies

The Wars, Timothy Findley

My Heart Is Broken (short stories), Mavis Gallant

Kamouraska, Anne Hébert

A Certain Mr. Takahashi, Ann Ireland

A Dream Like Mine, M. T. Kelly

Obasan, Joy Kogawa

The Stone Angel, Margaret Laurence

A Bird in the House (short stories), Margaret Laurence

Sunshine Sketches of a Little Town, Stephen Leacock

Such a Long Journey, Rohinton Mistry

Never Cry Wolf (semi-autobiography), Farley Mowat

Lives of Girls and Women, Alice Munro

Lives of the Saints, Nino Ricci

The Apprenticeship of Duddy Kravitz, Mordecai Richler

The Tin Flute, Gabrielle Roy

THE RESEARCH ESSAY

Prepared by Alan Baker

The process of writing a research essay is both similar to, and different from, the process of writing the "short essay," which we discussed in the opening chapter of this book. A research essay rests on the same foundations, but its structure is of course larger and more complicated.

The most obvious difference is length. While the research essay may sometimes be as short as four or five pages, it is often more like ten or fifteen. Another main difference is its purpose. While a "short essay" may be an informal expression of our own feelings or experiences, a research essay is a more objective argument: a methodical sifting of evidence to arrive at a valid conclusion. And in referring to this sifted evidence, we use the scholarly devices of quotations, name-page references and list of works cited.

Yet these differences do not change the fact that both the "short" and "research" essays require leaps of intuition, a focus and direction given by a thesis statement, unified development by example and argument, and serious revision. Since these foundations are common to the process of writing both essays, we will not repeat every aspect of our investigation into the short essay. Instead, we will focus mostly on the special challenges and the special rewards of the research essay.

If you have not already studied "Process in the Short Essay" (pages 2–29), please do so, as preparation for the more specialized essay we will investigate now.

Selecting and Focussing the Topic

What will you write about? Sometimes a teacher will erase all doubts by giving a very specific assignment: you will compare the imagery of two assigned poems by Margaret Atwood or analyze the Family Compact as a cause of the 1837 Rebellion or describe how a hamburger chain selects a certain corner for a business site.

When you are given a ready-made and specific topic like one of these, your job has already begun. You may know little about the subject, but at least you know the direction your research will take, and you'll waste no time on side issues.

More troublesome at first — but often rewarding in the end — are the more open assignments meant to be narrowed down. For example Jane, a student in

Writer's Workshop I, had a teacher who announced extremely broad subjects so that students would face the challenge of shaping their own topics. To do her research essay Jane could write on "pollution," "family violence," "health," "language" or "the supernatural."

Right away she liked the last choice, because for several years she had read occult books about subjects like vampires, ghosts, werewolves and witches, and her best friend consulted fortune-tellers. But how was she to cut down the overall subject so she could write, as her instructor said, "more about less"?

The teacher had made it clear that students were not to discuss all aspects of a subject as large as the supernatural. Just think what would be involved: Would they take an *historical* approach, discussing aspects of the supernatural among ancient and modern peoples? Would they take a *psychological* approach, showing the supernatural as a product of fears? Would they choose a *geographical* approach, showing how beliefs in the supernatural take different forms in various societies? Or would they take a *literary* approach, discussing "gothic" works by authors who wrote about the supernatural? The range of choice seemed enormous.

Certainly Jane could write a few lines on each of these matters and claim she had discussed the topic. But a superficial treatment is worthless: Why should anyone read what everyone already knows? To be satisfying, to be interesting, to be instructive, an essay must reach a certain depth. And unless we write an essay as long as a book, that depth is reached only by focussing the topic. To write about the supernatural, then, Jane could select any one of the subtopics just listed and investigate it in detail.

But how will she choose? Here we come to the rewarding aspect of general subjects like "the supernatural": there are so many possible subtopics that at least one should appeal to Jane's experience or interest. *She must find that one.*

Remember: When the topic is general, take time to find the right subtopic. Later, as you write the essay, your heightened interest and motivation will repay you that time and increase the quality of your writing.

If literature fascinates her, she might discuss the gothic novel. If her curiosity is raised by the friend who consults fortune-tellers, Jane might write about the popularity of astrology today. If she likes history, she could discuss the development of witchcraft. *Whatever her background and interests, she will do her best writing on matters that appeal to her. Therefore, within the limits of a given assignment, Jane and other writers should take special care to select a subtopic they like.*

Most people do this naturally. What many do not do, though, is enough preliminary reading and thinking to discover enough potential subtopics. Avoid this trap of denying yourself a choice.

Gathering and Ordering Information

Most of us can write "short essays" on topics we already know, without doing research in the library. But the major essays in a course are almost always research papers meant to teach students about subjects they are just now learning. In such cases there is work to do before the writing begins.

That work is not easy. In the library some people experience a form of paralysis: surrounded by more books and magazines than they could read in a dozen lifetimes, they stand looking about, thinking "Where do I begin?" If you do not have your own answer to that question, try this plan of action:

1. **Read enough to select one aspect of the subject.**
2. **Make a tentative thesis statement.**
3. **Do the main research, taking notes.**
4. **Make an outline.**
5. **Write the essay.**

Now let's examine each of these steps, as followed by Jane.

Step One: Read Enough to Select One Aspect of the Subject

A few people may know enough about the supernatural to omit this step. Since they already recognize the possible subtopics, they can choose one immediately and get to work. But if you are like Jane, you'll need to look up "supernatural" in a recent edition of any encyclopedia, or use the *Reader's Guide to Periodical Literature* and the *Canadian Magazine Index* to find magazine articles on the topic. At this stage Jane sought brief and general information that would show her the main aspects of the subject. She skipped over details, taking only the briefest of notes, because any that fell outside the research area eventually chosen would be a waste of time.

When she had uncovered a number of subtopics, Jane eliminated those that seemed unimportant. Then from the rest, she picked the one that most strongly appealed to her experience and interest. We know that Jane is intrigued by the supernatural. She noticed that one of the periodical indexes had the notation "See *Magic and witchcraft*" as a cross-reference under the main heading of "Supernatural." And that very evening at home she was startled to read in her local newspaper that a teacher had been granted paid religious leave from his job at a community college — because he was a witch.

At this stage, Jane thought a good subtopic might be witchcraft. But while checking references to "Witchcraft" in the encyclopedia, she saw still more choices to make. Would she discuss the entire practice of witchcraft in the Western world or describe only how a particular group practised witchcraft? She had to narrow the focus enough to permit good coverage of the subtopic, but avoid narrowing it so far as to get lost in one tiny area of specialization.

A sociologist might write a paper called "The Practice of Witchcraft Among Upper-Middle-Class Social Groups in Southern California" and send it to a professional journal for other sociologists. *But common sense tells us to make a compromise, avoiding both the broadness of an overly general subject and the narrowness of a greatly restricted one.*

Now Jane made her choice. She would concentrate on the practice of witchcraft today in North America, and in her essay would use the news item about the local witch. In her preliminary reading, Jane had seen that modern witchcraft developed in the nineteenth century and became popular in North America after World War II. She had also found that while modern witchcraft is often seen as a "cult," some witches claim it has direct links to earlier religions, and that it may even represent a new religion for today. From this information, Jane concluded that she would give enough historical background to introduce the topic clearly, but would focus on the development of witchcraft in modern times.

Step Two: Make a Tentative Thesis Statement

What about the development of modern witchcraft? Jane could describe it and give examples, but unless she made the facts pull together in the same direction — like a tug-of-war team pulling a rope — her readers would waste their time. "This is boring," they might think. "What's the point?"

Jane's job is to tell her readers that point, somewhere near the beginning of the essay. She could tell them that modern witchcraft is just a box of tricks, or that it is an important new faith, or that it is really one of many modern cult groups. Whatever Jane's message would be, she now had to put it into a *thesis statement*. As we saw on pages 7–8 of our chapter on the short essay, a thesis statement prepares the reader by *limiting the scope* and *focussing the purpose*. (It also prepares the writer to research effectively, avoiding time wasted on matters that will not be covered in the essay.)

At this early point, though, any thesis that Jane comes up with is a bit of a guess, like the hypothesis with which a scientist begins an experiment. Jane hopes her thesis will work out, because she hates wasting time. But only when she does the main research will she know for sure. After all, it is the research that will teach her the subject; once she does learn the facts, she might find that they disprove her initial idea — just as the results of the scientist's experiment may disprove the original hypothesis. *In the early stages, then, a thesis is tentative — open to change.*

Here is Jane's thesis statement, as it appears in paragraph 4 of her essay, which is presented in its entirety later in this chapter:

> A closer look at the development of modern witchcraft shows that its appeal is related to the current interest in cults and the supernatural rather than to its claim to be either an "old" or a "new" religion.

Step Three: Do the Main Research, Taking Notes

Some libraries still have the old card catalogue, which gives very full information on each book but can be tedious to use. Several years ago Jane's school moved to the microfiche system: the researcher puts a plastic card under a magnifier, then on the screen reads the main facts about each book and where it is shelved. More recently, her library also installed an on-line system through which students use a keyboard and terminal to find what is in the library, what the contents of each book are, where the book is shelved, whether it is there right now or is checked out and other useful facts. This system is so easy to use, fast and complete that Jane went straight to it to start her main research, *making a list of sources to consult.*

Instructions are normally posted by the side of these machines, and librarians are also available for help. Like both the card catalogue and microfiche systems, the online system catalogues library books by three categories: *author*, *title* and *subject*. Since Jane did not yet know authors or titles, she looked up the subjects of "witchcraft" and "magic." She identified the books that seemed most useful, rejecting those that were out of date, off-topic, too technical or too general. For each book that she intended to consult, she accurately copied down these facts:

1. The author's full name

2. The title of the book

3. The place of publication

4. The publisher

5. The year of publication

Some libraries have printers next to the monitors, which quickly and accurately reproduce at least some of this information. Check, though, to be sure *all* the above facts appear.

After using the online database to locate books, Jane was ready for magazines. She went to the table where her library kept its well-worn copies of the *Reader's Guide to Periodical Literature* and the *Canadian Magazine Index*. Starting at the most recent volume and working backwards a few years, she checked the headings of "witchcraft" and "magic," looking for useful articles. Each time she found one, she carefully wrote down all these facts:

1. The author's full name

2. The title of the article

3. The name of the magazine

4. The volume number and date of the issue

5. The beginning and ending page numbers of the article

(All the sources you actually use must appear in a list of "works cited" at the end of the essay. If you do not have these facts with you then, your carelessness will cost you an extra trip to the library.)

It will not take long to gather a list of sources: perhaps 5 or 10 for a short paper and 20 or 30 for a long one. If you have a long list, you may want to record each source on a separate filing card, for ease of organization. A short list like Jane's, though, is more easily kept on one page.

Jane's topic is familiar enough that she was able to locate numerous sources. For more-specialized topics, though, keep two other research tools in mind:

■ *Interlibrary loans* Your librarian will supply you with request forms on which you give the title, author and other information about a book or a magazine article that you need but that your own library does not have. The library will use its database system to see which other libraries do have the resource, and will order it for you, probably free of charge. Large research projects can hardly be done without the resources of additional libraries, but remember that the process takes a week or two. If you do not start your own project very early, you will be limited to the resources of your own library plus any others you actually visit.

■ *CD-ROM* Everyone has seen compact audio disks, which function with a laser. For several years the same technology has been in use to store huge amounts of data through CD-ROM (compact disk — read only memory). One such disk can hold the contents of almost 2000 floppy disks, and hundreds of databases are now available in this form.

Most postsecondary and public libraries have several useful CD-ROM indexes and other databases, which students can quickly learn to use. One favourite is ERIC, which indexes and abstracts the articles of about 900 journals in the fields of education and the social sciences. The user gets the disk from a librarian, slips it in its case into the CD-ROM disk drive, then pulls the case out. Through a user-friendly menu and through dialogue boxes, a student can then choose from a vast array of possibilities.

For example a "descriptor" (key word) such as "witchcraft" can be entered, to call up a list of all publications that include this subject. To narrow down the search, other descriptors such as terms that specify *where* or *when* may then be entered. The result is a "boolian search," which identifies only those sources in which the descriptors overlap — for example "witchcraft" only in "North America."

The bibliographical data and the descriptions of articles on screen can then be downloaded into the student's own floppy disk, to be printed out at home. Some libraries provide printers to do this on the spot.

CD-ROM does have one major disadvantage, though: unless you are a student at a large university, the journals which contain the articles you want are probably not in your library. Thus you must begin research early enough to request interlibrary loans (see above).

Your library may have databases other than ERIC. For example CBCA (*Canadian Business & Current Affairs*) is widely used because it indexes 200 Canadian business periodicals as well as 10 Canadian newspapers and 300 general Canadian magazines. Other databases provide not only indexing but the actual text of articles. For example the *Toronto Star* from 1989 to the present is now available on CD-ROM, one full year of issues on each disk. Students can conduct a boolian search, then either download articles onto their own formatted floppy disk or, if the facilities exist, print out on the spot.

Finally, at a fairly steep cost, many libraries offer on-line searches of any one of hundreds of databases that exist elsewhere. Librarians plan and execute this work carefully for the student, to keep on-line costs down.

Reference Sources

The on-line library catalogue, the *Reader's Guide to Periodical Literature* and the *Canadian Magazine Index* led Jane to all the sources she needed for her essay, especially since most articles and books that she consulted referred her to other writings on the subject.

In researching longer essays, though, or any essay on a more specialized topic, you may need to look further. Thousands of other reference sources cover almost any field you can imagine. These are a few that students have found useful:

General Sources

The Encyclopaedia Britannica. In general the most detailed and authoritative encyclopedia.

The Encyclopedia Americana. Easily read, with shorter articles than those of the *Britannica*.

The Canadian Encyclopedia. Very fully focussed on all aspects of Canadian history, culture, geography, commerce and public life.

World Almanac and Book of Facts. An annual collection of statistics and other facts on many subjects worldwide.

Canada Handbook. Covers most major aspects of Canada, from the point of view of the government.

Canada Year Book. A review of economic, social and political developments in Canada. Many statistics.

Canadian Almanac & Directory. An annual collection of facts about Canada.

Corpus Almanac & Canadian Sourcebook. An annual two-volume collection of facts about Canada.

The Corpus Administrative Index. A quarterly listing of telephone numbers for government agencies and officials (use these numbers to get information and materials).

The National Atlas of Canada. Contains maps and graphs that give a great amount of geographical, climatic, economic and social information.

The New York Times Atlas of the World. Maps of all parts of the world. Includes geographical, agricultural, industrial, commercial and social information.

The New York Times Index. News articles that appear in the *New York Times* are classified by subject, persons and organizations. Use the annual index to find when a story broke, then with that date find how other periodicals covered the same event.

The Canadian News Index. From 1977, indexes by subject the articles that appear in several major Canadian newspapers.

Canadian Magazine Index. A monthly index in print form; also widely available in CD-ROM through CBCA (*Canadian Business & Current Affairs*).

Facts on File: Weekly World News Digest with Cumulative Index. Accumulated weekly, in binders that each hold one year's indexing.

Canadian News Facts. An annual indexed "account of Canada's day-to-day news."

Bulletin of the Public Affairs Information Service. An international subject index of periodical articles.

Essay and General Literature Index. An author and subject index to collections of essays "with particular emphasis on materials in the humanities and social sciences."

Book Review Digest. Excerpts from reviews of books "published or distributed in the United States." Indexed by author, subject and title.

Canadian Book Review Annual. From 1975, short reviews of new Canadian books in many fields.

Bartlett's Familiar Quotations. An indexed collection of quotations on many subjects, from ancient to modern times.

Colombo's Canadian Quotations. Does for Canada what *Bartlett's* does for the world.

Dictionary of National Biography. Authoritative biographies of important persons in the United Kingdom, to 1900.

Dictionary of American Biography. Biographies of prominent Americans no longer living.

Dictionary of Canadian Biography. Biographies of prominent Canadians. (The last volumes, covering recent times, have not yet appeared.)

The International Who's Who. Concise biographies of "men and women who have achieved international prominence."

Who's Who in Canada. Concise biographies of prominent Canadians.

Science and Technology

Applied Science & Technology Index. A much-used cumulative subject index to English-language periodicals in a great many technical fields.

Chemical Abstracts. A mammoth international work that lists about 200 000 entries every six months. It summarizes conference papers, books and articles. Indexed in numerous ways.

Computer Literature Index. An annual index to articles, organized by subject, author and publisher.

Encyclopedia of Physical Science and Technology (15 volumes). Attempts to cover "the entire field of physical science and related technologies."

The Engineering Index. A much-used monthly index to conference papers and the major articles of hundreds of periodicals in all engineering fields. Indexed by author and subject. Available on CD-ROM as *Compendex*Plus*.

Index to IEEE Publications. An annual index to articles and conference papers in numerous areas of electronics.

The McGraw-Hill Encyclopedia of Science and Technology (7th edition, 1992). A 20-volume examination of the physical, natural and applied sciences. Index.

Pollution Abstracts. Published six times a year, it indexes and summarizes "world-wide technical literature on environmental pollution."

Science Citation Index. A multi-disciplinary index to the world's scientific and technical literature.

Social Sciences and Psychology

The Social Science Encyclopedia. In one volume, surveys the major social sciences.

Psychological Abstracts. Summarizes articles from the scholarly journals of many countries and indexes them by author and subject. Read the summaries to find which articles are worth looking up.

Sociological Abstracts. Summarizes articles from the scholarly journals of many countries and indexes them by author and subject. Read the summaries to find which articles are worth looking up.

Social Sciences Citation Index. "An international multidisciplinary index to the literature of the social, behavioral and related sciences." Annual.

Social Sciences Index. An author and subject index to English-language articles from a great many publications in anthropology, economics, geography, law and criminology, public administration, political science, psychology, social work and sociology.

Business and Economics

Business Periodicals Index. A monthly subject index to articles in a great many English-language business periodicals. Also indexes book reviews.

Canadian Business Index. Indexes articles in over 200 Canadian business periodicals, including *The Financial Post, The Financial Times of Canada* and *The Globe and Mail.* Indexed by subject, company name and personal name.

The Journal of Economic Literature. An international quarterly that has articles, book reviews, abstracts of major articles from other sources, and a subject and author index to itself. Geared to theoretical economics rather than current information about companies and trends.

PROMPT. A monthly index, begun in 1986, giving an overview of current markets and technology.

Canadian Business & Current Affairs (CBCA). On CD-ROM, offers three databases indexing 300 general magazines, 10 newspapers and 200 business periodicals.

The Humanities (Excluding Literature)

Humanities Index. An international author and subject index to articles in "archaeology and classical studies, area studies, folklore, history, language and literature, literary and political criticism, performing arts, philosophy, religion and theology." Also on CD-ROM under the same title.

Music Index. An international author and subject index of articles in music periodicals, including reviews of books and records.

Grove's Dictionary of Music and Musicians. An illustrated multi-volume work on composers, instruments, musical works, etc.

The Oxford Companion to Film. Discusses directors, actors, critics, individual films, techniques, etc. Illustrated.

Film Literature Index. A well-used index to many film periodicals.

New York Times Film Reviews. Reviews beginning 1913. Indexed.

Art Index. A much-used international author and subject index to periodicals in all major fields of art.

McGraw-Hill Dictionary of Art. A concise five-volume study of world art from its beginnings. Heavily illustrated.

Encyclopedia of Philosophy. Authoritative articles about philosophy and philosophers from the beginnings worldwide.

Encyclopedia of Religion. Published 1987 (15 volumes).

The Cambridge Ancient History, The Cambridge Medieval History, The New Cambridge Modern History. Detailed and authoritative coverage of these periods.

Literature

A Dictionary of Literary Terms. A good first source for research on genres or on technical aspects of literature.

The Oxford Companion to Canadian Literature. A concise and authoritative first source for most topics in the field. Covers authors, literary works, genres, criticism and more. Strong emphasis on Quebec.

Literary History of Canada, eds. Carl Klinck *et al.* Comprehensive and authoritative, but does not cover recent times.

The Oxford Companion to English Literature. Also in this series are *The Oxford Companion to American Literature* and *The Oxford Companion to Classical Literature.*

Literary History of the United States, eds. Robert Spiller *et al.* An authoritative examination of the subject from its beginnings.

The Feminist Companion to Literature in English, 1990 (1 volume).

MLA International Bibliography. The standard reference for serious literary research.

Canadian Literary Periodicals Index. Twice yearly from 1992, with annual accumulation.

Index to Canadian Literature. Yearly index to the important quarterly *Canadian Literature.*

Canadian Writers and Their Works. Large series of volumes with chapters on Canadian writers.

Contemporary Literary Criticism. A multi-volume work that gives "excerpts from criticism of the works of today's novelists, poets, playwrights and other creative writers."

Contemporary Novelists. Biography, bibliography and some criticism of important writers of English-language fiction.

Contemporary Poets. Gives the same material as above, except for poets.

Contemporary Authors. A multi-volume guide to current authors in all fields, including film and television.

The Oxford English Dictionary. The largest and most complete dictionary of English. Gives the fullest information on meanings, spellings and origins of words, illustrated by quotations from many periods. Now in its second edition (1989), with coverage of current terms as well.

The Oxford Companion to the Theatre. Briefly covers playwrights and their works, major movements in the theatre and technical aspects of theatre. Illustrated.

Having gathered her list of sources, Jane then conducted her research using the following guidelines given to her by her instructor:

As you begin the main research, be efficient. A few minutes spent checking a book's table of contents and index and perhaps leafing through the relevant chapters may save you hours. There is nothing more disappointing than laboriously collecting facts that are scattered through one book, only to find them collected in a few pages of the next book or even reduced to a graph or chart. Another waste of time is to collect facts from an old issue of a magazine, only to find that a newer issue with newer facts makes your notes obsolete.

When you have selected the most likely sources, begin taking notes:

■ The bulk of your notes should be a *summary* of facts or ideas that you think you will need. Be concise but accurate. Distinguish between fact and opinion, so that you can carry this distinction into your essay. Do not pick out facts that mean little by themselves, but record enough of the context to make sense of them.

 Use abbreviations that will be clear when you read your notes. (Avoid short forms like "comm," which could later be read as "communism," "communication," "commission" or other words.)

■ When you find a key idea stated so forcefully or eloquently that you could not possibly word it as well yourself, copy it *exactly*, putting quotation marks where the quoted words begin and end.

Take steps now to save time later:

■ Accurately record the page numbers of all summaries and quotations, because you will need them later for the references. *If you do not get them now, you will be back the night before the essay is due, leafing furiously through books and magazines.*

■ As you take notes, mark the items that seem most important, perhaps with an asterisk (*) in the margin. Later this step will help you to select the main points of your outline.

■ Although the main outline comes after the research, put together a *rough outline* of five or ten lines as early as you can. It may save you hours by channelling your reading and note-taking into exactly those areas that you will cover in the essay.

■ Use one of these systems for putting notes into the order that your main outline will require:

1. Write all notes on filing cards, one side only, with the subject labelled at the top. Do not waste time by recording all the reference information with each entry, but do list the author, the title — if you use more than one article or book by the same author — and the page number. Later, when writing the "list of works cited," you can look up the other facts in your list of sources. When all the cards are eventually placed in the order required by your outline, you write the essay from them. This system is considered essential for very long papers, and some people use it even for short ones.

OR

2. Write notes on sheets of paper, one side only. As above, record the author, title and page number with each entry and write a subject label above or in the margin. Later you can cut each item apart from the others with scissors, and arrange the items like note cards according to your outline. Since this system is not as neat as keeping note cards, it works best for shorter essays.

Step Four: Make an Outline

Jane knows that a research essay, like a house, is made from a plan. An outline, though, is not a blueprint. While almost every detail of a house should be planned in advance so that the builder will not add doors or windows during construction, the builder of an essay sometimes gets the best ideas in the middle of the job.

It is obvious that the outline for a research essay is longer and more detailed than the brief and tentative outline of the "short essay" discussed in our opening chapter. But even this longer outline should not be so complete that it strangles Jane's imagination as she writes, or so final that she cannot improve it if her discovery draft awakens valuable new ideas.

To begin forming her outline, Jane divides her notes into groups that seem to fit together. (She actually moves them into different combinations on the desk in front of her, like pieces of a puzzle.) Now she looks at them. Are there two main groups, one pro and the other con? Or does one group *cause* the material in another group? Are there three groups, and therefore three branches of her subject? Or are there four? Do her notes flow onward in time order from first to last, with divisions wherever one time period ends and the next begins?

If you examine your notes with an open mind, as Jane did, you will usually "find" rather than "choose" the form of your outline. Jane found a plan based mainly on time order, but which permits exceptions where necessary — for example, discussing the present in the introduction to awaken the interest of the modern reader.

OUTLINE

I. *Introduction*
   A. *Witchcraft: the most interesting of today's cult groups*
   B. *Difficulty of getting hard facts from the media*
   C. *Despite claims of some followers, witchcraft clearly a cult of the supernatural (THESIS)*

II. *Witchcraft as a Factor in Our Society*
   A. *Statistics*
   B. *The case of Charles Arnold, Toronto witch*

III. *The Historical Background: Three Categories of Witchcraft*
   A. *Sorcery*
   B. *"Diabolical" witchcraft*
   C. *Developments of the nineteenth and early twentieth centuries*
      1. *The Romantic movement*
      2. *Theory of Margaret Murray*

IV. *Revival of Witchcraft in the Postwar World*
   A. *Gardner the founder*
   B. *Gods, goddesses and magic*
      1. *Interview with L. Haze*
      2. *Description of a Witches' Sabbat*

V. *The Outlook for Witchcraft in Today's Society*
   A. *Prospects of recognition*
      1. *Charles Arnold's bid to conduct marriages*
      2. *Opposition in the United States*
      3. *The feminist appeal*
   B. *Conclusion*
      1. *Restatement of thesis*
      2. *Will witchcraft survive?*

Jane's outline has five main headings: a general introduction leading to her thesis, a closer introductory look at witchcraft in North America today, a section of early historical background, a section of more recent history leading to the present, and a closing "outlook" section on present-day witchcraft.

Outlines normally have at least three main headings, except for those that cast their topic in a "pro and con," "contrast" or "comparison" form. And few outlines have more than five or six main headings; more than this would probably mean the topic has not been well focussed.

Before we discuss the last step of writing an essay, read "Witchcraft in North America Today" so that we can refer to it as an example.

Reznik 1

Jane L. Reznik

Professor Martin

ENC 100

5 April 19__

Witchcraft in North America Today

1

If the 1960s was the decade of the "peace" generation and the 1970s that of the "me" generation, few would argue that the closing decade of our century is a time in which many young people are searching for meaning in life outside the framework of traditional religion. They may turn to one of the Eastern religions or may join one of the many cults that have so rapidly sprung up--and often just as rapidly disappeared--in recent years.

2

Perhaps the most interesting of these, witchcraft, is unlike most cults in that it has no "guru" or divinely appointed leader, no bands of fanatical followers and no mission to actively seek new members. Yet it does resemble cults in its closely guarded books of magic and its oath of secrecy taken by new members.

3

Hard facts about witchcraft are difficult to glean from the media. Reports tends to be sensationalistic, with stories of spells and "black magic," while most popular books and films on the subject deal with ghosts, spells or possession by devils and demons. Yet as more and more reports of witchcraft in North America appear, a serious debate has begun to assess the current status of the craft in today's society of competing faiths and beliefs.

Reznik 2

Some of its followers trace witchcraft back to ancient "pagan" pre-Christian beliefs, claiming that witches still communicate with gods of the "old religion." Others claim that modern witchcraft is really a new religion for our time. But <u>a closer look at the development of modern witchcraft shows that its appeal is related to the current interest in cults and the supernatural rather than to its claim to be either an "old" or a "new" religion.</u>

4

Thesis statement.

An estimated 5000 witches, both male and female, now practice in Canada (Delacourt A15). Jeffrey B. Russell, professor of history at the University of California and an authority on witchcraft, estimates that there are at least 15 000 witches in the United States, and writes that witchcraft is especially popular among those younger than 30, with women outnumbering men two to one (<u>A History</u> 140, 171). The irony is that this movement is spreading in a society whose art, books, movies and television still often depict witches as they were viewed in the Middle Ages: sinister old hags dressed in black cloaks and pointed hats, flying around on broomsticks on Halloween night, ready for mischief.

5

Since two works by Russell appear in the list of works cited, the title is given here. And since his name is mentioned in the text, it is omitted in the reference.

This stereotype of the evil witch is being attacked by modern practitioners such as Charles Arnold, clerical worker at a Toronto community college, who in December 1987 was granted religious leave on the basis of his membership in the Church of Wicca (pronounced "witcha"), a word which in Old English means "witch" or "sorcerer" ("Witchcraft" 604). Arnold, a second-degree high priest

6

An example brings life to the generalizations of the preceding paragraph.

and an Elder of Spendwick Coven in the Temple of the Elder Faiths (a group linking a number of Toronto covens, or witch congregations), said he was offended by popular portrayals of witchcraft, especially those that describe animal and even human sacrifices (Delacourt A15). He later testified that nothing links Wicca to Satanism or black magic (Slotnick A2). He denied that he used spells to win his case before an arbitration board which awarded him two days' paid leave to observe the Wiccan holidays of Samhain, the beginning of the Celtic New Year, and Belthane, the beginning of summer (Slotnick A1).

7

The arbitration board said that "Wicca is obviously a religion," while the lawyer for the Ontario Public Service Employees Union remarked: "You can't joke with somebody else's religion. These people have been persecuted for hundreds of years. They were burned at the stake in Salem"[1] (Slotnick A2). The board, which heard evidence from a professor of religion at the University of Toronto, concluded that Wicca is "the modern survival of the ancient pagan religions of Western Europe which were suppressed, following the conversion in Roman times, to Christianity" (A1). The Globe and Mail report includes a few details about the beliefs and practices of modern-day witchcraft such as its prayer rituals and the two major figures of worship, the goddess, or "Great Mother," and her companion the "Horned God." But the report gives only a superficial idea of what modern witchcraft is all about, and little or no information about its historical development.

Since Jane did not want to dwell on this point here, her content note offers further explanation after the last page of the essay.

Reznik 4

A more detailed account of witchcraft should begin by

showing how the term is applied to three quite different

though related phenomena: "The first is simple sorcery,^{2}

which is found in every period and culture. The second is

the alleged diabolical witchcraft of . . . Europe. The

third is the pagan revival of the twentieth century"

(Russell, "Witchcraft" 415).

Most historians of witchcraft would agree that its

origin lies in the practice of sorcery, "a web of beliefs

and practices whose purpose is to manipulate nature for

the benefit of the witch's client" (415). Sorcery has

been practiced since prehistoric times, and is still found

in areas such as Africa and the Pacific Islands.

According to Russell, sorcery

> is based on the assumption that the cosmos is a whole
> and that hidden connections therefore exist among all
> natural phenomena. The sorcerer attempts . . . to
> control or at least influence these connections in
> order to effect the practical results he desires.
> (A History 18)

Although sorcery was the main ingredient of

traditional European witchcraft, elements of pre-Christian

"pagan" religions, in which many gods were present at

once, also played a part. Eventually these lingering

Celtic and Teutonic religions and a rapidly spreading

Christianity clashed. The result was that many Christians

viewed witchcraft as a diabolical or devilish activity

that often inspired false interpretations of Christianity

itself. From about 1450 to 1650 and even later, witches

8

This is a whole
paragraph of transition,
introducing the
historical background to
witchcraft.

9

This material on sorcery
is the first major section
of historical background.

Quotations over four
lines long are indented.
In these cases, omit
quotation marks.

10

Second section of
historical background.

were hunted down, then tortured and killed by methods as cruel as burning at the stake. Today the only reminder of this period is the term "witch hunt," which describes political persecution.

11

In the eighteenth century the adoption of a more scientific world-view caused witchcraft to be considered a mere superstition, although witch hunting still occurred in rural areas. The execution of a "witch" was reported to have taken place in Germany as late as 1775. The last trial for witchcraft in England, in 1731, ended in acquittal.

12

It was not until the early nineteenth century that a revival of interest in the occult (from the Latin occultas, "hidden things") took place. Now the demonic and supernatural in general were taken up by artists and writers of the Romantic Movement in England, France and Germany. This period marks the birth of what we know today as modern witchcraft in its major "neo-pagan" form.

13

Third section of historical background.

As the occult movement gained strength during the late nineteenth and early twentieth centuries, its members made up a kind of modern folklore of witchcraft, including translations of "grimoires" or manuals of sorcery, and of the ancient Hebrew Kabbala (occult doctrines), magic number systems, spells, curses and love potions (Russell, A History 134).

14

This renewed surge of interest in witchcraft was given scholarly support by the theories of certain well-known anthropologists and folklorists of the early twentieth century. The most important of these was the

British anthropologist Margaret Murray, whose book <u>The</u>
<u>Witch-Cult in Western Europe</u> (1921) had a great influence
on the founders of modern witchcraft. Murray argued that
European witchcraft was derived from an ancient fertility
cult displaced by Christianity and founded on the worship
of a horned god called Dianus. Later researchers rejected
Murray's theory, but the idea of historical links between
European witchcraft and ancient religions was important in
setting the stage for the appearance of witchcraft as we
know it today.

The craft did not experience another revival until
after World War II, when it seemed to some that
established religions could not explain the chaos into
which the world had been plunged for the second time in
decades. This period of uncertainty spurred an interest
in the occult, which has only increased since that time
judging by the number of works on the subject to be found
in any bookstore. Many social scientists have described
this phenomenon: how in time of severe social stress
individuals may abandon trusted traditional beliefs to
seek meaning in the world of magic and the supernatural.
They have also described the unfortunate reality that
joining a sect or cult can backfire, leaving people
emotionally worse off than before (Benedict 39-44).

This post-war surge of interest in the occult led to
the magic formulations of Gerald Gardner, often described
as the father of modern witchcraft. Gardner, an
Englishman born in 1884, claimed to have been initiated
into the craft by an English witch in 1939. Russell

15

16

An ellipsis of three dots (...) replaces unnecessary words removed from the middle of a sentence. Four dots signal words removed from the end of a sentence.

explains that "Gardner used a variety of magical and literary sources to invent--or re-invent--a religion. . . . Gardner began to write a <u>grimoire</u> . . . still in existence in the Ripley's collection at Toronto. . . ."(<u>A History</u> 153)

17

Strongly influenced by the theories of Margaret Murray, Gardner introduced many "neo-pagan" elements into his credo, including the figure of the horned god, which owed something to Murray's Dianus image and the Greek nature god, Pan. Later, Gardner added a goddess modelled on figures such as Diana, the Greek goddess of virginity, and Isis, the Egyptian goddess of magic:

In a long quotation, the page reference comes after the final period.

> The chief deity of the witches is the Goddess, the deity of nature perceived as an earth Goddess, a moon Goddess, and a fertility Goddess. Witches emphasize the threefold nature of the Goddess: she is warrior maid; she is mother; she is hag of darkness and rebirth. . . . Some feminist witches worship the Goddess as their sole deity; most worship both the Goddess and her consort, the horned god. Some introduce a seasonal consideration, worshipping the Goddess in the spring and summer . . . and shift at Hallowe'en to worshipping the God during the autumn and winter. The worship of the God and Goddess represents the principle of duality, the belief that the cosmos is divided into doublets: male and female, light and darkness, negative and positive. The sexual union of the God and Goddess represents the principle of unification. (Russell, <u>A History</u> 158)

18

In his book <u>Witchcraft Today</u> (1954), Gardner completed his synthesis of ancient sorcery, pagan beliefs and his own poetic additions. Although most covens follow the teachings of Gardner, there are disagreements, with some groups claiming to be directly descendent from the master's coven and others downplaying the idea of links to an old religion,

Reznik 8

stressing instead the craft's poetical and psychological appeal (Russell, <u>A History</u> 154).

An interview with a young Toronto follower of Gardner, Leanne Haze, conducted by <u>Oh</u>!, a local college campus magazine, reveals some of the ideas of the modern urban witch. The authors begin their interview with Haze, a "second degree High Priestess," with the remark that "witchcraft is based on the manifestation of a 'higher self', symbolized in the ancient archetypes of gods and goddesses. Its origins are based . . . in man's first awareness of the powers of the mind." They go on to explain that the Wiccan Church of Canada has its headquarters in Toronto and that anyone can join in its "Sunday Circle" (sabbat ritual). "Our interview with Haze," they conclude, "is just another indication that witches are beginning to come out of the closet and let their views be known" (Snell and Morrissey 2).

Haze takes pains in the interview to disassociate herself from any form of diabolical or Satanic witchcraft. She explains that there are two kinds of magic:

> "Lunar magic works with the time of the year . . . and the solar magic works in the time of man. Lunar magic is earth magic, and is the one you do actual spells with. It's through your emotional and physical being and you affect your physical reality."

Haze explains that solar magic is different: "It's high magic and works with the times and movements of the planets. The time of man as opposed to the time of day" (10-11).

19

A quotation within a quotation is set off with single quotation marks.

20

Although indented quotations do not require quotation marks, this one does because it reports spoken comments quoted in the original article.

21   The usual witches' meeting or sabbat reflects this
notion of tapping the forces of cosmic energy for personal
benefit. Russell explains the symbolism: coven members
worship in the harmony of a ritual circle, usually
outdoors in a private place. At some meetings members are
naked, or "skyclad." "Some witches say that it increases
their contact with the powers of nature, others that it
erases class distinctions" (A History 169). An altar is
set up with a statue of the gods, an "athame," or daggar
used to invoke the god, a sword or wand, candles and wine.
Russell describes how the gods are invoked with ritual and
poetry, and the priestess sings, dances, or meditates, "in
a sense becoming the Goddess" (170). The coven creates a
"cone of power" representing "the combined will of the
group." Russell tells how:

> The members of the coven join hands and sing and
> dance in a circle. The High Priestess stands in the
> centre of the circle. When she feels the energy
> reach its peak, she knows that the cone of power has
> been raised. She signals for the coven to let go the
> power, focuses it with her will, and speeds it
> towards its destination. . . . The cone may be
> directed towards a spiritual and general end or
> towards a quite specific earthly purpose. Often the
> cone may be sent to heal the sick or to achieve some
> other good mutually willed by the coven.
>   The raising and release of the cone requires a
> great outpouring of energy, and this part of the
> ritual is followed by a period of meditation and
> centring, after which the coven takes communion with
> cakes and wine. . . . After communion ensues an
> informal, unstructured period for poetry, discussion,
> minor magic, song, games, or whatever seems
> appropriate. The rite is now almost over, but the
> circle must be broken, the sacred space returned to
> the mundane, and the Priestess brought back from
> her union with the divine. The guardian spirits
> and deities must be thanked. The Priestess breaks
> the circle by cutting across its circumference with

the tip of the sword, wand, or athame. The coven
members return to their ordinary lives as housewives,
students, bankers, librarians, or computer
technologists. (170-171)

A survey of Wiccan literature reveals that the
group's ethical code is a simple one: "Do whatever you
like so long as it doesn't hurt anyone else" (160). There
is a sense of taking responsibility for one's own actions,
and a warning that punishment will surely follow any evil
action. Witchcraft groups claim to create feelings of joy
and "positive magic." "Magic" in this context includes
astrology, divination of the future, and the casting of
beneficent spells. All this is so-called "white" magic;
"black" or negative magic is avoided.

On the subject of magic and spells, Charles Arnold,
the Toronto witch discussed earlier, said his success in
obtaining religious leave was foretold by his "spiritual
guides." But he denied using spells to obtain a
favourable result, saying that "a spell would have been a
bad move . . . because every bit of magic comes back to
the spell-thrower threefold." He added that he did not
use magic on this occasion because "It was a clear-cut
case," but did admit "using a little magic" to get the
house he and his wife now own in Toronto: "Of course, we
got it the next morning" (Delacourt A15).

Arnold is now trying to become "the first practising
witch in Canada to get a licence to perform marriages" but
is running into opposition, not only from the Ontario
Government (Tyler A6), but also from some Toronto covens

that object to "skyclad" weddings. The Toronto Star also reports practitioner Pat Phillips as saying that "attempting to have witchcraft recognized betrays the ancient and mysterious nature of the faith. Some covens want to remain low-profile." And not all witches agree on what they want. While high priest Jonathon Zotique claims that "Wiccans do not believe in marriage" except for unions of only "a year and a day," Wiccan Church of Canada chairperson Tamara James told The Toronto Star that though witches may observe an ancient religion, "many live in the modern world and want a permanent marriage" (A6).

25

This point refers again to the thesis.

Witchcraft is far from being accepted as a religion in North America, and has encountered official opposition on this score in the United States. Maclean's, for example, reported a case of American politicians wanting to deprive witches' churches of the tax-exempt status granted them as religious groups. Jesse Helms (Republican, North Carolina) claimed that "cults and witchcraft groups lead to violent and unlawful behavior." But Amber K., "a former first officer of the Berkeley, California-based Covenant of the Goddess," which represents about 70 American covens, said, "This is a throwback to the Middle Ages, when witches were equated with devil worship and all kinds of nonsense." Pointing out that "several organizations have been recognized as tax-exempt that espouse a system of beliefs, rituals and practices derived from pre-Christian Celtic and Welsh traditions which they label as 'witchcraft'," Secretary of

Reznik 12

the Treasury J.A. Baker refused to remove the tax-exempt status (Jussim 64).

Despite opposition in some circles, witchcraft   26
continues to grow in North America. This may be partly
because it is in tune with the feminist and other social
equality movements of the last few decades, as seen for
example in the promotion of a high priestess to coven
leader. Russell explains that some covens exclude men,
and that most worship a goddess rather than a god
(A History 156).

This feminist theme is seen in a recent proposal for   27
a film about the persecution of witches in early Nova
Scotia. In the movie, a group of witches in hiding
rescues other women accused of witchcraft. The producer
is Nanci Rossov and the female lead is Sonja Smits, star
of the weekly CBC series Street Legal. According to The
Toronto Star, the two realized the subject had yet to be
dealt with seriously by the movie industry. Rossov said
"It had either been trivialized or made fun of or made   This example supports
the point about
horrific," adding that "There's no question in my mind   feminism.
that one of the reasons this story hasn't been told is
because it is women's history" ("Burning" D5).

Despite the increase in such favourable publicity,   28
the current public image of witchcraft is problematical,
with practitioners seeking recognition of their "faith" by
a tolerant society, while at the same time attempting to
erase the old stereotype of the evil or mischievous witch
promoted for so long in books from the witch-hunting texts
of early times down to Shakespeare's Macbeth and beyond,

not to mention films such as Rosemary's Baby, The Exorcist, The Witches of Eastwick and others.

29   Works of art that have depicted witches have usually done so in a negative light, with a few exceptions such as Bernard Shaw's Saint Joan (1923) and Arthur Miller's The Crucible (1953). And most media coverage is negative, either through a sensationalistic or a humorous approach, as shown for example in a 1978 news report by syndicated columnist Jack Anderson, headed "Witches Invade the Military." It states that the American army "had taken steps to ensure that its chaplains would be willing and able to minister to the increasing number of personnel who were witches" (Qtd. in Russell, A History 8).

30   Despite bad press, witchcraft in North America is attracting more attention and gaining more adherents than at any time since World War II. Although some of its followers claim direct links to ancient religions, it seems clear that the main factor in its new popularity is the same thing that has attracted many people to other cults: the hope that a new and different belief will do more than traditional religion has done to satisfy the spiritual cravings of individuals who feel oppressed by the dangers and uncertainties of our time. It will be interesting to see whether witchcraft succeeds in gaining further public acceptance in this age of new faiths and cults, or whether, as so many of them have done, it will disappear from the public stage to surface now and then as an offbeat news item in the media.

Reznik 14

Notes

[1]In the infamous witch trials at Salem, Massachusetts
in 1692, nineteen persons were executed and more than a
hundred jailed as a result of accusations (later proved
false) by a group of hysterical young women and girls.
Arthur Miller's well-known play The Crucible was based on
this event, but actually referred to the persecution or
"witch hunt" of suspected communists at the McCarthy
hearings in the United States in the 1950s. Miller was
one of many writers accused in the so-called un-American
Activities Committee hearings.

[2]"Sorcerer" is derived from the French sorcier,
meaning both "sorcerer" and "witch." The term has always
been unclear: sometimes it refers to simple sorcery,
sometimes to diabolical witchcraft. Russell (A History
12) claims that "witch" does not come, as some think, from
the Middle English "wis," meaning "wise," which is instead
the origin of the term "wizard," a word also used after
about 1825 to denote a witch.

Reference to these explanatory content notes is made by raised numbers in the text. Use as few notes as possible, for they can interrupt the reader's train of thought.

Works Cited

Omit volume and page number when the reference book is arrange alphabetically.

Benedict, R. "Magic." Encyclopedia of the Social
    Sciences. New York: Macmillan, 1950.

Brian, Robert. "Child Witches." In Witchcraft:
    Confessions and Accusations. Ed. Mary Douglas.
    London: Criterion, 1970. 21-30.

"Burnings of Witches in Europe Spark Idea for a New
    Movie." The Toronto Star 12 Dec. 1987: D5.

Delacourt, Susan. "Adept at Casting Spells, but Magic Not
    in Cards at Hearing, Witch Says." The Globe and Mail
    11 Dec. 1987: A15.

Douglas, Mary, ed. Witchcraft: Confessions and
    Accusations. London: Criterion, 1970.

Gettings, F., ed. Encyclopedia of the Occult. London:
    Rider, 1986.

Jussim, Daniel. "Witchcraft." Maclean's 25 Nov. 1985:
    64.

"Occultism." The New Encyclopaedia Britannica:
    Macropaedia. Chicago: Macmillan, 1985.

Russell, Jeffrey B. A History of Witchcraft. London:
    Thames and Hudson, 1980.

---. "Witchcraft." Encyclopedia of Religion. New York:
    Macmillan, 1987.

Slotnick, L. "Witchcraft High Priest Must Get Holiday
    Pay, Humber College Told." The Globe and Mail 10 Dec.
    1987: A1-2.

Put no punctuation between name and date of a periodical.

After an author's first entry, three hyphens and a period represent the name in further entries.

Reznik 16

Snell, W. and J. Morrissey. "Old Religion in a New Age."

   Interview with Leanne Haze. <u>Oh! Magazine</u>. Toronto:

   Oakham House Societies, Ryerson Polytechnical

   Institute, Jan. 1988: 2-3.

Tyler, Tracey. "Trouble Brews over Witch's Bid to Perform

   Marriages." <u>The Toronto Star</u> 27 Feb. 1988: A6.

"Witchcraft." <u>Encyclopaedia Britannica</u>. 1973 ed.

You may omit city and publisher of a very familiar reference work.

Step Five: Write the Essay

Since the research essay is longer and more fully planned than the "short essays" discussed in our opening chapter, it is written in a less experimental way. We might still call the first version a "discovery draft," for the act of writing almost always triggers new ideas. Yet the extensive reading, note-taking and organizing done before the writing begins will strongly shape even the first draft.

Jane found herself writing more slowly and deliberately than in the "short essays" earlier in her course. She took fewer risks, staying closer to her outline, for any major shift of direction now would mean throwing pages of research into the garbage.

Since research papers are long and are revised through several drafts, word processing is a powerful tool in writing them. The Modern Language Association (MLA) recommends "saving" each draft under a different filename (for example "draft1," "draft2," etc.), so if the newest draft does not work out, you can go back to the previous one in memory.

The MLA also suggests recording quotations in separate files, so that rather than wasting time and risking error in recopying, you just retrieve them into your draft. Another suggestion is to keep a running bibliography in its own file, so that at any time you can check it so far, add new items, or delete items that were not useful.

As to format, the MLA advises that you not "justify" the right margin. It also suggests using a "running head" to produce your last name and the page number at the top of each page (see Jane's essay for exact format). In WordPerfect, for example, this is done through selecting "headers" either in the "Format" menu (in earlier versions) or in the "Layout" menu (in later versions).

The single-spacing of long quotations that you see in Jane's essay may be a bother once you have selected double-spacing. If you are computerized, why not adhere to the MLA's format of double-spacing all quotations (and indenting the long ones ten spaces — that is, approximately two "tabs").

Be sure to "save" drafts onto a backup disk; otherwise, you could lose a week or more of work if your hard disk crashes.

Yet if while writing she sensed that the facts were working *against* her tentative thesis, showing it to be wrong, like a scientist's experiment disproving her original hypothesis, the only honest response would be to interpret those facts all over, throw out the old outline and write a new one.

As Jane wrote her first draft, she followed these guidelines suggested by her instructor:

■ ***Put your thesis statement into an introduction*** An essay about a very familiar subject might have a short introduction with the thesis statement in the first paragraph, while one about a less familiar subject might begin with several paragraphs of introduction. Since few people know much about witchcraft, Jane's thesis statement comes at the end of the fourth paragraph.

In your introduction, whatever its length, *try to interest and prepare your readers.* Jane's reference to a spiritual search by young people is an appeal to the readers' prior knowledge: if they have already experienced one aspect of what is to be discussed, they will feel more hopeful about understanding the subject and will therefore be more likely to go on reading.

The contrast between witchcraft and other cult groups is meant to arouse further interest by showing that her topic, modern witchcraft, could be important. Finally, the mention of a growing controversy about the status of witchcraft today prepares readers by giving them a preview of the essay.

Other introductions use a quotation from a famous person, an amusing story, a frightening statistic or whatever else the author thinks will interest and prepare readers.

■ ***Connect the parts*** Just as the sentences of a paragraph are connected by transitions, so are the paragraphs of an essay. Use the transitions that we examined on page 39, especially at the beginning and end of a paragraph. Note, for example, how the first words of paragraph 26 signal a contrast from the previous paragraph: "Despite opposition in some circles, witchcraft continues to grow in North America." You may even use a whole paragraph, like paragraph 8 of Jane's essay, as a "bridge" between longer sections:

A more detailed account of witchcraft should begin by showing how the term is applied to three quite different though related phenomena: "The first is simple sorcery, which is found in every period and culture. The second is the alleged diabolical witchcraft of . . . Europe. The third is the pagan revival of the twentieth century" (Russell, "Witchcraft" 415).

Finally, larger organizational devices can help to keep the essay moving: Jane used a historical time line to trace the development of witchcraft. The momentum of this chronological order helps to move the reader from one section to the next.

■ *Write a meaningful conclusion* Do not end with a mere summary, although most research essays do have a summary near the end. Instead, try for a larger effect, as in musical compositions that rise at the end to a climax. Climax in an essay can be built in several ways. "Witchcraft in North America Today" uses the historical progression that we mentioned. It moves from early to modern times, carries the theme further by discussing the rise of modern witchcraft, and focusses the reader's attention on this theme. After a restatement of Jane's thesis, the essay then rises to a climax with a conclusion that speculates on the future of witchcraft.

Notice that Jane avoided loading her ending with false significance. If she had claimed that witchcraft would become a major religion or that someday everyone would have a witch in the family, the reader would doubt not only her conclusion but also the rest of the essay.

■ *Revise*, as the author of our "short essay" revised. Since we saw the whole process at work on pages 20–28, we will not repeat it here. What you have just read is a final draft, revised, edited and proofread — the product of the author's most careful work. It may still have flaws, but its writer sought to polish the argument as thoroughly as possible by "reseeing" it through several drafts.

In the last of those drafts, Jane scrutinized all suspicious-looking sentences and all words that just might be misspelled. It is in this final stage that she reached for the grammar book and the dictionary. (Why do so in the early stages, when words and sentences may later be changed or cut out in the process of refining the thought?)

Putting the editing and proofreading last does not diminish their importance. To many readers a grammatical error or spelling error is a stimulus that triggers an emotional response; some readers grasp such errors the way a hawk grasps mice — with a sense of victory. They positively gloat over the fact that some people cannot control the details of language as well as they can. It is for this reason that being careful with the details will pay off. Why distract a reader with faulty pronoun reference or spelling errors, when what you really want that reader to do is pay attention to your argument?

Final Form of the Research Essay

Few things are agreed upon by everyone, and essay form is no exception. If your teacher does not specify a particular set of rules, though, follow the form of our sample research essay, which is based on the name-page method of referencing recommended by the Modern Language Association (MLA) in its *MLA Handbook for Writers of Research Papers*.

This increasingly popular way of documenting replaces the old footnote or endnote system. Now brief references in parentheses, in the text of the essay, refer directly to items in a list of "works cited" (formerly called the "bibliography") at the end of the essay. Footnotes or endnotes, now called "content notes," are used only for explanations that are not important enough to appear in the essay itself.

Title Page?

Although some teachers still require a title page, the MLA no longer recommends it. See whether your own teacher wants one, and if so, what should be on it. Otherwise follow the MLA format, which replaces the title page with the following information on the upper left of the first page of the essay:

■ Your name

■ The teacher's name

■ Course designation

■ Date

The title appears just below this information, centred, and below it comes the first line of the essay. (See page 1 of Jane's essay for format and spacing.)

Page Format

Use standard-size paper, one side only, and leave standard margins so your teacher will have room to write comments. If you type or use word processing, double-space. If you write by hand, ask your teacher whether single- or double-spacing is preferred. If the teacher requires a title page, do not repeat the title at the top of page 1. In the upper right corner of each page, put your last name and the page number (see Jane's essay for exact format). Indent the first line of each paragraph five spaces if you type, further if you write by hand.

Quotations

Of course whenever you repeat someone else's exact words, you must signal that fact so the reader will not think the words are yours. **Quotations of up to four lines are put in quotation marks and incorporated into the body of your text. As for longer passages, we suggest either of two options:**

1. The MLA recommends that quotations longer than four lines be indented ten spaces all along the left margin and be double-spaced. However, this format, designed mostly for manuscripts that will be published, takes up a great deal of space. Many teachers prefer the traditional method below:

2. Single-space all quotations longer than four lines, and indent them five spaces from the left margin. (See Jane's essay, which follows this form.)

Note that with either method of spacing, *quotation marks are not used in a passage of more than four lines, because the indented format already identifies the passage as a quotation.*

■ *A quotation and the sentence in which it appears must make grammatical sense together* Avoid errors like this:

The author refers to the snow "It would fill the tracks in half an hour."

To correct this fused sentence, let's integrate the quotation with what comes before:

The author says that the snow ". . . would fill the tracks in half an hour. "

Note how the final quotation marks come after the period, not before. They would also come after a comma:

The author says that the snow ". . . would fill the tracks in half an hour," making the search more difficult.

■ *Where one quotation occurs inside another, enclose the inner one in single quotation marks* For example:

Then I said, "If this is what you call 'natural food,' I'll go back to TV dinners."

■ *You may omit irrelevant material from the beginning, middle or end of a quoted sentence by substituting an ellipsis (. . .) of three dots with a space between each* If the omission is from the end, add a fourth dot which is the sentence period. (See examples of both forms in paragraph 16 of Jane's essay.) The omission of one or more sentences from a passage is also signalled by four dots.

Even with omissions, the quotation as it appears in your essay must make sense. Don't attempt to save time by just quoting the beginning and end ("With a . . . it"), assuming your reader will find the rest in the book. Instead, the reader will just get lost.

Fairness to your source is equally important. An unscrupulous publisher might place on the back cover of a new paperback a quotation from a reviewer who said the novel is ". . . an excellent book. . . . ," when unfortunately the critic's full comment was ". . . an excellent book to throw in the garbage." An essayist who quotes out of context is falsifying as surely as if he or she had written the whole passage in the first place.

■ *You can sometimes make a quotation clearer by adding or substituting words in square brackets* (See the example and explanation on page117.) Use this technique sparingly.

Name-Page References

Quotation marks tell your reader when you are using another person's words, but not whose words they are or where the reader can find them in order to check the accuracy of the quotation or find more information on the subject. In a short informal essay it may be enough to introduce a quotation with a few facts: "As Margaret Atwood points out on page 75 of *Survival*. . . ." Your teacher will let you know if this is all the documentation required.

But in a formal research essay you need a fuller system of documentation. The standard used to be footnotes or endnotes, followed on the last page by a bibliography. This system did the job, but was not efficient: arranging and typing footnotes was laborious, and the notes and bibliography repeated too much of the same information.

For several years now the MLA has recommended a modernized system that delivers all the same information but in streamlined form. If your teacher prefers this approach, as most now do, study the following directions and see Jane's research essay for examples of their use.

The main feature of the name-page reference system is the way we now refer briefly, in the body of the essay, to sources used. Instead of adding a numeral that refers to a note elsewhere, we simply place, after a quotation or other borrowed material, the author's last name and the page or pages on which the information can be found. Note how both facts are put in parentheses, as in this example:

(Delacourt A15)

This brief reference is one part of your documentation of sources; the other is the corresponding entry in your list of works cited (formerly called the "bibliography") at the end of the paper. When we look there under the name "Delacourt," we find all the other facts we may need: the rest of the author's name, the title of her article, the fact that it appeared in the *Globe and Mail* and finally the date:

Delacourt, Susan. "Adept at Casting Spells, but Magic Not in Cards at Hearing, Witch Says." *The Globe and Mail* 11 Dec. 1987: A15.

Now we can look up the original article to verify Jane's accuracy, or to find more information.

The form of the name-page reference and the form of the entry in our list of works cited will both vary sometimes, depending on several factors. Study the guidelines that close this chapter, as well as the examples in Jane's essay, so you know what to do in each case. But first let's discuss the main question of documentation more fully.

When Do We Reference?

Some people worry about documentation, gloomily expecting to make a mistake and be accused of plagiarism. But most teachers can easily tell the difference between accidental and intentional plagiarism. The few students who deliberately present others' words or ideas as their own, in order to avoid the work of thinking, are frequently caught and then are harshly punished — perhaps by failure in the course or even by expulsion from school.

As for the honest majority of essay writers, observing the following principles should cover most cases of documentation. Even if your performance is not perfect, your teacher will note your honesty and will probably recommend improvements rather than blame you for "stealing" information.

■ *Reference whenever you quote an author's words or copy visual information such as a chart* If the borrowed passage is only part of a sentence, or even just a key word or two, it is still put in quotation marks and referenced.

■ *Reference whenever you summarize or paraphrase a source* In high school some students think that doing "research" means finding good passages in the encyclopedia and copying them out into their essay, shuffling a few words around to avoid plagiarism. What they fail to see is that not only words, but also ideas, can "belong" to the person who wrote them.

For example James Higgins, in his essay "Gabriel García Márquez: *Cien años de soledad*," published in Philip Swanson's 1990 book *Landmarks in Modern Latin American Fiction*, states the following on page 157:

The character with the acutest sense of life's futility is the disillusioned Colonel Aureliano. After undertaking thirty-two armed uprisings he comes to the conclusion that he has squandered twenty years of his life to no purpose and withdraws to his workshop, where he devotes himself to making the same little golden ornaments over and over again.

Suppose that a student doing an essay on the novelist García Márquez would write the following:

Colonel Aureliano is the character who shows the most acute sense of life's futility. After his 32 armed uprisings he realizes that he has squandered 20 years to no purpose and retreats to his workshop, where he spends all his time making the same little ornaments of gold over and over.

Do these thoughts still "belong" to Higgins? Despite the shifting of phrases and substituting of synonyms, a comparison of the two passages shows the whole progression of thought to be unchanged. A name-page reference should obviously follow the new version.

Furthermore, small groups of words such as "thirty-two armed uprisings" are identical in both passages. The essayist must either change all such passages, to produce a complete paraphrase, or put the borrowed parts in quotation marks to show who wrote them.

■ *Reference whenever you take from your source a particular idea or fact that is not common knowledge and that does not appear in other sources* (For example, the year of Shakespeare's birth, 1564, is not such common knowledge that most people could give it when asked. But since it can be found in thousands of sources, do not reference it.) But if critic X discovers an old trunk in an attic, containing documents which prove the year of birth to be not 1564 but 1565, and publishes an article about it, you must reference this information because it is the intellectual property of the author.

Kinds of Name-Page References

Reference to a Single Author

He denied that he used spells to win his case before an arbitration board which awarded him two days' paid leave to observe the Wiccan holidays of Samhain and Belthane (Delacourt A15).

Note how the period ending the sentence is placed *after* the reference. Note also that no comma appears between name and page, and that the word "page" or "p." is not used before the page number. This name-page reference leads us to the alphabetized entry under "Delacourt" in the list of works cited, where more information is given.

If you give an author's name in the text of your essay, you need give only the page number in the reference:

In her article, Delacourt explains that Arnold was granted paid leave for the Wiccan holidays of Samhain and Belthane (A15).

It is also possible to place the page reference directly after the author's name in the text:

Delacourt (A15) explains that Arnold was granted paid leave for the Wiccan holidays of Samhain and Belthane.

This method, though, may distract the reader. It is best used when the names of more than one author appear together in the text:

Both Russell (57) and Delacourt (A15) would agree that the arbitration board's decision was controversial.

When Two or More Titles by the Same Author are Listed in the "Works Cited"

The term "witchcraft" can be applied to three different phenomena (Russell, "Witchcraft" 415).

Since Russell is listed in the "works cited" as the author of a book, *A History of Witchcraft*, as well as an article, "Witchcraft," we avoid confusion by specifying the title between his name and the page number.

A Work That Has Two Authors

The editors of *Oh! Magazine* interviewed Toronto witch Leanne Haze (Snell and Morrissey 2–3).

If the names are already given in the text of your essay, give only the page number in the reference:

Snell and Morrissey's interview with Toronto witch Leanne Haze revealed much about her belief in magic (2-3).

Titled but Unsigned Articles

This feminist theme in witchcraft is seen in a recent proposal for a Canadian film ("Burning" D5).

With the B's in the alphabetized list of works cited can be found the full title: "Burnings of Witches in Europe Spark Idea for a New Movie."

List of Works Cited

Book

Russell, Jeffrey B. *A History of Witchcraft*. London: Thames and Hudson, 1980.

Essay from an Edited Book

Brian, Robert. "Child Witches." In *Witchcraft: Confessions and Accusations*. Ed. Mary Douglas. London: Criterion, 1970. 21–30.

Periodical Article

Jussim, Daniel. "Witchcraft." *Maclean's* 25 Nov. 1985: 64.

Note that no period separates the periodical from the date.

A Work by Two Authors

Snell, W. and J. Morrissey. "Old Religion in a New Age." Interview with Leanne Haze. *Oh! Magazine*. Toronto: Oakham House Societies, Ryerson Polytechnical Institute, Jan. 1988: 2–3.

The first and last names of the second author are not reversed, since the last name of only the first author appears in the alphabetical order of the list.

Note: The above examples will cover most cases. For more detail, consult the *MLA Handbook for Research Papers*, current edition, published in New York by the Modern Language Association.

Answer Key

Limiting the Scope: Exercise (p. 9)

This exercise is open-ended.

Making Thesis Statements: Exercise (p. 11)

This exercise is open-ended.

The "Main" Paragraph: Exercise (p. 43)

Answers to the first set of five questions are open-ended. The topic sentence answers to the next set of five will probably be close to these in theme:

1. Fast food is not nutritious.
2. The means of trade have advanced steadily.
3. Driving harms the environment.
4. Many houses waste energy.
5. Clearcutting forests harms the environment.

Topic Sentences: Exercise (p. 45)

1.	B	8.	C	15.	B
2.	C	9.	C	16.	C
3.	C	10.	A	17.	B
4.	A	11.	A	18.	C
5.	A	12.	A	19.	B
6.	C	13.	C	20.	C
7.	B	14.	B		

There could, of course, be alternatives to these answers, depending on how the topic sentences might be developed.

Unity in "Main" Paragraphs: Exercise (p. 47)

The revisions are open-ended.

Improving "Thin" Paragraphs: Exercise (p. 49)

The revisions are open-ended.

Economy: Diagnostic Exercise (p. 55)

1.	X	11.		21.	X	31.	
2.	X	12.	X	22.	X	32.	X
3.	X	13.	X	23.	X	33.	X
4.		14.	X	24.		34.	X
5.	X	15.	X	25.	X	35.	X
6.	X	16.	X	26.	X	36.	X
7.	X	17.		27.	X	37.	X
8.	X	18.	X	28.	X	38.	X
9.	X	19.	X	29.	X	39.	X
10.	X	20.	X	30.	X	40.	X

Economy: Exercise, Level 1 (p. 57)

Here are the most obvious corrections of these self-repeaters:

1. astounded
2. in the future
3. products of industries
4. the result
5. advantages
6. feelings
7. cheap
8. fascinating
9. a fact
10. at that moment
11. unique
12. merge
13. 8:00 a.m.
14. in the future
15. our environment
16. crucial
17. many countries
18. self-confidence
19. etc.
20. $150
21. obvious
22. fascinating
23. miserable
24. self-esteem
25. reappear
26. easily
27. obvious
28. 600 students
29. chaotic
30. crucial
31. rectangular
32. light green
33. impossible
34. in June
35. light brown
36. old people
37. unique
38. no alternative
39. competition
40. in my opinion

Economy: Exercise, Level 2 (p. 59)

These items are "correct": 4, 13, 15.
The revisions are open-ended.

Economy: Exercise, Level 3 (p. 61)

No items are "correct."
The revisions are open-ended.

Clichés: Exercise (p. 65)

These items are "correct": 3, 15.
The revisions are open-ended.

Euphemisms: Exercise (p. 71)

The answers are open-ended.

Euphemisms and Their Opposite: Words Biased Pro or Con (p. 73)

All answers are open-ended.

Jargon: Exercise (p. 77)

This exercise has no one set of correct answers.

Slang and Colloquialisms: Exercise (p. 81)

These items are "appropriate": 6, 23.
The revisions are open-ended.

Completing Sentences: Exercise (p. 87)

A great range of answers is possible.

Complete Sentences: Diagnostic Exercise (p. 93)

1.	F	11.	F	21.	F	31.	F
2.	F	12.		22.		32.	F
3.		13.	F	23.	F	33.	
4.	F	14.	F	24.	F	34.	F
5.	F	15.	F	25.	F	35.	F
6.	F	16.	F	26.	F	36.	F
7.	F	17.	F	27.	F	37.	F
8.	F	18.		28.	F	38.	F
9.	F	19.	F	29.	F	39.	F
10.		20.	F	30.	F	40.	F

Complete Sentences: Exercise, Level 1 (p. 95)

Items 3, 13 and 17 are complete. Also complete are items 6 (first word group), 14 (first word group), 16 (second word group), 21 (second word group), 22 (first word group), 23 (first word group) and 24 (first word group).

Complete Sentences: Exercise, Level 2 (p. 97)

Items 3 and 14 are complete. Also complete are items 2 (first word group), 4 (first word group), 7 (first word group), 9 (first word group), 10 (first word group), 12 ((first two word groups), 15 (first word group), 16 (first word group), 18 (first word group), 19 (first word group), 22 (first and fourth word groups), 23 (first word group) 24 (first and third word groups) and 25 (first word group).

Complete Sentences: Exercise, Level 3 (p. 99)

These items are complete: 1 (first word group), 3 (first word group), 6, 7 (first word group), 8 (first and third word groups), 9 (first and second word groups), 10 (first word group), 11 (first word group), 13 (first word group), 14 (first and third word groups) and 15 (first word group).

Comma Splice and Fused Sentence: Diagnostic Exercise (p. 103)

1.	CS	11.	CS	21.	FS	31.	CS
2.	FS	12.	FS	22.		32.	
3.	CS	13.	CS	23.		33.	FS
4.		14.	CS	24.	CS	34.	FS
5.	CS	15.		25.	FS	35.	CS
6.	CS	16.	CS	26.	CS	36.	FS
7.	FS	17.	CS	27.	FS	37.	
8.	CS	18.	FS	28.	CS	38.	FS
9.	CS	19.	FS	29.		39.	CS
10.	CS	20.	CS	30.	CS	40.	

Comma Splice and Fused Sentence: Exercise, Level 1 (p. 105)

These items are "correct": 3, 9, 15.
The revisions are open-ended.

Comma Splice and Fused Sentence: Exercise, Level 2 (p. 107)

These items are "correct": 5, 14, 16.

Commas: Exercise (p. 111)

1.   As I put my coat on, the dentist and receptionist had a brief discussion.

2. Sharon flirted outrageously with Michael, and Kenny and Jason flirted with her. OR: Sharon flirted outrageously with Michael and Kenny, and Jason flirted with her.
3. Ham radio has become my obsession.
4. The sediment on the ocean floor, hundreds of metres below sea level, is up to 300 m thick.
5. One of my math teachers helped me learn to achieve my goal in the subject, by spending a great deal of time working with me.
6. The activities of juvenile gangs are most noticeable in the increase of vandalism.
7. My brother, grandfather and I had been going to the races since before I could remember.
8. Correct.
9. I love to play hockey, but studies come first.
10. Patients must be fed when they are too weak to eat, themselves.
11. Our diet should contain dairy products rich in protein, and vegetables.
12. Correct.
13. If you can, use cash or make your payments promptly.
14. The peace that broke out when the Cold War ended did not last.
15. Harsh lighting produces harsh photographs.
16. Correct.
17. The last step is to record the time, drug and dosage on the patient's chart.
18. When rivers lose their velocity suspended particles of clay and silt are deposited, creating fertile soils in river deltas.
19. Correct.
20. People in Istanbul seem to think that hamburgers and fries are not worth eating.
21. Alcohol has become a problem for our schools, and teachers are deeply concerned.
22. Divorce, like birth and death, occurs every day.
23. The truth is that many alcoholics never seek help, resulting in their own destruction.
24. Correct.
25. Players who fight during a game should be suspended for the whole season.
26. Once I placed a couple of lines on the paper, some thoughts began to appear.
27. North Americans believe in eye contact.
28. The most sensible preparation for aging is a life well lived from the beginning.
29. Correct.
30. One thing that really bothers me is the idea of a large dog being kept in the city.
31. Once the needle is in, the plunger is retracted to check for blood.
32. Skiing has become the best way for city people to get into the country.
33. For hundreds of years English Canada has had social and political control over Quebec.
34. If you write a word without being completely sure of how to spell it, you may be making a mistake.
35. Although stubborn, Hagar is one of Margaret Laurence's most admirable characters.
36. Marriage is a big commitment.
37. Correct.
38. Erroll was a nice guy, but he was still immature.
39. The fastest sports are soccer, hockey, football, rugby and basketball.
40. While Dad was putting the lights on, my brothers and I started to place the star on the Christmas tree.

Semicolon, Colon, Question Mark and Exclamation Point: Exercise (p. 115)

These items are "correct": 3, 6, 12, 15, 30.
The revisions are open-ended, since there is often more than one way to eliminate the errors.

Run-on Sentence: Diagnostic Exercise (p. 119)

1.	ROS	11.	ROS	21.		31.	ROS
2.	ROS	12.		22.	ROS	32.	ROS
3.	ROS	13.	ROS	23.	ROS	33.	ROS
4.		14.	ROS	24.	ROS	34.	ROS
5.	ROS	15.	ROS	25.		35.	ROS
6.	ROS	16.		26.		36.	
7.	ROS	17.	ROS	27.	ROS	37.	ROS
8.	ROS	18.	ROS	28.	ROS	38.	ROS
9.		19.	ROS	29.	ROS	39.	ROS
10.	ROS	20.	ROS	30.		40.	ROS

Run-on Sentence: Exercises, Levels 1 and 2 (p. 121)

There are no "correct" items in these exercises.
The revisions are open-ended.

Pronoun Reference: Diagnostic Exercise (p. 131)

1.	X	11.	X	21.	X	31.	
2.	X	12.	X	22.	X	32.	X
3.	X	13.	X	23.	X	33.	X
4.	X	14.	X	24.	X	34.	X
5.	X	15.		25.	X	35.	X
6.		16.	X	26.	X	36.	X
7.	X	17.	X	27.	X	37.	
8.		18.	X	28.	X	38.	X
9.	X	19.	X	29.	X	39.	X
10.	X	20.	X	30.	X	40.	X

Pronoun Reference: Exercise, Level 1 (p. 133)

These items are "correct": 5, 11.

Pronoun Reference: Exercise, Level 2 (p. 135)

These items are "correct": 6, 14.

Agreement: Diagnostic Exercise (p. 141)

1.	X	11.	X	21.		31.	X
2.	X	12.	X	22.	X	32.	X
3.	X	13.	X	23.	X	33.	
4.	X	14.	X	24.		34.	X
5.	X	15.		25.	X	35.	X
6.	X	16.	X	26.	X	36.	X
7.	X	17.	X	27.	X	37.	X
8.		18.	X	28.	X	38.	X
9.	X	19.		29.		39.	X
10.		20.	X	30.	X	40.	

Agreement: Exercise, Level 1 (p. 143)

1.	is	14.	is
2.	he or she	15.	has
3.	was	16.	I
4.	us	17.	him or her
5.	was	18.	is
6.	its, it publishes	19.	their
7.	he or she has	20.	is
8.	is	21.	is
9.	were	22.	is
10.	is	23.	his or her life
11.	is	24.	is
12.	his or her	25.	you, your
13.	its		

Agreement: Exercise, Level 2 (p. 145)

These items are "correct": 6, 12, 18.
To some extent the revisions are open-ended.

Agreement: Exercise, Level 3 (p. 147)

Only item 6 is "correct."
The revisions are of course open-ended.

Equality of the Sexes in Language: Exercise (p. 151)

These items are "unbiased": 4, 13, 18, 25.
The revisions are open-ended.

Misplaced and Dangling Modifiers: Diagnostic Exercise (p. 155)

1.	Active sports involve a lot of competition, <u>such as soccer</u>.	MM
2.	Children flock to see Santa Claus <u>by the dozens</u>.	MM
3.	<u>Years ago</u> I think back when my friend offered me a cigarette at a party.	MM
4.	If you are like most people, a mortgage will be the largest debt of your lifetime.	
5.	I moved to Bayside with my parents when I was 13 years old <u>from the city of Ottawa</u>.	MM
6.	All students are <u>not</u> necessarily the same.	MM
7.	Pills are <u>virtually</u> used for everything.	MM
8.	By staying home you can save transportation money.	
9.	<u>As a child</u>, my father told me that the world is a cruel place to be in alone.	MM
10.	For many people, losing weight is a difficult problem.	
11.	A camera can <u>only</u> focus sharply on one object at a time.	MM
12.	Hailstones <u>only</u> reach 2.5 cm in diameter.	MM
13.	Since I was an only child, my parents wanted to protect me.	
14.	Car rental is <u>only</u> possible through credit cards.	MM
15.	Some programs of study are <u>only</u> available in community colleges.	MM
16.	It takes my mother only three minutes to drive to work.	
17.	Drinking is said to be a bad habit <u>by many doctors</u>.	MM
18.	When I was four, my parents and I moved into a new house.	
19.	There is no city that has no crimes at all <u>in this world</u>.	MM
20.	When I was a kid I lived with my grandmother, a lovely lady who would let me do anything I wanted to, <u>for a few months</u>.	MM

1.	<u>After waiting two hours in the lobby</u>, the doctor spent less than two minutes on me.	DM
2.	<u>Looking at my nephew watching television</u>, he seems to be in a trance.	DM
3.	<u>Living on the farm in southern Ontario</u>, winter tends to be cold and harsh.	DM
4.	<u>At the age of 13 years</u>, my entire life changed when my mother filed for a separation.	DM
5.	<u>After a few months of cleaning a dentist's office</u>, the dentist recommended me to her bookkeeper, so I was able to clean the bookkeeper's office too.	DM
6.	Dogs make good household pets because they are used for protecting the house <u>while away for the day</u>.	DM
7.	<u>After driving into the middle lane</u>, the truck slowed to a stop.	DM
8.	When I stroll down a busy city street, accompanied by a blaring walkman, my attention is distracted from my physical environment.	
9.	<u>After being introduced to the class</u>, everyone was nice to me.	DM
10.	Mothers tend to treat boys and girls differently <u>when small</u>.	DM
11.	<u>After hearing what had happened</u>, my blood began to boil as an irrational madness for revenge surged through my body.	DM
12.	<u>Going through Grade 12</u>, the teachers began to demand more work.	DM
13.	After I finish one or two drinks, my brain feels very light.	
14.	Loose bindings will cause the skis to fall off <u>while standing up and skiing</u>.	DM
15.	<u>By recycling paper</u>, thousands of square kilometres of forest will be preserved.	DM
16.	As I recalled my lessons, I didn't feel like attempting anything difficult.	
17.	<u>After spending three hours shivering and trying to stay warm</u>, the storm subsided and we quickly headed for camp.	DM
18.	<u>When feeling depressed or lonely</u>, a dog is always at your side wagging its tail.	DM
19.	<u>After writing tests and quizzes</u>, the board of education agreed to let me attend Grade 12 at York Memorial High School.	DM
20.	<u>When driving in a big city like Montreal</u>, parking is always a problem.	DM

Misplaced and Dangling Modifiers: Exercise, Level 1 (p. 157)

These items are "correct": 10, 18.
The revisions are open-ended.

Misplaced and Dangling Modifiers: Exercise, Level 2 (p. 159)

These items are "correct": 6, 12, 21.
The revisions are open-ended.

Parallel Form: Exercise 1 (p. 165)

1.	touching	11.	London
2.	heaviness	12.	after dinner
3.	speaking	13.	April
4.	skilfully	14.	intelligent
5.	large	15.	losing
6.	to roast	16.	planting the seeds
7.	shifted gears	17.	Harley-Davidson
8.	drinking too much	18.	angry
9.	going to the movies	19.	playing tennis
10.	to skate	20.	June

Parallel Form: Exercise 2 (p. 167)

These items are "parallel": 3, 12, 20, 29.
The revisions are open-ended.

Commonly Confused Words: Exercise (p. 171)

1.	accept	21.	its
2.	advice	22.	know
3.	effect	23.	led
4.	affect	24.	lose
5.	our	25.	morale
6.	bear	26.	passed
7.	breaks	27.	piece
8.	breathe	28.	personnel
9.	buy	29.	principal
10.	capital	30.	quiet
11.	clothes	31.	write
12.	course	32.	role
13.	council	33.	sight
14.	desert	34.	than
15.	due	35.	there
16.	immigrated	36.	they're
17.	farther	37.	through
18.	hear	38.	too
19.	heroine	39.	whether
20.	whole	40.	were

Apostrophes: Exercise (p. 179)

1. All pets should receive more sympathy than they do.
2. For entertainment Oshawa has movie theatres, ice rinks, roller arenas, nightclubs and all sorts of gyms to work out at.
3. The Beatles' influence and popularity will live as long as rock and roll exists.
4. The present art of producing with an assembly line system has come a long way since its introduction.
5. C
6. It's exciting to see a great horse thundering down the track.
7. The only way to reduce students' financial problems is to increase their grants and loans.
8. Students who are 18 and over are the ones who need money the most.
9. Thousands of people fish Ontario's lakes and rivers each year, but how many will take a minute to consider the results of fished-out waters?
10. Driving a motorcycle gives one a sense of independence, because the rider knows people are watching.
11. People who have no confidence in their own work will try to use others' ideas.

12.   Politics is what gets everyone talking and moving in this world.
13.   Parents' moral values are passed on to the next generation.
14.   My parents emigrated from Greece.
15.   C
16.   After each goal the team that was scored against gets possession of the ball behind its net.
17.   It's a holiday to escape from work and see who can catch the most fish.
18.   It's my parents' duty to take care of me; they are legally required to.
19.   She sees only his good qualities.
20.   C
21.   Solar systems have a sun and various numbers of planets.
22.   Are Canadians ashamed of their own country?
23.   C
24.   There are many owners' clubs for most sports cars.
25.   Newton's Second Law of Motion helps the swimmer to conserve energy.
26.   Illness can be the mind's expression to withdraw from life's stresses and strains.
27.   We'd go to my grandparents' house each year because it wasn't really Christmas anywhere else.
28.   The four-cycle system is what most automobile engines are based on.
29.   When Nick sees the Buchanans' reaction to Myrtle's death, he develops a sense of moral responsibility.
30.   Animals such as rabbits, monkeys and cats are being used for meaningless experiments.
31.   C
32.   It was Labour Day when all the delayed thoughts of moving finally hit home.
33.   When children see their favourite players using sticks to jab and spear other players, the next thing you know, the children are imitating.
34.   Anyone who has run for a few years on the road has no doubt experienced a deterioration of the knees.
35.   Elizabeth realized the faults of her parents' marriage.
36.   C
37.   True punk rockers wear safety pins through their noses or cheeks.
38.   A newborn child sees the light for the first time.
39.   My mother's parents don't travel at all.
40.   All over the world we are confronted with the same problems in women's lives.

Capitals: Exercise (p. 183)

1.   A friend of mine, Frank, once told me that he had been behind a Mac's store smoking a cigarette when all of a sudden a police officer approached and asked him where the pot was hidden.
2.   During the hockey game, the mother of one of the opposing players stood up from her seat and yelled as loudly as she could, "Kill that little worm!"
3.   In the first year of the program, students have to take accounting, economics, geography, mathematics, English, management, business law and psychology.
4.   Canadians have long been concerned with developing the North, but only recently with protecting it.
5.   My parents bought a house north of the business district, within a five-minute walk of an elementary school, a middle school, a high school, a Mac's Milk store and a shopping centre.
6.   On a bright summer morning, the first Monday of July, we got in our canoe and started down the Missinaibi River.
7.   Who has seen the wind?
        Neither you nor I;
    But when the trees bow down their heads
        The wind is passing by.
            — Christina Rossetti, 1872
8.   In high school one of my English teachers spent two months on *Hamlet*.
9.   In addition to containing beef and/or pork, wieners may contain water, flour, milk solids, salt and preservatives such as sodium nitrite, which has been known to cause cancer in laboratory animals.
10.   Cruise ships have many facilities such as bedrooms, swimming pools, lawn tennis courts, dancing halls, movie theatres and bars.
11.   Lady Macbeth, a strong-willed character who was capable of influencing Macbeth to murder his king, brought about her breakdown and death by her own ambitions.
12.   John Osborne was born on December 12, 1929, in London, England.

13. In today's modern society, people's morals and values are changing, so divorce, birth control and abortion are more easily accepted.

14. J. D. Salinger's best short story, "For Esmé — with Love and Squalor," shows how destructive war is to human feelings.

15. When I began high school I really got involved in soccer.

16. I arrived in Trinidad on Monday and began my search for a job on Tuesday.

17. Stephen Leacock once wrote, "The essence of humour is human kindliness."

18. In his *Biographia Literaria*, Coleridge refers to "that willing suspension of disbelief for the moment, which constitutes poetic faith."

19. Mackenzie King said, "The promises of yesterday are the taxes of today."

20. Blaise Pascal called humans "the glory and the shame of the universe."

21. The driver stopped the bus to jump out and take a look. He was immediately followed by the Spaniard, two Mexicans, Hugh, Geoffrey and Yvonne.

22. When the Canadian dollar sank in value, foreign automobiles such as the Volvo, Volkswagen, Toyota, Subaru and Honda rose sharply in price.

23. The National Hockey League Rules Committee brought in new rules which prohibited players from being overly aggressive.

24. My mother speaks French, Portuguese and English.

25. I have noted that math teachers do not dress as well as English teachers.

26. To depict their toughness, hockey players are given names such as "Hammer," "Battleship," "Tiger" and "Bulldog."

27. One of the fastest-growing religions in the world is Islam.

28. In each of Mordecai Richler's earlier novels, *The Acrobats, Son of a Smaller Hero* and *A Choice of Enemies,* the hero is an artistically inclined Canadian with a deep dislike of Canadian culture and a conviction that the society he lives in is a fraud.

29. As a faithful expression of the theme found in the play, the movie *Fortune and Men's Eyes* was the epitome of success.

30. "Well, Doctor," I said, "since you agree with the other doctors, I suppose we had better go ahead with the operation."

Abbreviations (p. 185)

1. CEO = chief executive officer
2. CPI = consumer price index
3. GIC = guaranteed income certificate
4. GST = goods and services tax
5. ICU = intensive care unit
6. NDP = New Democratic Party
7. RAM = random access memory
8. R&D = research and development
9. RN = registered nurse
10. SASE = self-addressed stamped envelope

INDEX